The Truth As It Is In Jesus

Comfort Ye My People

by

Mary Cleveland-Tepper

"Speak ye . . . [to the heart] of
. . . Jerusalem, and cry unto her,
that her warfare is accomplished,
that her iniquity is pardoned."

Isaiah 40:1, 2

TEACH Services, Inc.
www.TEACHServices.com

**PRINTED IN
THE UNITED STATES OF AMERICA**

World rights reserved. This book or any portion thereof may not be copied or reproduced in any form or manner whatever, except as provided by law, without the written permission of the publisher, except by a reviewer who may quote brief passages in a review.

The author assumes full responsibility for the accuracy of all facts and quotations as cited in this book.

Copyright © 2010 TEACH Services, Inc.
ISBN-13: 978-1-57258-650-5
Library of Congress Control Number: 2001012345

Published by
TEACH Services, Inc.
www.TEACHServices.com

This book is dedicated to
Dale Vaughn, who,
when I first found Christ, said to me,

"You've found something, and
I want to know what it is."

Acknowledgement

I have always regretted not being able to explain to Dale Vaughn what it was that I had found. My inability developed in me a deep desire to understand and to share what I continue to discover in Christ and the study of His Word. For this I am deeply grateful to Dale.

A special thank you goes to Robert J. Wieland. When he read my first attempt to put the thoughts of this book in writing, a rebuttal of Beyond Belief by Jack Sequeira and Beyond Belief: A Theological Picasso by Kevin Paulson, in a paper titled "There is a Third Option," he encouraged me to rewrite it as a statement of belief. He said, " I cannot see what you are seeing, but I believe you are seeing something."

I am greatly indebted to the untiring efforts of Tim Chapman who edited and re-edited the many early drafts of this book. He helped me keep the chain of thought, as it is easy to make leaps that many will not follow. He was always saying, "Clarify this. What are you trying to say?" or "How did you get from here to there?" or "Reference, reference, reference." Also the support of his wife Trish has been very special to me.

This book is being printed because I received a card from Teach Services, Inc. offering a free book review. They sent the card as a result of a note in their computer telling them I wrote this book. So, a special "thank you" goes to whomever it was that opened the door for this book to come out of the box it has been in for the past 12 years.

Unless otherwise noted, all scripture is quoted from the *King James Version Bible*.

The following books are referenced in this book and were authored by Ellen G. White:
- *The Acts of the Apostles*
- *The Adventist Home*
- *Child Guidance*
- *Christ's Object Lessons*
- *Counsels to Parents, Teachers, and Students*
- *The Desire of Ages*
- *Early Writings*
- *Education*
- *The Ellen G. White 1888 Materials*
- *Faith and Works*
- *The Faith I Live By*
- *The Great Controversy*
- *In Heavenly Places*
- *Mind, Character, and Personality*
- *The Ministry of Healing*
- *My Life Today*
- *Manuscript Releases*
- *Our Father Cares*
- *Patriarchs and Prophets*
- *Prophets and Kings*
- *Selected Messages*
- *Sermons and Talks*
- *The SDA Bible Commentary*
- *Sons and Daughters of God*
- *The Spirit of Prophecy*

- *Steps to Christ*
- *Testimonies for the Church*
- *Testimonies to Ministers and Gospel Workers*
- *Thoughts from the Mount of Blessing*

The following periodicals and pamphlets are referenced in this book and the articles were authored by Ellen G. White:

- *Redemption*
- *The Review and Herald*
- *The Signs of the Times*
- *The Watchman*
- *The Youth's Instructor*

Preface

Who am I to write a book such as this? I am simply a person whose heart has been touched by the love of God and is now compelled to share what He has shared with me. Allow me to tell you a bit about myself. I was baptized into the Lutheran Church as an infant but raised Southern Baptist (that was the only church that sent a bus into our neighborhood gathering up kids for Sunday school). As a teenager, I returned to the Lutheran Church to attend catechism classes. After that I joined the U.S. Air Force to serve my country.

Although many times I felt the call to go forward to the altar within the Baptist Church, I did not feel that those who were baptized made the changes in their lives that I had been taught they should. In catechism classes I learned about the commitment involved in baptism and knew I was not ready. As an adult I stopped going to church regularly, but I was always searching for what was "truth."

A friend gave me the book Project Sunlight by June Strong. It is the story of a woman's experiences as the last days of this earth draw near. Here I learned of a Saturday Sabbath and of people "sleeping" in the grave instead of going directly to heaven when they die. I also learned about "last day events." I had not heard any of this before, but somewhere deep in me I knew this had a ring of truth. I wanted to know more.

Over the next few months I read everything I could get my hands on concerning this "new truth." At home I found a special family Bible with all these great study helps in the back. I had received it as a gift the summer before when I purchased some children's Bible stories as well as some adult Bible readings authored by Ellen G. White. (Oh, how the Lord works!) For the first time in my life I knew I had to be baptized. It was time to make the commitment I had been putting off for so long.

I read Project Sunlight in March of 1982. I was baptized that August and introduced to the writings of A.T. Jones and E.J. Waggoner the following year in January. The first thing I read was The Third Angel's Message, a series of studies given by Jones at the 1895 General Conference. I could not put the book down. I wanted to know more about 1888 and also Waggoner.

I was invited to a special weekend gathering at a church where they would be looking at the history of the Seventh-day Adventist Church, including 1888. While at the meeting, someone in the back of the room made this statement, "If you are saved, you should know it." In my innocence I responded that the little seed of doubt kept me on my knees praying and kept me studying and striving to be what God wanted me to be. I could tell that many felt as I did. But over the next few days a real battle raged in me. Should I or shouldn't I know that I was saved? I cried out to the Lord for an answer.

The day after that prayer I was invited to a Bible study in Loma Linda. After only two Friday night Bible studies, I knew that God was providing the answer. I thanked Him and applied what I had learned concerning death to self. While wrestling in prayer, I knew I could say, "I am crucified with Christ, and yet I live, but the life I now live, Christ lives in me."

Interestingly enough, years later I looked back at the studies that led to this night of wrestling with self and I found that "self" was never once mentioned in either study. (I am an ardent note taker and have kept them all.) I tell you this because through this Bible study I was led to an "offshoot" movement. Through this movement I gained access to the many writings of Jones and Waggoner that were not then available within the mainstream church. When we are searching for truth, it is amazing where and how God will lead us.

This movement claimed to teach the message of Jones and Waggoner. I read everything this group printed. I am an avid reader and studier, and I was by now teaching an adult Sabbath School class in the mainstream Adventist church. I was learning and growing every day. Gradually a sense of unease crept in. The members of my church were tagging me as part of the "lunatic fringe" of the church, a "black sheep" because I focused on Jones and Waggoner and other pioneers. I had been writing to the leader of the offshoot movement with questions that he could not answer. I was seeing contradictions between his writings and those of Jones and Waggoner. I became aware that the mainstream church did not know, or seem to want to know, what I believed I was learning in these two men's writings. Although I had found no contradictions with Ellen White, many questions were being raised in my mind and much confusion was setting in.

Finally, when I could take no more, I claimed the Scripture, "You shall know the truth, and the truth shall set you free." I told the Lord that I knew He had led me to this point, so I would trust Him now. I said, "Take it all, Lord, everything I have learned. Take it all away. Give it back to me as you would have me to know it." And He did just that! Over the next days, weeks, months, even years, He took all these great truths I had learned and gave them back to me in new settings, forming new relationships, revealing things I had not seen before. He tied all the pieces together into a beautiful coherent whole. He showed me that much of the confusion was not necessarily truth versus error, but simply a matter of one's perception or point of view, and an unwillingness to see beyond one's own ideas (or established idea) of what is truth.

I believe the Lord took me beneath the surface of the many Bible stories, illustrations, church doctrines, and traditions to see the principles underlying them. Too often we get caught up in the outworking of the principle, basing a doctrine on the illustration used to reveal the principle, and we end up losing sight of the principle itself. A perfect example is in the early church when some honest members decided that immersion was a better way than sprinkling to illustrate the principle of "death and life in Christ." Unfortunately, a rift in the church and consequent separation was the result. Why? Because sprinkling, the illustration of a principle, had become the doctrine, or tradition, of the church, and the principle itself had lost its significance. As too often happens, the "mother church" could not, or would not, change. Time and time again this happens in churches and between individuals. Truth is not stagnant, and true principles can be demonstrated in numerous ways. This is a lesson we all need to learn.

This book is the result of what I believe the Lord did in giving me back the truths we all hold dear. You will find them presented in fresh new relationships and new settings, and in so doing I hope you will discover what I have found—a deeper level of faith and a firmer foundation upon which to stand, especially in consideration of the time in which we live and the events that are fast coming upon us. As I believe He gave it to me, I now give it to you.

Mary Cleveland-Tepper
May 2008

Table of Contents

Introduction 1

Chapter One   The Truth As It Is In Jesus 7
- *The first and the last Adam*
- *The impact of their choices*
- *Can death Hold you in the grave?*
- *Each Adam touches us today*

Chapter Two   Our Choices 27
- *The mustard seed*
- *In Christ by promise*
- *In Christ by faith*
- *Christ in you by promise*
- *Christ in you by faith*
- *Growing up in Christ*
- *Preparing to stand*
- *Seeing the unseen*
- *Hide and seek.*

Chapter Three   Familiar Stories Re-Examined 54
- *The man at the pool of Bethesda*
- *Israel in Egypt*
- *Babylonian bondage*

Chapter Four	The Law and The Gospel	66

- *Natural law in the spiritual world*
- *Two kinds of law*
- *Gravity, parachutes, and salvation*
- *Redemption is according to law*
- *Resurrection power*
- *Death before life.*

Chapter Five	Christ Meets Us Where We Are	85

- *Christ in the garden*
- *Christ as our example*
- *Dying with Christ*
- *The right action of the will*
- *What is faith?*

Chapter Six	Understanding The Battle Within	108

- *Drawing distinctions*
- *The man of Romans Seven*
- *A true self and a false self*
- *Defining sin*

Chapter Seven	Man's Spiritual Nature	134

- *As created by God*
- *As fallen by the sin of Adam*
- *As restored by the last Adam*
- *As it is in you and me*
- *The personal presence of Christ*

Chapter Eight	Rising To Where Christ Is	192

- *Secret prayer*
- *Christ is our only hope*
- *Vision of a finished work*

Appendix A	"The Third Angel's Message-No. 12"................. 213	

- *A study by A. T. Jones from the 1893 General Conference Bulletin*

Appendix B	Many Ways to Say the Same Thing..................... 227	

- *Drawing Distinctions*
- *Marriage illustration of Romans Seven*
- *The spirit of man:*
  - *Made in the image of God*
  - *God's image defaced*
  - *Image of God restored*
  - *Whose image is seen upon you?*
- *Two seeds, two soils*
- *Many ways to say the same thing.*

Introduction

"The word of God presents special truths for every age. The dealings of God with his people in the past should receive our careful attention. We should learn the lessons which they are designed to teach us. But we are not to rest content with them. God is leading out his people step by step. Truth is progressive. The earnest seeker will be constantly receiving light from Heaven. What is truth? should ever be our inquiry" (*The Signs of the Times*, May 26, 1881).

This statement was written by Ellen G. White in 1881. In 1888 God sent a "most precious" message to the Seventh-day Adventist Church through two men—A.T. Jones and E.J. Waggoner. It is now more than 120 years later and many in the church are still unaware of whom they were and the light bearing message that God sent through them to His people. I was introduced to their writings less than a year after finding the many books by Ellen White. I entered their writings with the same enthusiasm and openness to discover the truth as I had when I first began studying those of Ellen White.

I also enjoy studying about the sanctuary. I am fascinated in how thoroughly Christ is illustrated throughout. But for some reason my interest would tend to "dry up," and I would have to set it aside and come back to it another time. It was during one of these dry periods that I was asked to do a study on the sanctuary. Deeply concerned, I asked the Lord to make it come alive for me and for those who would come to the study. Imagine my surprise to find the truths I had learned through Jones and Waggoner depicted in the sanctuary!

The first thing I saw was how God had led the children of Israel through an "experience" of the sanctuary during their journey from

Comfort Ye My People

Egypt to Mount Sinai before He gave them the instructions for building the sanctuary. Then I began to see our own personal experience in the sanctuary and how our view of the gospel, as well as our understanding of our relationship to Christ, is progressive. The sanctuary took on a new life for me. I could see how God had been leading me, and leads all those who come to Him, through an "experience" of the sanctuary. By what we believe about Him, and the gospel of salvation, Christ knows exactly where we are in our spiritual journey through the sanctuary. He knows what the "stepping stone," or perhaps "stumbling block," is that lies next in our walk toward oneness with Him and His Father.

First, He draws the sinner to His cross. There we understand that He has paid the price to save us from our sins and how much He desires to give us eternal life instead of the death we deserve. All we have to do is confess our sin, acknowledge His atonement for us, and accept forgiveness. The now forgiven sinner returns home justified. The next time he sins he comes back to the cross and repeats the process again and again. The sinner does the best he can, and he trusts that Christ will make up the difference. This gospel message is represented in the courtyard at the altar.

Have you ever let it sink in that the sinner cannot go any further into the sanctuary than the altar? Only the high priest and his sons can officiate in the rest of the sanctuary. Only the priests can wash at the laver. Only the priests can go into the holy place. When I realized this, I understood that the "gospel" of the courtyard was for the sinner, but we need to move beyond that perception if we are to go any further in our walk with Christ. We need to stay focused on the One hanging on the cross, rather than on our sins. In so doing we come to understand that more is happening than simply a "transfer" of our sins to Christ. We are to be crucified there with Him, buried with Him in baptism. If this has been our experience, then we become a child of God. And if Christ is

Introduction

our High Priest, don't we become a "son" of the High Priest?

As a son we can wash in the laver; we can go into the holy place. We are also clothed in white linen, "covered" with the righteousness of Christ (not just "surrounded" as in the courtyard). Christ has become to us a very personal Savior, not just the Savior of the world. In the holy place we learn the lessons of the table of showbread, the candlestick, and the altar of incense. We can see the veil before the Most Holy Place, although we, as sons, cannot enter therein. We see the glorious robes of the High Priest and learn what we are to strive to be like. We have a work to do—inwardly we need to be like our High Priest, and outwardly, in the courtyard, we need to help others to find what we have found. When the "son" sins, he still needs the altar in the courtyard, but his focus becomes the work he has to do, the life he is called to live. By faith he seeks the power of God to do this work. As a "son," we enter into the work of sanctification, the "work of a lifetime."

On the Day of Atonement there was a special work to be done. (Please read Leviticus 16 to familiarize yourself with the services that took place once a year.) Notice that the high priest put off his garments of glory and put on simple white linen. Are not the sons wearing white linen? Is this not telling us that Jesus, our High Priest, is one with us as sons? Where He goes, we by faith can follow. In Him we can go into the Most Holy Place. Is this not what the third angel's message was designed to do, to show us the way into the Most Holy? On the Day of Atonement the high priest confessed the sins of his household upon the bullock and took the blood into the Most Holy Place and sprinkled it there. Those who have had a true experience in the three angels' messages will claim the mercy of God and, by faith, enter in with their representative, the High Priest.

Next we have the offering of the goat. There are no sins confessed upon this offering, which is for the people. This told me two things. This goat represents the perfect life of Christ, and this perfect righteousness of Christ was for all people—He is one with all humanity, not just the sons or the children of Israel! I believe this goat represents the message, "Christ our Righteousness," that was sent to God's people in 1888, especially in the understanding of Christ as the last Adam. The blood of the goat—the perfect life of Christ given to all humanity in the second Adam—is brought into the Most Holy Place and is sprinkled down upon those who entered in by faith under the messages of the three angels. This new message will judge us and challenge us to see if we are truly willing to "follow the Lamb withersoever He goeth" (The Acts of the Apostles, p. 591). Our appropriate reaction to this message is revealed by what was done with the two bloods in the Most Holy Place. This is revealed later in this book and explained in principle very clearly by Jones and Waggoner, but suffice it to say that we are to experience that "oneness" with our heavenly Father that Christ has already accomplished within Himself.

Notice that Leviticus 16 tells us that there is "no man" in the courtyard—is this not saying to us that, for the children of Israel, the work of the courtyard is a "finished work"? There are no "sons" in the sanctuary either. Is the work of the holy place also a "finished work"? (Read the chapter titled "A Firm Platform" in Ellen White's book Early Writings.) In Christ the ministry of these apartments is a finished work. Is not Sabbath rest all about the "finished work" of God?

The mixed blood is carried out of the Most Holy Place to cleanse the rest of the sanctuary, just as the loud cry will go forth to call all, who will, to enter into the Most Holy Place while the censor still burns within. There is much more to this day, but I hope you can see where the message of Jones and Waggoner comes into play and is a necessary part of the truths we need to finish the work God has called us, as Seventh-day Adventists, to do.

Introduction

There is also another level of faith revealed on the Day of Atonement. Ellen White tells us that when the work of the Most Holy Place is finished Christ will take off his priestly garments, put on His garments of glory, and come to this earth. He will at that time place all the sins of His people upon the head of the "scapegoat," and they will be sent to the "land of no remembrance." It is an interesting thing to note that during the services of the Day of Atonement the sins are placed on the head of the scapegoat and sent to the wilderness before the high priest changes his garments back to the garments of glory. Is this an error on the part of Ellen White? At first I wondered, but not any more. I believe that the services of this day were given especially to God's people to strengthen their faith. What Ellen White saw was the "outworking" of the "finished work" revealed in the sanctuary. Jones and Waggoner both talk about this level of faith—laying hold of a work as already done, before it can be manifested!

Contained in the services of the Day of Atonement are the messages for us today, the deeper understanding of gospel truths necessary to get us through what is coming, a clearer understanding of who we are in Christ and who He is in us. As sinners we need the gospel of the courtyard. As sons we need the gospel of the holy place. But, as a people living in the last days, we need the gospel of our "oneness" with Christ and the Father, which is only found within the Most Holy Place. Much more is revealed in these services, but enough of Jones' and Waggoner's message is there to encourage us to know what the truths were that God sent to us through them. I can only pray that the things I share with you in this book will encourage you to seek that "oneness" with Christ, and thereby meet the Father face-to-face. They have been waiting long enough. It is time for God's glory to rise and shine in His people!

Comfort Ye My People

Chapter One

The Truth As It Is In Jesus

"In the beginning was the Word, and the Word was with God, and the Word was God. The same was in the beginning with God. All things were made by him; and without him was not any thing made that was made. . . . And the Word was made flesh, and dwelt among us" (John 1:1-3, 14).

This verse refers to the Son of God, Jesus Christ, whom the Father sent to this world to be with us. Through His Son, the Father wished to make Himself known.

"God, who at sundry times and in divers manners spake in time past unto the fathers by the prophets, Hath in these last days spoken unto us by his Son, whom he hath appointed heir of all things, by whom also he made the worlds" (Heb. 1:1, 2).

Here we see that it is the Father who wishes to speak to us, as He did in the past through the prophets, but now does so through His Son.

"At the Saviour's baptism, Satan was among the witnesses. He saw the Father's glory overshadowing His Son. He heard the voice of Jehovah testifying to the divinity of Jesus. Ever since Adam's sin, the human race had been cut off from direct communion with God; the intercourse between heaven and earth had been through Christ; but now that Jesus had come "in the likeness of sinful flesh" (Romans 8:3), the Father Himself spoke. He had before communicated with humanity through Christ; now He communicated with humanity in Christ. Satan had hoped that God's abhorrence of evil would bring an eternal separation between heaven and earth. But now it was manifest that the connection between God and man had been restored" (*The Desire of Ages*, p. 116).

When I first caught the impact of what Ellen White says here, I was stunned into silence. I had always been taught that Christ is the go-between for us and the Father. We in our sin cannot be in the presence of God because His glory would consume us. But here we are told that in Christ we communicate with the Father Himself!

In the beginning, God spoke directly to Adam and Eve. Sin broke down that communion and God communicated with us through His Son. I believe our heavenly Father still desires to speak directly with you and me. When God said to Moses, "let them make me a sanctuary, that I may dwell among them" (Ex. 25:8), I was always shown how Christ is represented there. Now I believe the sanctuary was also given to us by God the Father to show us the way to come back into communion with Him through and in Christ. It is interesting to note that the first article of furniture that God showed Moses was the ark of the testimony, the place where He said He would commune with Moses and Aaron. (See Exodus 25:8, 22 and *Patriarchs and Prophets*, p. 67.) Unfortunately, the sin of Nadab and Abihu limited Aaron's approach into the Most Holy Place to once a year, and even then only with special preparations. (See Leviticus 16:1-6.) With this added limitation, God was trying to bring home to Israel (and to us today) the absolute holiness of God, that sin cannot exist in His presence and that something more was needed before we could again commune with Him face-to-face. Even Moses had to be hid in "a clift of the rock" and was covered by God's hand as God passed by (Ex. 33:22). Christ is that "rock" into which we are to be "hidden" that we too may be able to once again communicate with God the Father.

"Men in sin cannot meet God alone and exist. This is shown in

Rev. 6:13-17" (A.T. Jones, *The 1895 General Conference Bulletin*, p. 216). We tend to look at Christ as the one who stands between man and God. We are told that He is the Mediator, as the one interposing between two extremes—us in our sin and God in His purity. We see Jesus as our advocate, our friend in the court, who pleads mercy for us before a stern judge. Have you ever looked up the word advocate as found in 1 John 2:1? *Strong's Concordance* defines it as "intercessor, consoler," translating it as "advocate, comforter." It is the same word used to describe the Holy Spirit in John 16.

But the most interesting thing is found when you look up the often overlooked word "with." This word denotes a closeness that goes beyond the one in the "middle," or even the one who is "beside, near, or in close vicinity to." It says that our Advocate, our Comforter—Jesus Christ—is in "union" with the Father, in "companionship" with Him, in "resemblance" to, in "addition" to, in "completeness" with the Father. We all know that the Holy Spirit is the Comforter sent to us after Christ ascended to heaven. This verse tells us that Christ is also our Comforter in addition to the Father! How many of us view God as a Comforter in the same way as we see Jesus or the Holy Spirit?

It is true that we in our sinfulness (without our Advocate, Jesus Christ) cannot approach God without being destroyed, so it is easy for us to view Jesus as the one who goes to the Father "for" us. Even Revelation 1:1 tells us that when God wants to reach us He sends His message through the Son. But, in the quote from *The Desire of Ages*, page 116, I hope you too caught the fact that when Ellen White refers to the time God spoke at Christ's baptism she tells us that He was revealing to the world that the connection between God and man "had been" restored, that in Christ, God and man met together! "To wit, that God was in Christ, reconciling the world unto himself" (2 Cor. 5:19).

"God's holiness is pure, that is true; it is such holiness that sin cannot bear the presence of it. It is holiness of such transcendent purity and power as to be a consuming fire to sin. Its consuming power upon sin is because of its wondrous purity; and therefore, because of the wondrous purity, and the power of that wondrous purity, of the holiness of God in Jesus Christ, he longs to come in contact with those who are laden with sins, who are permeated through and through with sins, in order that this holiness, finding an entrance, shall consume the sin, and save the soul. That is Christ's holiness.

"It is one of the most blessed truths in the Bible, that our God is a consuming fire because of his holiness. For, then, in Jesus Christ, we meet him whose holiness is a consuming fire to sin; and that is the pledge of our salvation in perfection from every stain of sin. The brightness, the glory, the all consuming purity of that holiness, will take every vestige of sin and sinfulness out of the man who will meet God in Jesus Christ" (A.T. Jones, *The 1895 General Conference Bulletin*, p. 312).

"Whereas, out of Christ, in himself, alone, no man can see God and live. In Christ, out of himself, no man can see God and not live. In Christ, to see God is to live; for in him is life, and the life is the light of men" (Ibid., p. 217).

This, I believe, is the underlying message of the two Adams—all that the first Adam lost the last Adam has redeemed. In Christ we can again find direct communion with God. True, our heavenly Father must first reach fallen humanity through His Son. But He is ever seeking to draw us, by faith, into the Son. He knows that His glory will consume sin out of us if we will abide, by faith, in Jesus Christ. He desires so much to commune with us again, face-to-face. In fact, God so loved the world that He gave us His Son, the Word of God, in three basic forms:

1. The Written Word – the Bible, and all inspired messages, testify of Jesus.
2. The Created Word – the world around us that Jesus, the spoken Word, has made.
3. The Living Word – Jesus Christ came to this earth and is now in heaven.

When we find a truth that can be explained in harmony with all three of these, we shall have the truth as it is in Jesus; for He is the Word—written, spoken, and "made flesh" to dwell among us (John 1:14). All three forms will be used to show the depth revealed in the type versus anti-type of the two Adams and its meaning to us today. May this study of His Word draw you into oneness with Christ that you may find that blessed oneness with the Father that the Scriptures speak of in John 17.

The First and the Last Adam

The only story we have of the first Adam is his creation and subsequent fall. Read Genesis 1-3. Adam was created perfect. He was tempted by the voice of Satan through his beloved Eve. Adam made the choice to listen to that voice instead of the voice of God, hoping that God would understand. He disobeyed a direct command of God. "The wages of sin is death" (Rom. 6:23). If this sentence of death had been fully executed that day, there never would have been another human being on earth, unless God started over again with another Adam. The potential human race would have died in the first Adam. Even though Adam did not die immediately, his one sin impacted all subsequent humanity.

"Wherefore, as by one man sin entered into the world, and death by sin, and so death went over all men: *in whom all men have sinned.* For unto the time of the Law was sin in the world, but sin is not imputed, while there is no law. But death reigned from Adam to Moses, even over them also that sinned not after the like manner of transgression of Adam, which was the figure of him that was to come" (Rom. 5:12-14, Geneva Bible, 1599 edition, italics added).

Adam had knowingly violated a direct command of God, the consequences of which was death. In these verses we are told that death was reigning even over those who had not sinned as Adam, over those who had never even heard of the law, those who lived before the Law was given at Sinai. If sin is not held to one's account while there is no law (Rom. 4:15, 5:13), then why is death reigning? Note that the Geneva Bible (the precursor to the King James Version) specifically states that sin and death entered into the whole world and affected all men because all sinned in Adam.

"And so it is written, The first man Adam was made a living soul; the last Adam was made a quickening spirit. Howbeit that was not first which is spiritual, but that which is natural; and afterward that which is spiritual. The first man is of the earth, earthy; the second man is the Lord from heaven" (1 Cor. 15:45-47).

This verse draws the contrast between the two Adams, but wherein was Adam the "figure of him that was to come"? Concerning the two Adams, A.T. Jones asks these questions:

"Wherein was Adam the figure of Him? In his righteousness?—No; for he did not keep it. In his sin?—No; for Christ did not sin. Wherein, then, was Adam the figure of Christ?—In this: That all that were in the world were included in Adam; and all that are in the world are included in Christ. . . .

"Does the second Adam touch as many as did the first Adam?—And the answer is that it is certainly true that what the second Adam did, embraces all that were embraced in what the first Adam did.... Suppose Christ had yielded to temptation and had sinned. Would that have meant anything to us?—It would have meant everything to us....

The first Adam's righteousness would have meant all to us, and the second Adam's righteousness means all to as many as believe. That is correct in a certain sense; but not in the sense in which we are studying it now. We are now studying from the side of the Adams" (*The 1895 General Conference Bulletin*, p. 268, 269)

Jones recognizes that there is a point at which the choices that each Adam made embraced all of humanity. He also recognizes that there is a point where the righteousness of the second Adam embraces only the believer. But first, before moving to the believer, he explains in more detail what each Adam's choices meant to all of humanity. We will do the same.

The Impact of Their Choices

Ellen White says, "His [Christ's] arm encircles the whole human race....We are in Christ Jesus by His covenant of promise" (*The SDA Bible Commentary*, vol. 5, p. 1143). She is not referring to believers only, because in the very next paragraph she asks, "Are we in Him by living faith?"

She also tells us that Christ wrought out redemption for man. "This was not done by going out of Himself to another, but by taking humanity into Himself. Thus Christ gave to humanity an existence out of Himself. To bring humanity into Christ, to bring the fallen race into oneness with divinity, is the work of redemption" (*The SDA Bible Commentary*, vol. 7, p. 927). The Scriptures also declare: "That in the dispensation of the fullness of times he might gather together in one all things in Christ, both which are in heaven, and which are on earth; even in him" (Eph. 1:10). Here we are told that Christ took "all humanity into himself," but the question is, "Are we in Him by living faith?" The work of redemption is to bring those who are "out of" Christ by unbelief "into Christ" by faith.

The one thing both Adams have in common is that all of humanity is included in each of them. The choices each Adam made had an impact on the entire human race, for the entire human race is represented in each of them. To understand the significance of this relationship, we need to understand the biblical principle brought out in Hebrews 7.

"And to say as the thing is, Levi also, who receiveth tithes, payeth tithes in Abraham. For he was yet in the loins of his father, Abraham, when Melchisedec met him" (Heb. 7:9, 10, Geneva Bible)

First, let me say that in this verse we are not told that Levi had any choice in what Abraham did. It also does not say that Levi was in any way responsible for what Abraham did. It does not say that what Abraham did was as Levi, or instead of Levi. The Lord is simply saying that Levi did what Abraham did for he was yet in Abraham's loins.

Paul is using the principle laid out in these verses to prove that the priesthood of Christ was greater than the Levitical priesthood. Having established that Christ is of the order of Melchisedec, he states that the lesser is blessed of the greater. Paul shows that even though Levi receives tithe he paid tithe while in the loins of Abraham, when Abraham met Melchisedec. The choice Abraham made in paying tithe to Melchisedec had an impact on Levi; it made the Levitical priesthood the lesser to be blessed of the greater—the priesthood of Christ. Applied to the two Adams, the use of the principle remains the same. What these two Adams did, the choices they made, had an impact on everyone accounted as being in them, naturally in the first Adam, by promise in the last Adam.

Today, this biblical principle gives us an insight into how God looks at things. That is, in His eyes the whole human race (yet in Adam's loins) did as Adam did and reaped the results of Adam's sin. Most everyone accepts this in one fashion or another. The question that often arises is, "Can the same thing be said of the last Adam?

Does Christ, as the last Adam, represent the whole human race or only those who believe?" The answer lies in this: To what extent do His choices affect all of mankind?

Before attempting to answer these questions concerning Christ, let us look at the first Adam and the impact of his decision upon our lives today. The whole human race is born mortal (subject to death) with "the law of sin...in my [our] members" (Rom. 7:23) without any choice of our own. Why? What the first Adam did we are accounted as having done in him, for we were yet in his loins (Heb. 7:9, 10). Adam's disobedience brought the results of sin to the whole human race (Rom. 5:12). It came from nowhere else. You and I were there in his loins, and we reaped the same as Adam did. It is called "heredity." Today, babies are being born addicted to heroin. How? While in the womb they did as their mother did, only without their choice. Yet, they reap the results of their mother's actions.

We tend to look at the law of sin simply on a spiritual level, but death is its physical counterpart. You and I are born subject to the first mortal death, without any choice of our own. We may have the choice of how we will die, but not as to whether we will die. In fact, at the cellular level, our physical bodies begin to die the moment we are born.

Besides the power of death, there is another power at work at the cellular level from the time of our birth. Whenever a cell dies, there is a new cell created to take its place. What law is this? If the law of death came from the first Adam's choices, what law brings this new life? Did you choose to have either of these powers at work in your physical body? If physical death is the counterpart of spiritual sin, does this power that provides a new living cell to replace the death of the old also have a spiritual counterpart?

"By the casting of grain into the earth, the Saviour represents His sacrifice for us. 'Except a corn of wheat fall into the ground and die,'

He says, 'it abideth alone: but if it die, it bringeth forth much fruit.' John 12:24. Only through the sacrifice of Christ, the Seed, could fruit be brought forth for the kingdom of God. In accordance with the law of the vegetable kingdom, life is the result of His death" (*Education*, p. 110).

"Rightly interpreted, nature is the mirror of divinity" (*The Review and Herald*, September, 18, 1900).

Here we find that the law by which Christ would die and live again has its counterpart in the natural world we live in. The Created Word and the Living Word are in harmony, speaking as one. In 1 Corinthians 15:36 the written Word of God states: "Thou fool, that which thou sowest is not quickened [made alive], except it die."

"The seed dies, to spring forth into new life. In this we are taught the lesson of the resurrection" (*Education*, p. 110). Ellen White also refers to the flowers that die in the fall and come back in the spring as a lesson of the resurrection. (See *The Review and Herald*, November 8, 1898.) These illustrations speak of the physical life. There would be no life, plant or human, were it not for the death and resurrection of Jesus Christ. In *The Desire of Ages* and Romans 8:2, we find that this resurrection power is "the Spirit of life in Christ Jesus" (p. 466). Romans 8:2 goes on to say that the "Spirit of life in Christ Jesus" is that which sets the believer free from the "law of sin and death."

"Christ is the 'Light which lighteth every man that cometh into the world.' John 1:9. As through Christ *every human being has life [physical], so also through Him every soul receives some ray of divine light.* Not only intellectual but *spiritual power, a perception of right, a desire for goodness, exists in every heart* [the conscience?]. But against these principles there is struggling an antagonistic power. The result of eating the tree of knowledge of good and evil is manifest in every man's experience. There is in his nature a bent to evil, a force which, unaided, he cannot resist. To withstand this force, to attain that ideal which in his inmost soul he accepts as alone worthy, he can find help in but one power. That power is Christ. Co-operation with that power is man's greatest need" (*Education*, p. 29, italics added).

"That Christ is in all men is evident from the fact that they live; but he is so held back and kept down that it is difficult to discern Him. Nay, in most men the opposite character is revealed, the mere fact of living and breathing being in many cases the only evidence that Christ is there. Yet he is there, waiting to be revealed,—longing for the time to come when the Word of God may have free course and be glorified, and the perfect life of Jesus of Nazareth be manifested in mortal flesh" (E.J. Waggoner, *Glad Tidings*, p. 35, 36).

As a result of the first Adam's choice to transgress God's word, the human race was brought into the bondage of sin and Satan. At that moment Adam no longer had a clear perception of truth. (See A.T. Jones, *The 1895 General Conference Bulletin*, p. 190-192.) His focus was self-preservation from Satan's perspective, which is to protect self at all cost, cast blame on everyone possible before bringing self into the picture. His will was in the control of Satan. Communion between God and man was broken. (See *Patriarchs and Prophets*, p. 67.)

Christ stepped in to help man in his hopeless situation. First, He secures for us our physical life, and then He gives us His "spirit of life"—the light that lights every man, "spiritual power, a perception of truth, a desire for goodness, exists in every heart." How? He becomes the second man—the enmity put between the serpent and the woman, between the seed of the serpent and the seed of the woman. (See Genesis 3:15 and Galatians 3:16.) Jesus Christ, the word made flesh, was the seed of the woman whose heel would be bruised by the serpent. But, as the last Adam, Christ brought to humanity the enmity against Satan that would finally bruise the head of the serpent.

As the last Adam, Jesus Christ stands as the only other human being to represent the entire human race. He meets man where he is in his fallen condition. He came "made of a woman, made under the law" (Gal. 4:4). What does this mean to us? He was born with the law of sin in His members, the same "bent to evil" that is in our members (*Education*, p. 29). Also, the law of death was at work in Him as it is in every human being born of a woman. He was subject to the same physical death that all humanity received through the disobedience of the first Adam.

Unlike the first Adam, this last Adam never chose the voice of Satan over the voice of God. He always listened to the voice of His Father. By that, He "abolished in his flesh the enmity" (Eph. 2:15). The enmity that existed between Jew and Gentile in Christ's day was only the outworking of the enmity that Satan had placed between God and man. Christ came to tear down this wall between the Jew and the Gentile by making "one new man" (Ibid.)—a joining of man to God in himself, abolishing the enmity in the flesh that kept not only God and man apart, but kept Jew and Gentile apart.

"Abolished," according to *Strong's Concordance*, means, "to be [render] entirely idle [useless]" (p. 2673). The "enmity in his flesh" was not destroyed, done away with, removed, or taken out of the flesh. It was rendered useless, made entirely idle. Due to the law of heredity, a certain trait, weakness, or potential can be passed down to us from our ancestors. Our environment and our own choices play a great part in whether or not these things we inherit will ever be fully manifested in us. The life Jesus lived shows us that the enmity in his flesh, the "law of sin which is in my members" (Rom. 7:23), "the lower corrupt nature" (*The Adventist Home*, p. 127), "the wisdom of the flesh" (Rom. 8:7, Geneva Bible) need never be seen in our lives. He "rendered entirely idle" the law of sin in his members.

"Satan is the great originator of sin; yet this does not excuse any man for sinning; for he cannot force men to do evil. He tempts them to it, and makes sin look enticing and pleasant, but he has to leave it to their own wills whether they will do it or not" (*Testimonies for the Church*, vol. 2, p. 294).

"The strongest temptation cannot excuse sin. However great the pressure brought to bear upon the soul, transgression is our own act. It is not in the power of earth or hell to compel anyone to do evil. Satan attacks us at our weak points, but we need not be overcome. However severe or unexpected the assault, God has provided help for us, and in his strength we may conquer" (*Patriarchs and Prophets*, p. 421).

Not once in the entire life of Jesus could Satan cause Him to falter. On the cross the last Adam died. Did this death that Christ became subject to from the first Adam hold Jesus in the grave? No! Why? Death could not hold Him, because Jesus had never sinned. The law of sin in His members, that "bent to evil" in his flesh, never controlled the choices of Christ. He did not deserve death and death could not hold Him. The enmity in His flesh had been destroyed, rendered entirely idle, during His lifetime and was now slain on the cross—killed outright (Eph. 2:16). The enmity in His flesh (that is now in yours and mine) did not rise with Him when He came forth triumphant from the tomb.

Can Death Hold You in the Grave?

This is the big question. Can the death you have received from the first Adam hold you in the grave? Think carefully before you answer. We know that we have all sinned, whereas Christ did not. So, can the death passed on to us by the first Adam hold you and me in the grave? The answer is "no"!

"For since by man came death, by man came also the resurrection of the dead. For as in Adam all die, even so in Christ shall all be made alive" (1 Cor. 15:21, 22).

The choices we make today will determine in which resurrection we rise, but we do not have a choice to rise! Just as we received physical death from the choice of the first Adam, we receive physical resurrection from the choices of the last Adam. The death the first Adam gave to humanity was a death from which there was no resurrection and would have remained so if Jesus Christ had not stepped in and earned the right to rise again. Only because we will all be made alive again, in Christ, is there even a place for what is called the "second death." Some try to say that Christ died the "second death" upon the cross. What the death of the first Adam, before Christ stepped in, and the second death have in common is no consequent resurrection. The death that Christ died was a death from which He could see no resurrection. He alone turned the death of the first Adam into a death from which we will all rise.

The last Adam passes this resurrection on to us, just as the first Adam passed death to all men. The power of death and the power of the resurrection are at work in us today, by no choice of our own. Our cells die because of the first Adam's choice. New cells take their place because of the last Adam's choices. In God's eyes all of humanity was there in each Adam. We all did as they did. Through Jesus Christ, God, in His great love and mercy, balanced the scales. Spiritually, because of his fall into sin, the first Adam passed to all humanity the enmity in the flesh, enmity against God. The last Adam puts within the heart of every man a "spiritual power" that is enmity against Satan. Christ, as the last Adam—the quickening spirit—may sustain us physically without our choice. But Jesus, as the second man—the Lord from heaven—gave the "spirit of man" another chance to choose which voice it will listen to, which authority it will follow, which "enmity" will be in control. (See A.T. Jones, *The 1895 General Conference Bulletin*, p. 192.)

Each Adam Touches Us Today

The first Adam touches us today. The last Adam touches us today. We receive mortality and its spiritual counterpart—the law of sin in our members—by no choice of our own. Likewise, we receive resurrection and its spiritual counterpart—the law of the spirit of life in Christ—by no choice of our own. I have come to believe that the law of the spirit of life in Christ Jesus is to be found in the conscience of every man, just as the law of sin is in the spiritual flesh of every man. Each law strives to be in control of the thoughts of man, and consequently the higher powers of the soul. The conscience waits for voluntary submission of the will, while the spiritual flesh seeks to rule by any means possible. Could this be why Satan seeks so desperately to take away our freedom of conscience? (See *The Great Controversy*, p. 591.)

Through the writings of Ellen White, I discovered that the conscience is the "voice of God" to man; it is the "spiritual eye of the mind," the "inner light." Choosing to sin causes iniquity to triumph over the conscience, and the lower passions blind the conscience. Sin and selfishness sears, blackens, and crisps the conscience. (See *Testimonies for the Church*, vol. 2, p. 305; vol. 4, p. 31; vol. 5, p. 120, 177; and *The SDA Bible Commentary*, vol. 7, p. 765.)

The spirit of life is in the conscience just as the germinating principle of life is in the seed. It is buried within the hard shell of self, which is created by our sins. The conscience is awakened by the Holy Spirit at conversion. (See *Christ's Object Lessons*, p. 97, 98 and *The Review and Herald*, April 1, 1890.) It is quickened, made alive and active, with the death of self, the right action of the will, and the true exercise of faith. (See *The Signs of the Times*, October 17, 1906; *Testimonies for the Church*, vol. 7, p. 195; and *The Desire of Ages*, p. 691.)

"Justification means the saving of a soul from perdition, that he may obtain sanctification, and through sanctification, the life of heaven. Justification means that the conscience, purged from dead works, is placed where it can receive the blessings of sanctification" (*The SDA Bible Commentary*, vol. 7, p. 908).

In Jesus "the law of the spirit of life" in His conscience was ever awake and active. Whereas, "the law of sin," in His members, was ever dormant, rendered idle. For us, the reverse is more often the case. The hard shell of self must be purged from the conscience. Then the conscience is educated through the daily study of the Word, that it may receive the blessings of sanctification. As the conscience, the voice of God to man, takes its proper place of authority in our lives, we begin to reveal the Christ-like life. The law of sin in our members, the voice of Satan, will then be rendered idle in us as it was in Jesus, the second Adam.

We can easily fail to catch the significance of how each Adam touches us today if we try to bring in our own personal choices too soon. The two Adams, the choices made by them and the consequent effects of those choices on the entire human race, must be seen as they stand type versus anti-type, one the figure of the other.

Brother Jones said it well: "The question is, Does the second Adam's righteousness embrace as many as does the first Adam's sin? Look closely. Without our consent at all, without our having anything to do with it, we were all included in the first Adam; we were there. . . . What that first Adam, what that first man, did, meant us; it involved us. That which the first Adam did brought us into sin, and the end of sin is death; and that touches every one of us, and involves every one of us.

"Jesus Christ, the second man, took our sinful nature. He touched us "in all points." He became we and died the death. And so in him, and by that, every man that has ever lived upon the earth, and was involved in the first Adam, is involved in this, and will live again. There will be a resurrection of the dead, both of the just and the unjust. Every soul shall live again by the second Adam, from the death by the first Adam.

"'Well,' says one, 'we are involved in other sins besides that one.' Not without our choice. When God said, 'I will put enmity between thee and the woman, and between thy seed and her seed,' he set every man free to choose which master he would serve; and since that, every man that has sinned in this world, has done it because he chose to. 'If our gospel be hid, it is hid to them that are lost: in whom the god of this world hath blinded the minds of them which believe not,'—not them who had no chance to believe; the god of this world blinds no man until he has shut his eyes of faith....

"Therefore, just as far as the first Adam reaches man, so far the second Adam reaches man. The first Adam brought man under condemnation of sin, even unto death; the second Adam's righteousness undoes that, and makes every man live again. As soon as Adam sinned, God gave him a second chance, and set him free to choose which master he would have. Since that time every man is free to choose which way he will go; therefore he is responsible for his own individual sins. And when Jesus Christ has set us all free from the sin and death which came upon us from the first Adam, that freedom is for every man; and every man can have it for the choosing" (A.T. Jones, *The 1895 General Conference Bulletin*, p. 269).

Now listen to Ellen White as she speaks of the fall of man and Christ's present role:

"By rebellion and apostasy man forfeited the favor of God; not his rights, for he could have no value except as it was invested in God's dear Son. This point must be understood. He forfeited those privileges which God in His mercy presented him as a free gift, a treasure in trust to be used to advance His cause and His glory, to benefit the beings He had made. The moment the workmanship of God refused obedience to the laws of God's kingdom, that moment he became disloyal to the government of God and he made himself entirely unworthy of all the blessings wherewith God had favored him.

"This was the position of the human race after man divorced himself from God by transgression. Then he was no longer entitled to a breath of air, a ray of sunshine, or a particle of food. And the reason why man was not annihilated was because God so loved him that He made the gift of His dear Son that He should suffer the penalty of his transgression. Christ proposed to become man's surety and substitute, that man, through matchless grace, should have another trial—a second probation—having the experience of Adam and Eve as a warning not to transgress God's law as they did. And inasmuch as man enjoys the blessings of God in the gift of the sunshine and the gift of food, there must be on the part of man a bowing before God in thankful acknowledgment that all things come of God. Whatever is rendered back to Him is only His own who has given it.

"Man broke God's law, and through the Redeemer new and fresh promises were made on a different basis. All blessings must come through a Mediator. Now every member of the human family is given wholly into the hands of Christ, and whatever we possess—whether it is the gift of money, of houses, of lands, of reasoning powers, of physical strength, of intellectual talents—in this present life, and the blessings of the future life, are placed in our possession as God's treasures to be faithfully expended for the benefit of man. Every gift is stamped with the cross and bears the image and superscription of Jesus Christ. All things come of God. From the smallest benefits up to the largest blessing, all flow through the one Channel—a superhuman mediation sprinkled with the blood that is of value beyond estimate because it was the life of God in His Son.

"Now not a soul can give God anything that is not already His.

Bear this in mind: 'All things come of Thee, and of Thine own have we given Thee' (1 Chronicles 29:14). This must be kept before the people wherever we go—that we possess nothing, can offer nothing in value, in work, in faith, which we have not first received of God and upon which He can lay His hand any time and say, They are Mine—gifts and blessings and endowments I entrusted to you, not to enrich yourself, but for wise improvement to benefit the world" (*Faith and Works*, pp. 21, 22, italics added).

Summary

1. In Christ we meet the Father face to face.
2. In Christ the Father's holiness will consume sin out of us.

So, how do we get "in" Christ? We don't! We are already in Christ by promise.

1. When Adam sinned, we, being in his loins, did as he did and reaped the results—the law of sin in our members and a physical death from which there was no resurrection—by NO CHOICE OF OUR OWN.
2. Jesus Christ becomes the second Adam, taking all humanity into Himself by promise. When this last Adam lived a life of righteousness, we, being in Him by promise, did as He did and reaped the results—the spirit of life in Christ in our conscience and a physical resurrection from the death we received from the first Adam—by NO CHOICE OF OUR OWN.
3. In the first Adam we lost everything, even the right to breathe.
4. In the last Adam we gained everything back, even the promise to rise unto everlasting life!
5. After Adam sinned he could no longer choose for himself, his will was in Satan's control.
6. When Christ stepped into humanity, by promise, He set

man's will free to "choose you this day whom ye will serve" (Joshua 24:15).
7. The second Adam, Jesus Christ, demonstrated that by HIS CHOICES the results of what the first Adam did could be reversed, and they were.
8. By OUR CHOICES can the results of what the second Adam did also be reversed?

Chapter Two

Our Choices

All things are given us in the gift of Jesus Christ. But not every human being experiences all the "blessings" of the gift. As the last Adam, Christ balanced the scales as to what we lost through the sin of the first Adam by no choice of our own. As the second man He brings even greater blessings, and these blessings "every man can have . . . for the choosing" (A.T. Jones, *The 1895 General Conference Bulletin*, p. 269). Now the choices we make become relevant. Now the righteousness of the last Adam means all to everyone who believes. Now comes the understanding of how the last Adam can be "not as" and "much more" than the first Adam (Rom. 5:15-19). Christ not only balanced the results of Adam's sin, He also made provision for every man that will ever choose to commit sin, knowingly or unknowingly. It took only one man's choice to sin to bring condemnation of death to all. It took one man's entire life of choosing not to sin to give life back to all. We, through our own choices, have committed many offenses worthy of death. Jesus' perfect life is offered to us to give us eternal life in place of the second death we deserve. The blessings of this provision can be ours only by our choice, through the exercise of faith.

In Matthew 9:22 Christ said, "Thy faith has made thee whole." When I first became an Adventist, I was taught that we should ask for the gift we need and believe that God will give it to us if it is according to His will. I found that Waggoner believed that "faith does not make facts; it only lays hold of them" (The Glad Tidings, p. 199). I sought for harmony between these two ways of understanding faith. I found that the first is describing how we see faith at work; the second is describing how faith truly works, beneath the surface, where we can see only through the eyes of faith. The first also tends to insinuate that faith is a work that we do that moves God to do something for us. Waggoner's comment insinuates that God's work is already done and our exercise of faith only provides a channel through which He can dispense the blessings that He has for us.

For clarity let us look at the lesson that nature reveals—one half of what is needed for life is already in the organism (the mighty oak in the acorn); the other one half is found in the environment (water, sun, soil, air, etc.). The point at which these two halves meet is where our choices and the exercise of faith come into play.

The Mustard Seed

I looked at the scriptural lesson of faith as revealed in the story of the mustard seed told in Matthew 17:20. We tend to focus on the size of the mustard seed as compared to the mountain to be moved. Why? Because we are often too quick to judge truth by what we see, rather than look beneath the surface at what cannot be seen with the physical eye. Let us take a look at "how" the mustard seed grows. What manner of faith would the seed exercise that could enable it to move the mountain of dirt that lies above it?

When the mustard seed was created, the whole of the parent's life was planted therein, just as the mighty oak is in the acorn—the one half of life that is in the organism. The tiny mustard seed, by faith, lays hold of the fact that it is destined to be a mustard tree. It trustingly submits itself to be worked by its environment—the one half of life found without—even though it means death to the seed itself. The rain will soften the hard shell, causing it to fall away and enabling the life within to be brought forth. The fragile new life, so easily crushed between the fingers, has a vitality and a purpose that pushes the young plant upward, moving great obstacles out of its way.

"The seed has in itself a germinating principle, a principle that God Himself has implanted; yet if left to itself the seed would have no power to spring up" (*Christ's Object Lessons*, p. 63). "The germ in the seed grows by the unfolding of the life-principle which God has implanted. Its development depends upon no human power" (Ibid., p. 77).

Faith did not make the seed a mustard seed: "God giveth it a body as it hath pleased him, and to every seed his own body" (1 Cor. 15:38). Faith does not implant the germinating principle of life within the seed. God, through the parent tree, has done that beforehand. To become like its parent, the seed itself must consent to be softened, broken, and to fall away; a seed cannot be "quickened, except it die" (verse 36). The seed cannot destroy itself. It is the exercise of faith that enables the seed to be worked by the powers without—the rain, soil, sunshine, and air. The seed trusts that these powers from without will work within to bring forth the life that the parent planted therein—the two halves brought together as one. Note also that it is God who implanted the germinating principle in the seed, and it is only God who can bring that life forth. So it is with us.

"When the mustard seed is cast into the ground, the tiny germ lays hold of every element that God has provided for its nutriment, and it speedily develops a sturdy growth. If you have faith like this, you will lay hold upon God's word, and upon all the helpful agencies He has appointed. Thus your faith will strengthen, and will bring to your aid the power of heaven" (*The Desire of Ages*, p. 431).

Laying hold of God's Word is the laying hold of the facts as they really are—the mighty oak in the acorn. Laying hold upon the helpful agencies is our submitting our life to be worked by God, to allow His power from without to bring forth His "life principle" that lies buried within each of us.

"Consider, says Jesus, how the lilies grow; how, springing from the cold, dark earth, or from the mud of the river bed, the plants unfold in loveliness and fragrance. Who would dream of the possibilities of beauty in the rough brown bulb of the lily? But when the *life of God, hidden therein,* unfolds at His call in the rain and the sunshine, men marvel at the vision of grace and loveliness. *Even so will the life of God unfold in every human soul* that will yield itself to the ministry of His grace, which, free as the rain and the sunshine, comes with its benediction to all" (*Thoughts from the Mount of Blessing*, p. 97, italics added).

"That in the ages to come he might shew the exceeding riches of his grace in his kindness toward us through Christ Jesus. . . . For we are his workmanship, created in Christ Jesus unto good works, which God hath before ordained that we should walk in them" (Eph. 2:7, 10).

The Written Word and the Created Word are trying to tell us what the Living Word has already revealed to us: that the life we long to have put into our hearts is already in our possession. Our heavenly Parent, who loves everyone equally, has given it to us. We have before us, in the Written Word and the Living Word, a complete picture of who our Parent is and what His life was, as the "surety" of what we can become. But power must come from without "to call forth" the life within.

Find the spiritual counterparts to the rain (Holy Spirit), sunshine (the Sun of Righteousness), soil (the Word of God, Jesus Christ, love of God), air (atmosphere of heaven through continual attitude of prayer), and conditions of life (submission, rest, peace, openness to receiving and being worked on), and you shall find the "how" of reproducing the life of our Parent—as revealed through Jesus Christ. This is another whole study in itself.

Our Choices

The focus of the two Adams is to reveal to us the unseen facts about God and Christ and their relationship to us. By faith we must lay hold of these truths before we will trustingly submit to be worked upon completely from without.

In Christ by Promise

Jones looked at Christ as the last Adam, and he saw all humanity represented there. He taught that whatever Christ did, all humanity has done in him. Whatever Christ received, all humanity received in him. For example, in lesson 15, given at the General Conference Session of 1895, Jones presents Christ in the Psalms. He shows "how entirely the Psalms mean Christ, and that the one whose experience is recorded there is Christ" (*The 1895 General Conference Bulletin*, p. 299). Then Jones asks these questions in reference to Psalms 23:

"Who? Me, a sinner?—one laden with sins? Will he lead me in the path of righteousness?—Yes. How do you know? He did it once. In Christ he led me in the paths of righteousness once, for his name's sake, a whole lifetime. *Therefore I know that in Christ he will lead me,* a sinful man, again and ever in the paths of righteousness for his name's sake. That is faith" (Ibid., p. 300, italics added).

A few pages later he finishes his thought:

"But who was he [Christ]? He was ourselves. Then God has demonstrated once in the world, and to the universe, that he will so come to me and you; and so live with us, as we are in the world to-day; and will cause his grace and his power to so abide with us; that, in spite of our sinfulness, in spite of all our weaknesses, the righteousness and the holy influence of God will be manifested to men, instead of ourselves and our sinfulness" (Ibid., p. 302).

As Christians we desire to have Christ's life developed in us. But we tend to forget the balance of being in Christ. A plant does not say to the soil, "Give me what I need, that I may go my way." Likewise, we are not to come to Christ, get what we need, and then go our way until another need arises. No. As the plant must abide in the soil, so we are to abide in Christ and remain in Him by faith. Only in Him can we reap the blessing of what He has done for us as the last Adam, just as a plant must develop deep roots in the soil to grow to full maturity.

Listen to Jones:

"First of all I would call especial attention to that expression 'in him.' This expression is not used in the Scriptures and I shall never expect to use it, in any such sense as that it is in him as in a receptacle, or a reservoir, to which we are to go and take out what we may need, and put it upon us, or apply it to ourselves. No, no, no! That is not it. It can never be gotten in that way....

"No; it is in him, and we ourselves are to be in him, in order to have it. We are to sink ourselves in him. Our self is to be lost in him. Then he has us....

"Many people make a mistake here. They say, 'Oh yes, I believe on him. I know it is in him, and I get it from him.' And they propose to take it from him and apply it to themselves. Then soon they become quite well satisfied that they are righteous; they are holy; and they get so far along at last that in their estimation it is a settled fact that they are perfect, and just cannot sin, and are even beyond temptation. Such a view is certain to bring only such a result; because it is out of him. And it is themselves who are doing it.

"But that is not the way; that is self still; because it is out of Christ.... No; we are to go to him for it, there is where it is; and when we go to him, we are to enter into him by faith and the Spirit of God, and there remain and ever 'be found in him.' Phil. 3:9" (*The 1895 General Conference Bulletin*, p. 217).

In Christ by Faith

Ellen White also states how important it is to abide in Christ. "Our first and highest duty is to know that we are abiding in Christ. He must do the work; but we are to seek to know what saith the Lord, yielding our lives to his guidance . . . every invitation he gives to us to seek the Lord, is a call to abide in him. It is an invitation not merely to come to him, but to remain in him" (*The Review and Herald*, September 18, 1900).

We are in Christ Jesus by His covenant of promise, but the question is, "Are we in Him by living faith?" The seed can be in the soil, but if the rain is not allowed to do its work, the seed maintains its hard shell and the life of the parent remains buried within. Without the work of the Holy Spirit, the hard shell of self in us remains untouched. The germinating principle of the spirit of life within remains only a promise. Once the rain has softened the hard shell and the life is being brought forth, can a plant continue to exist if you uproot it from the soil? No! It must remain in the soil or lose its life.

The following texts speak to this truth:

"I count all things but loss for the excellency of the knowledge of Christ Jesus my Lord: for whom I have suffered the loss of all things, and do count them but dung, that I may win Christ, And *be found in him*, not having mine own righteousness, which is of the law, but that which is through the faith of Christ, the righteousness which is of God by faith" (Phil. 3:8, 9, italics added).

"Even the righteousness of God which is by faith of Jesus Christ unto all and upon all them that believe" (Rom. 3:22).

The righteousness of God, which was revealed by the faith of Jesus, may be unto all, but it is only upon all who believe. As we abide in Christ by faith, His righteousness will be seen upon us. In the unbeliever the righteousness of God remains hidden within the hard shell of self—for they "hold the truth in unrighteousness" (Rom. 1:18).

Christ in You by Promise

Waggoner said that "Christ is in every man . . . He is in the sinner, in order that the sinner may have every incentive and facility for turning from sin to righteousness. . . . But, although He is in every man, not every man has His righteousness manifested in his life; for some 'hold down the truth in unrighteousness.' Rom. 1:18. R.V. . . . The difference, then, between the sinner and the Christian is this: that, whereas Christ crucified and risen is in every man, in the sinner He is there unrecognized and ignored, while in the Christian He dwells there by faith" (The Glad Tidings, pp. 88, 89).

"'As many as received Him, to them gave He power to become the sons of God, even to them that believe on His name.' John 1:12. That is, as many as believed on His name received Him. To believe on His name is to believe He is the Son of God; to believe that He is the Son of God, means to believe that He is come in the flesh, in human flesh, in our flesh, for His name is 'God with us;" so to believe on His name means simply to believe that He dwells personally in every man,--in all flesh. We do not make it so by believing it; it is so, whether we believe it or not; we simply accept the fact, which all nature reveals to us" (Ibid., pp. 80, 81).

Christ is said to be the "gift" given to this world from God, our loving Father. (See John 3:16.) I once heard a sermon where it was shown that many of the truths of God have their parallels in the law of the land. For instance, the definition of "pardon" in a book of law can sound amazingly "scriptural," as if taken from the Bible itself. In this sermon the speaker (a professor of law at a nearby university) defined the qualifications that a "gift" must meet before the law will recognize it as a true "gift." The qualifications are:

1. Must be donated—given with no required return of payment or compensation.
2. Must be delivered.
3. Must be received.

Far too often the gift of Christ is presented as separate from us and there is something we have yet to do in order to receive Him into our hearts. This sermon showed me that in order for Christ to be, by law, a true gift, He must not only have been given but also delivered and received! The proof that He has been given, delivered, and received lies in the very fact that we have breath in our nostrils and a beat in our hearts. (See Romans 10:6-8.)

If I were to give a juicer to someone who is ill and in need of fresh juices, of what value is the gift if it is put upon a shelf, hid in a closet, and never seen? What value is the gift if it is displayed prominently and proudly upon the kitchen counter, but never used? The full value of the gift is only realized as the receiver allows the gift to become an integral part of his life. And so it is with the gift of Christ. Although given to all, only those who by faith value the gift and allow it to be appropriated into their life can reap the full blessings of the gift—character transformation and eternal life.

If the gift of life were not already there in the seed, it would be infertile, impossible ever to be a living plant. God gave this principle of Christ's life to every human being. Not to do so would be to uphold the idea that God has already predetermined those who are to be saved and those who are to be lost—that some can never be saved no matter what they do!

Christ in You by Faith

Being no respecter of persons, God has given the life of His Son to every human being born of the loins of the first Adam. Nature tells us that just because a seed has the germ of life within there is no guarantee that every fertile seed will find good soil, take root, and grow into a mature plant. But the life within is its only hope of ever being like its parent—"Christ in you, the hope of glory" (Col. 1:27). Remember, there are conditions that must be met before the life within can be manifested. Here is where our exercise of faith enters the picture. Here lies the difference between the believer and the unbeliever—not who has Christ and who does not, but who exercises faith and who does not.

Waggoner stated that the reason "nine hundred and ninety-nine thousandths of the preaching of the gospel" in his day "did not reach the people" was that the "connection between God and man," between Christ and man, "was not made" (*The 1897 General Conference Bulletin*, p. 85). There was always a space left for us to close, a gulf for man to cross. The message of the Lord, through Jones and Waggoner, closed this gap.

Jones clearly taught that all humanity is in Christ, by no choice of our own. Waggoner taught that Christ is in all humanity, by no choice of our own. Not to recognize that every seed was once in the "loins" of its parent is to deny the principle revealed by the Spoken Word of Genesis 1:11. Not to give the life of Christ to all humanity is to deny the very laws of the natural world. But always remember that the life God has given only He can bring forth: "As in nature, so in grace" (*Christ's Object Lessons*, p. 65). The same principles found in the Created Word have their parallel in the Written Word.

"The seed has in itself a germinating principle, a principle that God Himself has implanted; yet if left to itself the seed would have no power to spring up. . . . There is life in the seed, there is power in the soil; but unless infinite power is exercised day and night, the seed will yield no returns. The showers of rain must refresh the thirsty fields;

the sun must impart warmth; electricity must be conveyed to the buried seed. The life which the Creator has implanted, He alone can call forth. Every seed grows, every plant develops, by the power of God" (*Education*, p. 104).

Read this quote again, this time with its spiritual counterparts:

The conscience of man has in itself a germinating principle, the spirit of life in Christ, a principle that God Himself has implanted. Yet if left to itself, the conscience has no power to be awakened and quickened. There is life in the conscience, there is power in the Word of God, but unless infinite power is exercised day and night, through the prayer of faith, the conscience will yield no return. The Holy Spirit must refresh the mental faculties and soften the hardened heart, the stubborn will. The Sun of Righteousness must impart warmth, the power of God must be conveyed to the dormant spirit of life within the conscience. The life that the Creator has implanted, He alone can call forth. Every conscience grows; every conscience develops (conversion and character development) by the power of God.

To put the life of God into every human soul is not pantheism. To say that man can get in touch with this life within and bring it forth of himself is a pantheistic concept. Only God can call forth the life He has implanted. Also, to refer to this "life" as an essence or as an entity of some sort is also pantheism. This "life" implanted within is a principle, a power, and/or a presence. But it is not an entity with an existence of its own, in or out of the physical body, nor is it an essence with the attributes that belong only to God such as eternal (self) existence, creative power, infinite intelligence, etc.

"The theory that God is an essence pervading all nature is one of Satan's most subtle devices" (*Testimonies for the Church*, vol. 8, p. 291). Truth says that God is "the Presence that pervades all created things" (*Education*, p. 100). Ellen White also wrote, "A mysterious life pervades all nature...The same power that upholds nature, is working also in man" (Ibid., p. 99).

In the parable of the sower and the seed (Matt. 13:3-9), we usually focus on the Word of God as the seed that is planted in the soil of our hearts. There are great truths to be learned from this perspective. Ellen White brings them out very well in *Christ's Object Lessons*, pages 33-89. But, in the same context, Ellen White also reveals another perspective. She sees the seed as our self and Christ as the soil: "As the plant takes root in the soil, so we are to take deep root in Christ. As the plant receives the sunshine, the dew, and the rain, we are to open our hearts to the Holy Spirit" (p. 66).

She recognizes a dual application, but does not expound upon it. The message that Jones and Waggoner were presenting she called "the matchless charms of Christ" (*The Ellen G. White 1888 Materials*, p. 348). In their teachings she recognized a familiar note and commented, "every fiber of my heart said, Amen" (Ibid.). Jones and Waggoner elaborated upon this second application with great clarity. Jones focused on the assurance of what the seed (humanity) was, is, and can become as revealed by its parent—Jesus Christ. Waggoner focused on what the seed was, is, and can become as revealed in what the parent gave to the seed—the whole of Christ's life, the germ of life within. Both men understood the condition of faith, trust, and obedience before the life of the parent could be revealed.

Growing up in Christ

A seed will go through many changes as it grows from a young sprout into a mature, fruit bearing plant. I noticed that I too was going through changes in my view of Christ and what I laid hold of by faith. When I first came to Christ, I found myself in the "courtyard" experience of the sanctuary. Jesus Christ was held up before me as the Lamb slain—as my Substitute. I learned that Christ accepted me just as I am.

My faith laid hold of a work done for me by Christ. I came to the cross a sinner, and I returned free from condemnation, forgiven and full of peace and joy. My focus was upon Christ who loved me enough to die a horrible death just for me. I was now justified—declared innocent. My past was wiped clean, and I was ready to live my life for Christ.

Having by faith taken my place as a member of God's family, a child of the High Priest, I could now go into the holy place of the sanctuary. Every article of furniture there depicted a close walk with Jesus. As I looked at the High Priest, I found Christ lifted up before me as my Example. His garments of glory revealed a life of perfect obedience to His Father, and He was calling me to become like Him. My faith laid hold of a work to be done in me by Christ. My focus was now upon Jesus Christ and the righteous life He lived and wanted to live in me. I sought the Holy Spirit to empower me to do as He did, to sanctify me—to cleanse me and make me pure. I entered into the process of sanctification.

How this work is to be done continues to be a big question for many today. We study the life of Christ, the pattern set before us, and we strive to be like Him, asking God to give us the wisdom and the strength to do what is right. We find many sincere people telling us all about *what* we are to be. But few are telling us *how* to be like Him. Ellen White gives us an insight:

"It is the Holy Spirit, the Comforter, which Jesus said He would send into the world, that changes our character into the image of Christ; and when this is accomplished, we reflect, as in a mirror, the glory of the Lord. That is, the character of the one who thus beholds Christ is so like His, that one looking at him sees Christ's own character shining out as from a mirror. *Imperceptibly* to ourselves we are changed day by day from our own ways and will into the ways and will of Christ, into the loveliness of His character. Thus we grow up into Christ, and *unconsciously reflect His image*.

"Professed Christians keep altogether too near the lowlands of earth. Their eyes are trained to see only commonplace things, and their minds dwell upon the things their eyes behold. Their religious experience is often shallow and unsatisfying, and their words are light and valueless. How can such reflect the image of Christ? How can they send forth the bright beams of the Sun of Righteousness into all the dark places of the earth? To be a Christian is to be Christlike.

"Enoch kept the Lord ever before him and the Inspired Word says that he 'walked with God.' He made Christ his constant companion. He was in the world, and performed his duties to the world; but he was ever under the influence of Jesus. He reflected Christ's character, exhibiting the same qualities of goodness, mercy, tender compassion, sympathy, forbearance, meekness, humility, and love. His association with Christ day by day transformed him into the image of Him with whom he was so intimately connected. Day by day he was growing away from his own way into Christ's way, the heavenly, the divine, in his thoughts and feelings. He was constantly inquiring, Is this the way of the Lord? His was a constant growth, and he had fellowship with the Father and the Son. This is genuine sanctification" (*The SDA Bible Commentary*, vol. 6, p. 1097 and *The Review and Herald*, April 28, 1891, italics added).

Jesus says to consider the lilies, how they grow, they neither toil nor spin (Matt. 6:28). Ellen White sees that this change in our character, which we so desire, happens "imperceptibly" and "unconsciously." So how does the lily grow?

In Lessons on Faith, pages 15-44, Jones took faith to a depth I had not seen before. In the story of the centurion, there is revealed a faith that laid hold of the fact that when Christ spoke there was power in the word itself to accomplish what it said. Jesus Himself called this "great faith" (Matt. 8:4-10). Jones taught that when we read the Bible and learn to "hear" God speak to us, then faith can lay hold of that "spoken" word and know "it is done" in us. Three years later, again commenting on the creative power in the Word of God, Jones said:

"We are his workmanship, created in Christ Jesus. Then the first step, you see, in Christianity, the first step in the course which God would have men take, can be taken only by creation, can be taken only by our being created....

"And the great beauty of that truth is that it is so easy for it all to be done. For when we have it settled that it can be done only by creation, self is utterly lost, you see: he knows that there is no source of creation in him: he simply has to quit. And when he knows that it can be done only by creation, and is brought face to face with the Creator, then it is easy; for God can create simply by speaking the word, 'He spake, and it was....'

"We become Christians only by creation; we remain Christians only by creative power; we grow in Christian grace only by successive creations of God. There is no development in Christian life except by the direct creative power of God from heaven, through his word, by the Holy Spirit...

"O when we know that the true progress, the true growth of the Christian life, the true development of the Christian heart, is by the successive creations of God, through His spoken word in the Spirit, then all that is needed is to find the word; and it is done. Here is the true remedy" (*The 1901 General Conference Bulletin*, pp. 103, 104).

"The plant grows by receiving that which God has provided to sustain its life. It sends down its roots into the earth. It drinks in the sunshine, the dew, and the rain. It receives the life-giving properties from the air" (*Christ's Object Lessons*, p. 66). When these right conditions for growth are met, the lily "unfolds in loveliness and fragrance."

As "the life of God, hidden therein, *unfolds at His call* in the rain and the sunshine" a series of successive creations of new cells take place, and "men marvel at the vision of grace and loveliness" (*Thoughts from the Mount of Blessing*, p. 97, italics added).

I looked beneath the surface of how you and I grow from babies into adults and realized it was by successive creation and re-creation of new cells. I believe our Christian growth must also be accomplished through constant creative power, re-creating us new at each stage of development, as we yield ourselves "to the ministry of His grace, which, free as the rain and the sunshine, comes with its benediction to all" (Ibid.). To grow into the full stature of Christ we must simply meet the conditions of life. The growing will come naturally. Creation is not our work; it is God's. Our work is to "be still, and know that I am God"—to rest and be open to receive. Remember, "by beholding, we are changed" and "in Christ we are a new creation." Here I have found great power and experienced many victories.

Preparing to Stand

Up to this point in my Christian walk I had been looking at the Christ who walked this earth and the Christlike life I was trying to live for Him. One day, while in prayer, these words came to me: "You are looking to the wrong Christ!" This set me back on my heels in shock. What did God mean I was looking to the "wrong Christ"? Over the next few days I found my attention being drawn to the Christ who now stands in heaven above.

The first and second angel's messages of Revelation 14, with the midnight cry of 1844, were "to prepare them to enter with Jesus by faith into the most holy place of the heavenly sanctuary" (*Early Writings*, p. 260). The third angel's message was to show "the way into the most holy place" (Ibid.).

Our Choices

The anti-typical Day of Atonement has arrived. We are to be in the Most Holy Place of the heavenly sanctuary today, by faith, "cooperating with Christ in the work of preparing our souls to reflect the divine image" (*The SDA Bible Commentary*, vol. 7, p. 933).

"This is the great day of atonement, and our Advocate is standing before the Father, pleading as our intercessor. In place of wrapping about us the garments of self-righteousness, we should be found daily humbling ourselves before God, confessing our own individual sins, seeking the pardon of our transgressions, and cooperating with Christ in the work of preparing our souls to reflect the divine image. *Unless we enter the sanctuary above, and unite with Christ* in working out our own salvation with fear and trembling, we shall be weighed in the balances of the sanctuary, and shall be pronounced wanting" (Ibid., italics added).

As I studied into the Most Holy Place, I found that another picture of Jesus Christ and another level of faith began to emerge. Only here, in the Most Holy place in the heavenly sanctuary, did I find the message I believe will lead God's people to lighten the earth with God's glory. Jones and Waggoner are said to be the beginning of the loud cry of the third angel which is to prepare a people "to stand in the hour of temptation, which they are soon to meet" (*Selected Messages*, vol. 1, p. 363, and *Early Writings*, p. 277). Looking into the "Most Holy Place" I caught the same revelation of Christ and His Oneness with humanity as I saw in their writings. With this increased depth of knowledge of Christ's relationship to man, through the understanding of the two Adams, also came another level of faith. Listen to Jones as he comments on Galatians 2:20.

"We hear people so many times say, 'I want self to be crucified.' Well, we turn and read the text to them, 'Knowing this, that our old man is crucified.' And they respond: 'Well I wish it were so.'" Turn to the next text, and read: 'I am crucified with Christ.' It says I am. Who is? Are you? Still they answer: 'I don't see that I am. I wish it were so; but I cannot see how I am crucified, and I cannot see how reading that there, and saying that that is so, will make it so.' But the word of God says so, and it is so because it says so, and it would be true and everlastingly effectual if that were all there is to it. But in this case it is so because it is so. God does not speak that word to make it so in us; he speaks that word because it is so in us, in Christ....

"Our old man is crucified; yet when God sets forth his word that it is so, we accepting that word, and surrendering to it, it is so to each one who accepts it because the word has the divine power in it to cause it to be so. And by that means it would be everlastingly so, even if that were all there is to it. But that is not all there is to it; because in Jesus Christ human nature has been crucified on the cross, actually, literally; and that is my human nature, that is myself in him that was crucified there....Therefore, we can say with perfect freedom,—it is no boasting, it is not presumption in any sense; it is simply the confession of faith in Christ—'I am crucified with Christ'" (*The 1895 General Conference Bulletin*, p. 351).

Waggoner also writes about this level of faith:

"For every soul the victory has been gained, and the enemy has been disarmed. We have only to accept the victory which Christ has won. The victory over all sin is already a reality; our faith in it makes it real to us. The loss of faith puts us outside the reality, and the old body of sin looms up again. That which is destroyed by faith is built up again by unbelief. Remember that this destruction of the body of sin, although performed by Christ for all, is, nevertheless, a present personal matter with each individual" (The Glad Tidings, p. 38).

Through the messages of Jones and Waggoner, Jesus Christ was lifted up before me as my Surety, my Righteousness. They directed my faith to lay hold of a finished work in me in Christ. My focus became the Christ who now stood before the throne of God in glorified humanity. My need was to sink myself into Him by faith. Then, hidden in Him, I could also stand before the throne surrounded by the glory of God. My faith would truly be the channel for that glory to consume sin out of me and reveal God's glory upon this earth through the instrument of my humanity.

Henry Soltau, in his book *The Holy Vessels and Furniture of the Sanctuary*, printed in 1851, says it very well:

"The teaching of the Spirit of God is (if we may use the expression), from heaven to earth, and not from earth to heaven. He would fix our faith steadfastly on the fact that 'old things are passed away, and all things are become new.' He would instruct us as to the entire destruction of the flesh in the death of Jesus for us, and in our consequent life and resurrection with Christ risen and glorified; and having fastened our souls on these blessed facts, and thus rooted and grounded us in Christ, He would then make these truths to be the practical power of our walk and conduct on earth; so that we come back again to earth from heaven, to walk here below as a heavenly people, following the steps of that blessed one who came forth into the world from the Father. Unhappily too much of the teaching of the present day is of the reverse order—an attempt to lead to heaven by means of a clean walk on earth, instead of presenting a clean walk on earth as the result of being already 'seated in heavenly places in Christ'" (p. 120).

Seeing the Unseen

Through the work of the Holy Spirit, I had come to Christ seeing myself as a slave to sin, full of guilt and condemnation. I came in search of forgiveness and deliverance. My faith laid hold of what He did for me upon the cross. As He forgave me, I experienced great joy and found a new sense of freedom. Now, I see that what I experienced at that point was the "blessings" of what Jesus Christ had already accomplished for me in His own life, death, and resurrection. My faith did not make it a fact; it only enabled me to experience the blessings of what Christ Jesus had already gained for me in Himself.

In my Christian walk, I had been exercising faith by trusting in God to do a work in me. At my baptism He had revealed to me the power of the Holy Spirit. He met me at Sinai as I, like the children of Israel, determined to do all that He said to do. He then took me to Creation and there I learned that the change I so desired could only be accomplished by His creative power. All the time He was working with me, drawing me ever nearer to see the deeper truth—sanctification is also a finished work in Jesus Christ. It is a work of a lifetime as lived out in us during our walk upon this earth—we have much yet to learn and faith must be constantly exercised through our freedom to choose. It takes time for the seed to develop to the full maturity as revealed in the parent. But Christ is our sanctification, just as truly as He is our justification. (See 1 Corinthians 1:30.) In our humanity that is in Him, it is a finished work.

In the Most Holy Place I began to see where justification and sanctification came together as a perfect whole, where "mercy and truth are met together; righteousness and peace have kissed each other" (Ps. 85:10). Here *Faith and Works* found their true relationship. We need to learn about these concepts individually before we can grasp the whole picture. Much of our present understanding of these terms is based upon our own experience, which is only natural. But now is the time to think as a man, to put away childish perspectives, to learn to see beneath the surface, to judge truth, not by what we see, feel, and hear, but by what God sees, feels, and hears. We need to learn to walk in the Spirit and not in the flesh. We need to learn to see the unseen and to live as though that were the only truth.

For example, by sight we see the sun rise in the east and set in the west. The earth appears flat as far as the eye can see. At one time in this earth's history these "observations" were held to be "facts of truth." Scientists have since discovered the earth is round and revolves around the sun. Many of our ancestors thought Columbus was a fool. By "observation" only the world still appears flat. But, in the face of scientific discovery, today you and I would be thought a "fool" if we still believed as our ancestors once did.

If we are to get through the exceeding darkness of sin that is fast coming upon this earth, we need to discover the true facts concerning the "unseen" kingdom of God. Only then will we be able to stand when the whole world, caught up in the deceptions of sin, declares us the "fool." To judge truth, at that time, by our own experiences and observations will be to our eternal ruin.

"If ye then be risen with Christ, seek those things which are above, where Christ sitteth on the right hand of God. Set your affections on things above, not on things on the earth" (Col. 3:1, 2).

Hide-and-Seek

This idea of a changing perspective of truth and an ever-expanding understanding of the gospel can also be demonstrated through a game familiar to all—hide-and-seek. Assuming, as children, we have all played the game, or at least have heard of the game, how would you play hide-and-seek with an infant or a small toddler? The underlying principle will remain the same, but the game takes on a new name with the rules altered slightly. We call it peekaboo. The infant or toddler cannot possibly enter into the game as older children will, so the one doing the seeking is also doing the hiding. The child has only to watch and enjoy.

Think it through and this is how we relate to the gospel in the courtyard. We are infants in Christ. We are simply observing, and Christ is the one doing all the work. As we "behold" and rest in His love, we enjoy the blessings of His work of redemption for us.

As the child grows older he or she starts to take an active part in the game, now referred to as hide-and-seek. The game is first played in the home. Next might be the backyard. Children may play the game at school or even in the park. Each level and place requires greater physical participation and mental exercising on the part of the child.

Just so, as we grow up in Christ, we find our role becomes more active and our minds expand in wrestling with the Scriptures. Our witnessing and Christian influence begins in the home and extends to school and friends, to the workplace, to different parts of the city, and even to other countries. Our focus changes from Christ doing all the work for us to the work we have to do in cooperation with Him. It is in the holy place we find symbolized what God will do for us and what He expects to be revealed in us as we seek to become one with Him.

When we become adults we cease to play hide-and-seek. We may still play peekaboo with toddlers and hide-and-seek with our children, but the game is generally not played among adults. Perhaps I should say the child's "game of fun" becomes a "game of life" when "played" by adults, such as a child being protected from an abusive parent, a wife seeking shelter from an abusive husband, or a witness hiding from a potential killer. As an adult you would not "play" hide-and-seek, and definitely not peek-a-boo, with someone who wishes you bodily harm. On the converse, you could not "play" witness protection with an infant or even a small child. They could not possibly understand what you are doing.

So it is with the gospel. God reaches us at the level at which we can understand and enter into a relationship with Him. As He draws us closer to Him, we grow in understanding and the simple gospel of the courtyard takes on a previously unseen breadth and depth. Eventually there will come a time in our Christian walk when, like Paul, we must say, "When I was a child I spake as a child, I understood as a child, I thought as a child: but when I became a man, I put away childish things" (1 Cor. 13:11). "Therefore, leaving the principles [beginnings] of the doctrine of Christ, let us go on unto perfection" (Heb. 6:1).

As adults, the principle of the game hide-and-seek may remain the same, but the name changes to Child Protection Agency or perhaps Home for Battered Women. This game of life finds its fullest expression in what is called the Witness Protection Program. The one doing the hiding changes his name, alters his appearance, takes on a new occupation, and moves to a new location. The one doing the seeking must stretch every faculty of his mind if he wants to find the one hiding.

Today, God is calling us to "seek ye the LORD while he may be found" (Isa. 55:6). God did the seeking to find us when we were infants in spiritual things. Now He is calling upon us to stretch our mind to find Him where He and His Son are now.

In AD 32 Jesus Christ changed His name from Lamb of God to High Priest. He changed His appearance from a man with sinful flesh, to a man with holy flesh. His occupation changed from sacrificial Lamb to Mediator, and He moved from this earth to heaven. In 1844 He moved again, this time into the Most Holy Place of the heavenly sanctuary. What many Adventists fail to recognize is He changed His garments just as Aaron did. In Leviticus 16 Aaron is instructed to put off his garment—the garment of glory—and to put on the holy linen garments—the simple white robe similar to those worn by the sons of the high priest. The Son of God, also the Son of Man, would not enter the presence of His Father radiating His own glory. He came before His Father wearing the white robe of the righteousness of Christ woven in heaven by His Father while Jesus walked this earth, the robe woven without one thread of human devising.

Note again, the garment the high priest is wearing is very similar to the white robe that the sons wear. Here we see that Christ, our High Priest, stands as the representative of all those who have believed in His mercy and by faith are seeking to follow Him. As a sinner we could enter the courtyard, but we could go no further into the sanctuary. Having by faith taken our place as "sons" of the High Priest, we can venture into the holy place and learn the many lessons there. But only the High Priest can enter into the Most Holy Place. Only as we become one with Him, hidden in Him by faith, can we enter therein, having also shed the garments of our own glory and wearing only the white robe of Christ's righteousness. We must exercise every faculty of our being to find Christ where He now is. We must "know" His name (character), what garment He wears, and the work He is doing, as well as where He is located.

Christ is not "hiding" from us, but He knows a much greater work is yet to be done in and through us. What was done with the blood on the Day of Atonement gives us an insight to this work. I believe the blood of the goat—an offering for sin but with no sins confessed upon it—represents the message of Christ's righteousness that comes in to judge God's professed people. It falls only upon those who have found their way into the Most Holy Place, those who came in through the three angels' messages. Those who are resting solely in the mercy of God as represented by the blood of the bullock—a sin offering upon whose head all the sins of the household of the high priest were confessed.

I have come to believe it is a grave mistake to start the services of the Day of Atonement with the blood of the goat, thinking the blood of the bullock is simply a preparatory service for the high priest. In the

Our Choices

Mishna there is told what was done with both of these bloods while the high priest was officiating in the Most Holy Place. After the sprinkling of the goat's blood, over the same places as was sprinkled the blood of the bullock earlier in the day, the container with the blood of the bullock was emptied into the container with the blood of the goat. The now mixed blood was poured back into the empty container that had held the blood of the bullock. The container with the now mixed blood was carried out to make atonement in the rest of the sanctuary.

How fitting a symbol is this! Those who have entered into the Most Holy Place claiming the blood of mercy (represented by the bullock) hear the message of Christ's righteousness (represented by the goat) and willingly stand up to be judged by that message. Consequently they empty their life entirely by faith into Jesus Christ. Once emptied completely of self—the glory of man laid in the dust—Christ now fills them with His life of perfect righteousness and He carries them forward to do the final work prior to His coming to the earth a second time.

Where are you in your Christian walk? Are you still in the courtyard playing peekaboo, crying, "Christ did it all at the cross, I only have to believe"? Or are you in the holy place all caught up in the part you have to play, the work you have to do? Christ is now in the Most Holy Place in the heavenly sanctuary, and if you have not entered therein, you will need to stretch every faculty of your being to find Him while He may yet be found—while the censor still burns.

Soon the final atonement will have been made and Christ will be changing His name again from High Priest to Lord of Lords and King of Kings. He will put off His priestly garments and put on the garments of wrath. He will return to this earth, and His work will be to reward His faithful waiting ones with life everlasting and to silence the wicked and bring an end to sin. Will you, by faith, be following

Christ when He comes? (See Revelation 14:15, 17.) Or, will He find you among those who are still running and hiding from Him? (See Revelation 6:15-17.)

Summary

1. All humanity is in Christ by promise; the question is, Are you abiding in Him by faith?
2. Christ is in all humanity by promise, but does He abide in you by living faith?
3. Our view of Christ and the gospel is progressive:
   a. Justification: Christ did it all for me—I only have to believe.
   b. Sanctification: Christ is my example—He empowers me to do as He did.
   c. Glorification: In Christ the "work is finished"—I rest in Him and He works in me. (Christ "walked this earth as one already glorified," should we not do the same? Are we to wait for the resurrection to experience glorification?)
4. Our view of *Faith and Works* is progressive:
   a. We are saved by faith alone without works—courtyard experience
   b. We are saved by faith with works (obedience to the ten commandment law)—holy place experience
   c. Salvation is a "finished work" in Christ, which I lay hold of by faith. As I abide in Christ by faith, He works out His righteousness in me for all to see—Most Holy Place experience
5. Each statement in #3 and #4 are true in their place. But the question is, Where does our focus need to be for the times we are now living in? What "truths" do we need to get us through

the trying times that lie ahead for God's people?
6. What is your understanding of the gospel? What is your view of the relationship between *Faith and Works*? Do you know where you are in the sanctuary?

Chapter Three

Familiar Stories Re-Examined

A major portion of Ellen White's work was to show us the way into the Most Holy Place as she uplifted the message of the three angels of Revelation 14. The message of the angel of Revelation 18 is to prepare a people to stand in the hour of temptation that is coming upon this earth. This trial will require an even greater depth of faith than we have heretofore exercised. Ellen White recognized this level of faith. It apparently was not her work to speak or write upon it as clearly as did Jones and Waggoner. Although it is woven into her writings, it can easily be overlooked. Read the story of the man at the pool of Bethesda presented in *The Ministry of Healing*, pages 81-85.

The Man at the Pool of Bethesda

Christ comes to the man in his crippled condition, and He asks, "Wilt thou be made whole?" (John 5:6). For a moment hope came to the man's heart. Then he remembers how often he had tried to reach the pool, how often he had failed, and that no one had been there to help him. He turns away wearily. Jesus commands him, "Rise, take up thy bed, and walk" (verse 8).

Ellen White tells us:

"Jesus had given the palsied man no assurance of divine help. The man might have said, 'Lord, if Thou wilt make me whole, I will obey Thy word.' He might have stopped to doubt, and thus have lost his one chance of healing" (*The Ministry of Healing*, p. 84).

"Of ourselves we are no more capable of living a holy life than was the impotent man capable of walking. Many realize their helplessness; they are longing for that spiritual life which will bring them into harmony with God, and are striving to obtain it. But in vain" (Ibid.).

Why do we strive in vain? Many are waiting until they "feel" they are made whole before they will believe that God will give, or has given, them the power to obey.

"But no, he believed Christ's word" (Ibid.).

What "word" did the sick man believe? The only words Christ spoke were "Wilt thou be made whole?" and "Rise, take up thy bed and walk." As the sick man looked into the face of Jesus, he caught a glimpse of what we have yet to learn. You and I need to look steadfast into the face of Jesus until we see what this man saw. We need to behold the love and power he saw there. We need to learn the depth of what he learned. Because he "believed that *he was made whole*; immediately he made the effort, and God gave him the power; he willed to walk, and he did walk. Acting on the word of Christ, *he was made whole*" (Ibid., italics added).

"Love and power seem to breathe from His [Jesus'] very presence" (Ibid.). The sick man knew Jesus would not command him to do something which that love had not already made him capable of doing. He knew the power he saw in Jesus was just waiting for an opportunity to work in him. He did not wait to "feel" that he was made whole. His faith laid hold of the fact—the promise hidden in the command—that healing was already his. As the man chose to act upon that belief, God, the Father, gave the power and it was manifested for all to see—the man was made whole. Can we, by faith, do as this man did?

Take a glance at Ephesians 1 and catch just a glimpse of what is already ours in Christ:

"Blessed be the God and Father of our Lord Jesus Christ, who hath blessed us with all spiritual blessings in heavenly places in Christ: According as he hath *chosen us in him before the foundation of the world, that we should be holy and without blame before him in love: Having predestinated us unto the adoption of children by Jesus Christ* to himself, according to the good pleasure of his will, To the praise of the glory of his grace, wherein *he hath made us accepted in the beloved.* In whom *we have redemption through his blood, the forgiveness of sins,* according to the riches of his grace; Wherein he hath abounded toward us in all wisdom and prudence; Having made known unto us the mystery of his will, according to his good pleasure which he hath purposed in himself: That in the dispensation of the fulness of times he might gather together in one all things in Christ, both which are in heaven, and which are on earth; even in him: In whom also we have obtained an inheritance, being predestinated according to the purpose of him who worketh all things after the counsel of his own will: That we should be to the praise of his glory, who first trusted in Christ. In whom ye also trusted, after that ye heard the word of truth, the gospel of your salvation" (Eph. 1:3-13, italics added).

The acorn is "predestined" to be a mighty oak tree, but that is no guarantee it will ever become an oak tree. It is only the promise hidden within the hard shell, totally dependant upon the "conditions of life" being met. So it is with us.

Israel in Egypt

This principle of seeing a work that we believe has yet to be done as already being done came to my attention even before the Lord showed me the depth of the two Adams. I had been studying the story of the children of Israel, when they were in bondage to Egypt. I was reading in *The Spirit of Prophecy* about a new king that arose over Egypt who did not want to lose the labors of the Israelites so he had set taskmasters over them. I came across this sentence: "They compelled their women to work in the fields, as though they were slaves" (*The Spirit of Prophecy*, vol. 1, p. 161). The words "as though" seemed to leap from the page. What did this mean—"as though they were slaves"? I was always taught that the children of Israel were slaves.

Upon further study I discovered that the Israelites had gone into Egypt a free people by invitation, not having been conquered in battle; in fact, they were "more and mightier" than the Egyptians. During the famine they never sold their possessions, or themselves, into slavery as many Egyptians had done. Then I found this: "The children of Israel were not slaves" (Ibid., p. 159). (See also *Patriarchs and Prophets*, pp. 231-233, 281 and Exodus 1:9.)

The final, eye-opening fact concerning their condition of slavery came just as the Israelites were about to leave Egypt, following the last plague—the death of the firstborn sons. I read that they "spoiled" the Egyptians (Ex. 12:36). How?

"The Egyptians had been enriched by the labor unjustly exacted from the Israelites, and as the latter were about to start on the journey to their new home, it was right for them to claim the reward of their years of toil" (*Patriarchs and Prophets*, p. 253).

Since when can slaves claim a reward for their labor? I realized that the children of Israel were in truth a free people who had simply been deceived into slavery. This bothered me until I understood its implications. If they had been conquered in battle or sold into bondage, then their problem was their taskmasters. The solution was to break the power of Egypt so they could be free. But, if they were truly a free people, who had only been tricked into slavery, then their problem was not their slave-master; it was their own ignorance and their own fear. (See Hebrews 2:15.) They had lost sight of who the true God was to them and who they really were when they had entered Egypt. The first step toward a solution was knowledge: "Ye shall know the truth and the truth shall make you free" (John 8:32). And the second step was the assurance of God's power: "God is love . . . but perfect love casteth out fear" (1 John 4:16, 18).

God, in His mercy, met them where they were in what "they thought" was their need. He sent Moses, as their deliverer, and the power of Egypt was broken. The children of Israel went out free from temporal bondage. But was their real problem ever solved? (Read Psalms 105 and 106.) No, Israel constantly forgot their God. They had much to learn concerning God, His love for them, and their spiritual bondage to sin. (See *Patriarchs & Prophets,* p. 371.)

"Many years had the children of Israel been in servitude to the Egyptians....And being surrounded with idolatry, many of them had lost the knowledge of the true God, and had forgotten his law....Everything around the children of Israel was calculated to make them forget the living God....many of the Hebrews were content to remain in bondage rather that go to a new country and meet with the difficulties attending such a journey....The task of Moses would have been much easier had not many of the Hebrews become corrupted, and been unwilling to leave Egypt" (*The Spirit of Prophecy*, vol. 1, pp. 180, 181).

For many years we have been in servitude to the prince of this earth. Surrounded by idolatry we, too, have lost the knowledge of the true God and His law. Everything around us is calculated to make us forget the living God. Many today, even of God's professed people, are content to remain in bondage rather than face the difficulties that lie ahead.

Man tends to look at sight and circumstances to determine what is truth. To all outward appearances, the children of Israel were slaves in need of deliverance from their Egyptian overlords. They only had to believe that God sent Moses, obey all of God's commands, and wait till they could go out free. God sees beneath the surface of sight and circumstance. He is trying to get us to fix our eyes on the unseen truths. (See 2 Corinthians 4:18.) God knew all along that Israel was a free nation. Through the spoiling of the Egyptians, He tried to show them that which their years of ignorance and fear had hidden from their view. He tried to open their eyes to see the deception they had been under.

Have we opened our eyes? Or, like the Israelites, do we still think we are born "literally, in true fact," slaves to sin? Do we only have to believe that God sent Jesus as our deliverer, obey all His commandments, and wait for Him to lead us out of the bondage of sin? This may have been true when God "met us where we were" in bondage to "spiritual Egypt." But, today God calls His professed people to come out of Babylon, not Egypt!

Babylonian Bondage

They left Egypt with a certain level of love for God and trust in His power as a temporal Savior. But they did not yet exercise faith in Christ as a personal Savior from their own personal spiritual bondage. Many acknowledge Christ as the Savior of the world but do not allow Him to be to them a personal Savior. In not understanding their true problem, they eventually found themselves in bondage again—this time to Babylon, a nation representing a false religion. The light that Jones and Waggoner had is said to be the beginning of the message of the angel of Revelation 18, "Babylon the great is fallen, is fallen" (*The Review and Herald*, December, 6, 1892). There is a voice from heaven that comes as a result of this message: "Come out of her, my people, that ye be not partakers of her sins, and that ye receive not of her plagues" (Rev. 18:4).

We cannot come out of the bondage of spiritual Babylon with the same understanding of slavery as we had when we, by faith, came out of spiritual Egypt—when we knew little, if anything, of God. We need a depth of understanding that will open our eyes to see our real problem, our actual need, and the true solution. Our present understanding may be enough to keep us from falling back into the world but is it enough to get us out of Babylon—the confusion within the churches and in our own minds?

Jones wrote, "It is written that the people said to one another: 'Let us build us a city and a tower.' And the name which they gave the city was 'Babel.' At that time the meaning of the word 'Babel'—its original meaning—was 'Gate of God.' Accordingly, they said: 'Let us build us a city and a tower, whose top may reach unto heaven.'

"But, because of their pride and self-exaltation, their whole enterprise was turned so utterly into confusion that the word 'Babel' lost its original meaning of 'Gate of God,' and bore only the meaning of 'confusion.' And thus, that which originally meant the 'Gate of God' became only a symbol of 'confusion.'

"And this original meaning of 'Babel'—'Gate of God'—with its new meaning of 'confusion,' carries a lesson all the way through the whole subject of Babylon. It has its lessons now, in the phase of the threefold message which speaks of Babylon and her fall" (The Great Nations of Today, p. 137).

In reference to the second angel's message of Revelation 14, Ellen White says:

"The term Babylon, derived from Babel, and signifying confusion, is applied in Scripture to the various forms of false or apostate religion. But the message announcing the fall of Babylon must apply to some religious body that was once pure, and has become corrupt. It cannot be the Romish Church which is here meant; for that church

Familiar Stories Re-Examined

has been in a fallen condition for many centuries. But how appropriate the figure as applied to the Protestant churches, all professing to derive their doctrines from the Bible, yet divided into almost innumerable sects. The unity for which Christ prayed does not exist. Instead of one Lord, one faith, one baptism, there are numberless conflicting creeds and theories. Religious faith appears so confused and discordant that the world know not what to believe as truth. God is not in all this; it is the work of man,—the work of Satan" (*The Spirit of Prophecy*, vol. 4, p. 232).

The angel of Revelation 18 will repeat the message of the second angel of Revelation 14. If history is going to repeat itself, will another "once pure" church have become "corrupt"? Confusion is on every side, even within our own beloved Seventh-day Adventist Church. The world looks upon us and knows not what to believe as truth.

There is a poem about several blind men who went to see an elephant. Each had an opportunity to "see" a part of the elephant. Later, they argued long into the night as each tried to limit the whole of the elephant to only the part they, individually, "saw" and understood.

Are we doing the same? Can we not step back and let God give us a picture of the whole gospel, to see as He sees? Only God can bring the parts together as a perfect whole and put them in their proper place. Only as we sink deeper into Christ can we learn to see as God sees.

The illustration of the Emancipation Proclamation, signed by President Lincoln on January 1, 1863, can be used to help us grasp the significance of the message of the last Adam. That proclamation broke the power of the taskmaster over the slaves in the South. It "declared free all persons held as slaves within any state or part of a state then in armed rebellion" (World Book Dictionary). Not all slaves wanted to be free. Some slaves were kept ignorant of the proclamation. These "free persons" remained in bondage, some willingly, some unknowingly.

When the news of the proclamation came to the slave, he had a choice to make: to believe or not to believe in the validity of the proclamation. If believing it to be true, he had to choose to trust in the power behind that proclamation to uphold the freedom claimed for him. Did the slave have to wait for the power of the government to come down where he was and literally escort him off the field of slavery? No! Based on the declaration of the proclamation, the slave simply had to believe that he was a free man. Acting on that belief, he could choose to walk off the field of slavery—not to become free, but to experience the freedom that was already his.

Should the taskmaster refuse to allow the slave to leave and choose to whip him and cast him into a dark place bound in chains, what will be the reaction of the slave? If he thinks that his belief in and acting upon the proclamation is what "gained" his freedom for him, he will lose hope and sink into despair. But, if he walked off the field of slavery because he knew he was free, then, like Peter, he can sing even though imprisoned—they may destroy the body, but they cannot touch his spirit. Could this be the secret of rejoicing while in tribulation?

Christ is said to have signed our "emancipation papers" with His own blood. (See *The Ministry of Healing*, p. 90.) Although that blood was literally shed on the cross 2,000 years ago, we are told that Christ is the "Lamb slain from the foundation of the world" (Rev. 13:8). When the first man sinned, the second man, the Lord from heaven, immediately stepped on the scene. Those papers were signed, by promise, and every man was declared free in Christ—free to choose whom they will serve. For us, the question is, "Are you in Him by faith?"

"There is not a single soul that is bowed down with the weight of sin which Satan hath bound upon him, whom Christ does not lift up. Freedom is his; he has only to make use of it. Let the message be sounded far and wide. Let every soul hear it, that Christ has given

Familiar Stories Re-Examined

deliverance to every captive. . . . The thing is true, whether we believe it or not. . . . The message to us is that our 'warfare is accomplished,' our iniquity is pardoned. Is. 40:2" (E.J. Waggoner, The Glad Tidings, pp. 21, 22).

Waggoner refers to verse 2 in Isaiah 40. The first verse of that chapter says, "Comfort ye, comfort ye my people, saith your God." Ellen White tells us the last message of mercy to be given to the world is "behold your God," which is found in Isaiah 40:9. (See *Christ's Object Lessons*, p. 415.) Isaiah 40 also documents the message of John the Baptist: "The voice of him that crieth in the wilderness, Prepare ye the way of the LORD" (verse 3). He came in the spirit of Elijah, whose spirit is to sound once again in these last days to prepare the way of the Lord. (See Matthew 11:7-15 and Malachi 4:4-6.) The message of Isaiah 40 is to be spoken "comfortably" to Jerusalem (speak to the heart—the feelings, the will, and the intellect)—cry unto her that her "warfare is accomplished," her "iniquity is pardoned". Our emancipation papers have been signed! Can you hear the "comforting" sound?

Our own "taskmaster" may be Satan, the law of sin in our members, the guilt of sins committed, the fear of death, or our own ignorance of truth. (See John 8:32, 16:11; Hebrews 2:14, 15; Romans 7:23; and Colossians 1:2.) Whatever we think holds us in bondage to sin its power has been broken! However, we have been tricked and deceived into believing we are "literal" slaves with a taskmaster over us, whose power has yet to be broken. Too many of us are still looking for a deliverer to come and lead us out of bondage.

There was no Moses who came and delivered the children of Israel out of Babylon! The prophesied time arrived and the message was: "Who is there among you of all his people? his God be with him, and let him go up to Jerusalem . . . and build the house of the LORD God of Israel . . . which is in Jerusalem" (Ezra 1:3). Has not our prophesied time come? Are we not, by faith, traveling to the heavenly Jerusalem? Are we not being called today to do the same thing—to become living stones in the living temple of God? The voice from heaven says, "Come out of her my people."

How many times have we heard the call to "come out" defined as to separate from your church and come apart and join our church because we have the truth and your church does not? Notice, it is a "voice from heaven" that gives this call, not the "angel" who came down from heaven. God, Himself, will call "his people" to "come out of her." (Come out of the confusion that is Babylon.) It is not for us, as God's professed people, to call His people out of Babylon. In fact, the Bible itself defines what it means to be separated. Listen to what God says to Moses as they talk together on Mount Sinai.

"And he [God] said, My presence shall go with thee, and I will give thee rest. And he [Moses] said unto him, If thy presence go not with me, carry us not up hence. For wherein shall it be known here that I and thy people have found grace in thy sight? is it not in that thou goest with us? so shall we be separated, I and thy people, from all the people that are upon the face of the earth. And the LORD said unto Moses, I will do this thing also that thou hast spoken" (Ex. 33:16).

In 1844 the Midnight Cry that attended the second angel's message was "Behold, the Bridegroom cometh; go ye out to meet Him" (*Early Writings*, pp. 238, 242, 248, 249). Jesus said, "Come unto me, all ye that labour and are heavy laden" (Matt. 11:28), "come to me, that ye might have life" (John 5:40), and I and My Father are one (see John 17). To come out of Babylon is to come unto Jesus, which is to have God's presence with us making us a separated people, even though we are still in the midst of physical Babylon as was Daniel and his three friends. A time may come when God will call us to physically separate from our individual churches, but our present focus must be "knowing" we abide in Christ, with its consequent union with God, no matter where we are.

"Our truest unity, with other people, is our sole loneliness with God. Our truest fellowship, our sincerest love, our tenderest sympathy, our interaction with all people is found only in standing absolutely alone, separate from all things, with God." (*The 1901 General Conference Bulletin*, p. 103)

Summary

1. We need to "behold our God" until we see what the paralytic saw:
   a. A love that would not command us to do something that God's love had not already enabled us to do.
   b. A power that is just waiting to reveal Christ's "finished work" in us.
2. We need to lay hold of a "finished work," revealed in Christ, and choose to act as if that were the only truth, no matter what may be the "apparent reality" here on earth. When we do so, God will manifest that finished work in us for all to see.
3. There will be no "Moses" to lead us out of Babylon. It is our choice to act upon the command to "go up to Jerusalem and build the house of the Lord."
4. To "come out of Babylon" is to come unto Jesus, to find our "sole loneliness with God."
5. What barriers may stand in our way to laying hold of this "finished work" with the level of faith needed?

Chapter Four

The Law and The Gospel

I have come to believe that it will be difficult to get out of Babylon and find that perfect union with God until we better understand how the law and the gospel relate to one another. Ellen White tells us that the law and the gospel are to be bound together as a perfect whole. (See *Testimonies to Ministers and Gospel Workers*, p. 94.) Because the gospel deals with the "supernatural," we tend to think that it operates under "supernatural" laws that we cannot comprehend, making it a mystery and leaving us with a level of uncertainty.

When you wake up in the morning do you worry about, or even question, that the sun will rise in the east and set in the west? Do you give thought to the fact that when you get out of bed that your feet will land on the floor? If you have a garden and choose to plant corn, will you get tomatoes instead? When I came to understand the reason behind the answers to these questions, I found that my faith began standing with the same level of surety.

"Because that which may be known of God is manifest in them; for God hath shewed it unto them. For the invisible things of him from the creation of the world are clearly seen, being understood by the things that are made, even his eternal power and Godhead; so that they are without excuse" (Rom. 1:19, 20).

"Men could learn of the unknown through the known; heavenly things were revealed through the earthly; God was made manifest in the likeness of men. So it was in Christ's teaching: the unknown was

The Law and The Gospel

illustrated by the known; divine truths by earthly things with which the people were most familiar" (*Christ's Object Lesson*s, p. 17).

The origin of sin may be a mystery but the "mystery which hath been hid from ages and from generations" is now "made manifest to his saints" (*The Signs of the Times*, March 25, 1897). To a great extent this mystery can be understood simply by looking at the natural laws we tend to take for granted. A glimpse into the way I view the relationship of the law and the gospel to one another will be revealed in the next two illustrations. The first one will clearly show how the gospel operates according to very fixed and surprisingly familiar laws. The second will illustrate a relationship that exists between the law of God and the gospel of redemption that, I believe, is unlike anything we are accustomed to.

Natural Law in the Spiritual World

The first deals with a natural law called the "Law of Biogenesis." Simply stated, it means that life comes only from life. Something that is dead cannot be made alive unless something that has life already comes into play.

Perhaps, before we begin, death itself ought to be defined. We tend to limit our definition of death to the complete cessation of life—the grave. Christ said of Lazarus, after he had died, that he only sleeps. (See John 11:11-14.) What is it that a person sleeping and a person in the grave have in common? Neither of them is actively "corresponding" with their respective environments. The one is breathing; the other is decaying; but neither is actively living, moving, and having their being in their surroundings. (See Acts 17:28.)

"For the living know that they shall die: but the dead know not any thing, neither have they any more a reward; for the memory of them is forgotten. Also their love, and their hatred, and their envy, is now perished; neither have they any more a portion for ever in any thing that is done under the sun" (Eccl. 9:5, 6).

This verse is telling us that the dead are no longer a part of the land of the living. As a principle it is here applied to a person in the grave—no correspondence with the living world either in action or thought. Applying the same principle to a person sleeping—not actively moving, and to all appearances not hearing, seeing, or smelling—one could describe a sound sleeper as "dead to the world."

By principle a person can be dead in part. A blind person is unable to correspond with the world of sight. Although, as a rule, their sense of hearing is in greater correspondence to the world of sound than most sighted people—dead to sight but alive to sound. The Bible says that a woman who lives in pleasure is "dead while she liveth" (1 Tim. 5:6). How can this be? While she actively participates with the pleasures of this world, she is not partaking of the pleasures of the heavenly world—while alive in one world, she is dead to the other.

This brings us to the phrase, "dead in trespasses and sins" (Eph. 2:1). We can be said to be dead for two reasons: (1) We are actively participating in disobedience to God's laws. In other words, we are not in correspondence with the environment of God. We are alive unto sin and dead unto God. (2) "The wages of sin is death" (Rom. 6:23). The "end of sin" is separation from Him who is Life, which results in death. Complete separation from God is inevitable unless something intervenes to save us.

Let us take a look at James 1:14, 15 with key words defined by *Strong's Concordance*:

"But every man is tempted [tested], when he is drawn away [dragged away *from point of origin*] of his own lust [longing, heart's desire], and enticed [entrapped, deluded, decoyed, tricked]. Then when lust hath conceived [clasped, seized, captured, made a union], it bringeth forth sin: and sin, when it is finished [complete entirely, *separation is complete*], bringeth forth death" (italics added).

Did you notice that it is our own desires that are drawing us away from our point of origin? And what is that origin? It is God, who created us in His image. Unlike us, He has never forgotten our point of origin. How often do we struggle to find God in the first place, rather than realize we need only to come back to Him?

Today we are being called to "awake to righteousness, and sin not" (1 Cor. 15:34). We need to stop sleeping, to come out of our stupor, and begin to correspond actively with the spiritual environment of God. The Father wants us to come into obedience to His spiritual laws before our connection to Him is completely severed. Our being spiritually dead, asleep to righteousness, calls for an application of the Law of Biogenesis. Something that has life must come and make us spiritually "alive"—must come and wake us up. This process is illustrated in the natural world.

A mineral in the soil is said to be inorganic, which is another way of saying "it is dead to the organic world." If a child should eat a mud pie, the inorganic mineral has no correspondence with the organic life of the body. The mineral passes through immediately or gets stored in the body until it can be passed out later. There is a barrier that stands between these two worlds. The inorganic mineral, in and of itself, can do nothing to pass from its world into the organic kingdom above.

This idea was expounded upon by Henry Drummond, a Scottish geologist and religious writer (August 17, 1851–March 11, 1897), who devoted much attention to science, and in 1877, was appointed lecturer on natural science in the Free Church College in Glasco. His most remarkable work was Natural Law in the Spiritual World (1883), and it was in this book where I was first introduced to the Law of Biogenesis and its spiritual counterpart. The Lord used this book to open my eyes to look at nature and its relevance to the correct understanding of spiritual principles. The written word alone can, and has been, interpreted a thousand different ways. But, when the Created Word and the Written Word are found to speak the same "Word," we find truths that become solid, dependable, and unchanging. As the natural world began to harmonize with the spiritual, and the spiritual with the natural, my faith found a solid foundation to stand upon.

Drummond wrote, "No change of substance, no modification of environment, no chemistry, not electricity, nor any form of energy, nor any evolution can endow any single atom of the mineral world with the attribute of life. Only by the bending down into this dead world of some living form can these dead atoms be gifted with the properties of vitality; without this preliminary contact with Life they remain fixed in the inorganic sphere forever. It is a very mysterious Law which guards in this way the portals of the living world" (Natural Law in the Spiritual World, p. 61).

"In the Word of God, the first thing that strikes the eye is a great gulf fixed. The passage from the Natural World to the Spiritual World is hermetically sealed (completely sealed, esp. against escape or entry of air) on the natural side. The door from the inorganic to the organic is shut, no mineral can open it; so the door from the natural to the spiritual is shut, and no man can open it. This world of natural men is staked off from the Spiritual World by barriers which have never yet been crossed from within. No organic change, no modification of environment, no mental energy, no moral effort, no evolution of character, no progress of civilization can endow any single human soul with the attribute of Spiritual Life. The Spiritual World is guarded from the next in order beneath it by a law of Biogenesis—*Except a man be born of the water and the Spirit, he can not enter into the kingdom of God.* John 3:5

"The exclusion of the spiritually inorganic (flesh and blood) from

The Law and The Gospel

the kingdom of the spiritually organic is not arbitrary, nor is the natural man refused admission on unexplained grounds. *His admission is a scientific impossibility"* (Ibid., p. 64, italics added).

How does the inorganic (dead) mineral become an organic (living) mineral? Only by a living plant coming down into the inorganic world (roots growing down into the soil) and reaching out to the dead mineral in the earth. The "dead" mineral is absorbed into the root and thereby becomes a "living" mineral within the plant. (See Psalm 104:14.) How does the natural man become a spiritual man? Only by Christ, who has spiritual life, coming down from the spiritual world into this natural world, reaching out to touch every human being. As we consent to be absorbed into Him—buried with Him, hidden in Him—He transforms us and translates us into His kingdom above. "No man hath ascended up to heaven, but he that came down from heaven, even the Son of man which is in heaven" (John 3:13).

"Rightly interpreted, nature is the mirror of divinity" (*The Review and Herald*, September 18, 1900). This idea, of "moving" from one world into another, finds its almost perfect parallel in Christ's conversation with Nicodemus. Many tend to view the new birth as the time when Christ came into their hearts, as if the parallel is to be found in the conception of a child in the womb. True, we first begin to "experience" Christ in the heart when we are born again, but in reality, the parallel is the birth process—the "bringing forth" of the child from the womb. The infant who is alive in the womb is now moving into a world which before he was "dead" to (in principle), just as the dead mineral in the soil moves into the living plant.

Behold, all things become new, old things are passed away. The infant takes on an entirely new existence. When we are born again, we move from being alive to sin and dead to God, to being "dead indeed unto sin, but alive unto God through Jesus Christ our Lord" (Rom.

6:11). We are the ones being "brought forth" into an entirely new existence as we are transformed and translated into the kingdom of God—today by faith, soon in reality. Again, we may think it is Christ that enters us at the new birth, but notice what Nicodemus asked, "Can a man be born when he is old? can he enter the second time into his mother's womb, and be born?" (John 3:4). The focus of Nicodemus was on the child coming forth from the womb a second time. Take a look at these verses in 1 John:

- "Every one that doeth righteousness is born of him" (1 John 2:29).
- "He that saith he abideth in him ought himself also so to walk, even as he walked" (1 John 2:6).
- "Whosoever is born of God doth not commit sin" (1 John 3:9).
- "Whosoever abideth in him sinneth not" (1 John 3:6).

Two things equal to the same thing are equal to one another, are they not? Being born of God and abiding in Christ are one and the same! Go back and look at all the familiar verses we use to describe the new birth experience and you will find the focus is our "moving into Christ," not Christ moving into the believer. (See Galatians 3:27; 2 Corinthians 5:17; Ephesians 2:4-6; Colossians 2:9-13, 3:1-3; and Philippians 3:8, 9.) We may be "experiencing" Christ in our hearts for the first time but we are the ones doing the moving into Christ by faith (experiencing what Christ has already done by promise).

Conception took place for every human being when the One who has Life came from the heavenly world into this spiritually dead world and touched each and every one of us. Only when faith is come can the birth process begin (Gal. 3:23-4:6). As we by faith rest in the soil of Christ and are watered by the Holy Spirit, the power of God will then be able to bring forth the dormant germ of Christ's spirit of life that lies buried within each of us. Being born of God is actually a lifelong process (on this earth) of being brought forth from death to life, from sin to righteousness, from bondage to freedom, from earth to heaven, from a "child under tutors" to an "heir of God through Christ." But only because we have so much yet to learn.

Two Kinds of Law

The second illustration also will use objects and laws with which we are very familiar. To begin, we must first define what is meant by the term the law of God, not in the sense of the Ten Commandments, but in the sense of being "law."

In this world there are two kinds of laws: the natural laws in God's created world and the governmental laws drawn up by man. The natural laws are constant and unchanging, whereas man's laws are provisional and temporary. The natural laws describe for us how the powers in God's created world function, showing us how we are to relate to those powers. Governmental laws, on the other hand, are designed by man and draw the lines as to how those in positions of authority, and those they govern, are to relate to one another.

Did you notice the difference? Natural laws help us understand how natural powers function; they do not tell the powers how they are to operate. Man-made laws, on the other hand, do tell those holding governmental powers, and those they govern, how they are to function. The natural laws are fixed and unchanging because the powers they describe are fixed and unchanging. The instability of man always causes the governmental laws to change, to be temporary.

Natural laws are no respecter of persons as the natural powers relate to everyone equally. Those in positions of power will use governmental law to favor one group over another. Natural powers can never operate outside their divinely assigned boundaries. Those given authoritative power tend to be arbitrary—"not regulated by fixed law, can be determined as the occasion arises, based on ones own wishes or will" (Defined by World Book Dictionary).

Having looked at "law" itself, which kind of law defines the law of God known as the Ten Commandments? Is it like unto the natural laws of God's created world? Or, being the foundation of God's government, is it like unto our governmental laws? (See *Patriarchs and Prophets*, p. 66.) I believe the biggest problem in understanding the true character of God lies right here. We have not understood the true relationship of the law of God and the government of God. We tend to view them both in the same light as we see our own government and the laws we make. It is time we let the Created Word have its say. "Rightly interpreted, nature is the mirror of divinity" (*The Review and Herald*, September 18, 1900). The law of God is like unto a natural law. God's government operates according to the principles of natural law.

Gravity, Parachutes, and Salvation

The Ten Commandments, being a transcript of God's character, are simply the Laws that explains how we are to relate to God, who is love, as well as to our fellow human beings, as an expression of God's love. To better understand this power of love and how to relate to it, let us look at the power of gravity. It is very beneficial to us in many ways. Life as we know it could not exist without it. Should a person fall from the roof of a 10-story building, does gravity continue to benefit him? No! In fact, you could say, "He is a dead man!" Why? Because the law of gravity has taught us that gravity is going to do what it does naturally—it is going to hold things to the earth. We know that the rate at which the man is falling, and the distance he will fall,

The Law and The Gospel

is going to prove detrimental to the physical body when he finally reaches the ground.

Is the power of gravity at fault? No. Does a fault lie in the law of gravity? No. Then what is wrong? Why is gravity now destroying the man instead of benefiting him? The only thing that changed is the man's relationship to the power of gravity. Having left the roof of the building, the man "transgressed" the law of gravity. Being no respecter of persons, and being unchanging, gravity could do nothing else than what it is designed to do. This unfortunate relationship between the falling man and gravity will surely end in disaster unless something comes into the picture to change the man's present condition.

With that foundation laid, let us go up 10,000 feet in an airplane. The first Adam's violation of God's law was like jumping out of an airplane without a parachute. Skydivers would call it "terminal velocity"—the end of the fall is final. Likewise, "the wages of sin is death" (Rom. 6:23). There is quite a distance you have to fall before you reach the ground. Because the end of sin is not immediate, we tend not to grasp the reality of the consequences that lie ahead. When a person leaves an airplane without a parachute there is nothing he, of himself, can ever do to put himself back into a safe, life-sustaining relationship to the power of gravity. Neither could Adam, of himself, get back into a life-sustaining relationship to God. Someone or something, from outside himself, had to come to his aid.

The last Adam, a quickening spirit, is like unto the parachute. No one in his right mind would jump from a plane without one. God knows that the first man violated His law of love not fully comprehending the consequences. He knows that man will soon not even know that God has a law and will break His law in ignorance. In His mercy God will allow no man to jump without a parachute in place and ready to go to work when called upon. Having a parachute in place may be the only hope of salvation from the fall, but it is no guarantee that "terminal velocity" will not take place.

There are "conditions" that must be met before the parachute is of any value to the wearer: (1) He must become aware that he is in a dangerous situation, or he will not realize his need of a parachute. (2) He must come to see that there is nothing of himself that he can do to break his fall, or he will never totally depend upon the parachute to save him. (3) He must know what the parachute is designed, to do or he will not trust it to do what is needed. (4) He should know about, and understand the necessity of, pulling the ripcord, or the parachute will never open. (5) He must know that there is a parachute already in place, ready to go to work. (Ignorance of this one fact can have the same result as not having a parachute at all.) I trust the spiritual counterparts to these conditions can readily be seen.

To enable the parachute to work, all he has to do is pull the ripcord. What does it mean to pull that cord? You are saying, "I will put my trust in the parachute to do for me what I cannot do for myself." How do you know you can trust the parachute? "Faith does not make facts, it only lays hold of them" (E.J. Waggoner, The Glad Tidings, p. 199). Pulling the ripcord does not make the parachute work; it only enables it to go to work, to do what it was designed to do. At some time in our lives we have seen a parachute at work bringing its precious cargo safely to the ground. The life Jesus lived, as a man in sinful flesh, is the assurance we have that the "spirit of life" in us will do for us exactly what it did for Him. Here is where faith in the last Adam is revealed. When we truly lay hold of the facts, we will "pull the cord" and watch the principle God has implanted go to work.

"Receiving and believing is his [man's] part of the contract. He is to receive Christ as his personal Saviour, and is to continue to believe in him. This means abiding in Christ, showing in him, at all times and under all circumstances, a faith that is a representation of his character—a faith that works by love, and purifies the soul from all defilement" (*The Review and Herald*, April 24, 1900).

"It [faith] is the act of the soul by which the whole man is given over to the guardianship and control of Jesus Christ. He abides in Christ and Christ abides in the soul by faith as supreme. The believer commits his soul and body to God and with assurance may say, Christ is able to keep that which I have committed unto Him against that day. All who will do this will be saved unto life eternal" (*Mind, Character, and Personality*, vol. 2, p. 531).

"Now unto him that is able to keep you from falling, and to present you faultless before the presence of his glory with exdeeding joy, To the only wise God our Saviour, be glory and majesty, dominion and power, both now and ever. Amen" (Jude 1:24, 25).

Redemption is According to Natural Law

There is an even greater depth to this illustration. The law of gravity has educated us to know that the man who is falling is in a life-threatening relationship to the power of gravity. Man has transgressed God's law and the written Word informs us that we are in a life-threatening relationship to God, whose power of love is a consuming fire to sin. (See *Thoughts from the Mount of Blessing*, p. 62.) Remember, the problem was not with gravity, nor is it with God. The falling man knows he must come into a right relationship to gravity, just as we know that God calls us to obey His law.

Some think that the gospel of Christ has done away with the need to keep the law. Does the parachute do away with the law of gravity? Without gravity, the parachute could never bring the man safely back to the earth. Some think that obedience to the moral law will save us. There is not a single movement the falling man can perform, even if given supernatural power, that will bring him back into a safe relationship with gravity.

In the beginning, the rule for Adam was the law of salvation: "They could obey and live, or disobey and perish" (*Patriarchs and Prophets*, p. 53). The same terms applied to the old covenant formed at Sinai: "All that the Lord hath said will we do" (Ibid., p. 371). Neither Adam nor the children of Israel maintained obedience, so God had to provide a new covenant. Why? "They could not hope for the favor of God through a covenant they had broken" (Ibid.). Having violated its law, neither can the falling man hope for favor from gravity. This new covenant, the law of redemption, was based on better promises—God's, not ours. It simply called for the sinner to trust in another to do for him that which he could no longer do for himself. (See E.J. Waggoner's Bible Studies on the Book of Romans pages 82 and 83.) In our illustration, the man must put his trust in the parachute to do for him that which he cannot do for himself. And that is to bring him back into a life-sustaining relationship to gravity.

Now, catch this carefully, the parachute is, itself, operating under another law—aerodynamics, using another power—air—to accomplish its mission of putting the falling man back into a proper relationship to gravity. God's plan of redemption had to operate according to law. (See *Testimonies for the Church*, vol. 5, p. 575.) God knew He could not save man from his inevitable end using only the law and power man had violated. The "mystery, which from the beginning of the world hath been hid in God" (*Testimonies to Ministers and Gospel Workers*, p. 292)—the hidden depth of God's love—was about to be revealed. (See Colossians 1:26, 27; Ephesians 3:9, 19; and *The Desire of Ages*, p. 22.) He needed a law and a power that could override the consequences of the law that man had broken and, at the same time, bring man back into obedience to the very law he had transgressed!

Knowing what that law and power was, God needed someone who was willing, and able, to come to this earth and operate under this other law. In so doing He could provide a way of salvation for those who were in violation of the first law and bring them back into a life-sustaining relationship with divinity.

"The Lord saw us in a sad condition, and sent to our world the only messenger that he could trust with his great treasure of pardon and grace. Christ, the only begotten Son of God, was the delegated messenger. He was ordained to do a work that even the angels of heaven could not accomplish. He alone could be trusted to do the work required for the redemption of a world all seared and marred with the curse. And in this gift the Father gave all heaven to the world" (*The Review and Herald*, February 15, 1898).

His "great treasure of pardon" is redemption from the consequences we deserve—eternal death—just as the parachute saves the falling man from "terminal velocity." The "great treasure of grace" is the power to again bring us into harmony with God's love through obedience to His moral law, just as the parachute brings the falling man back into harmony with gravity. So, what other law and power is brought to light through Christ? What hidden depth of God's love is revealed through the Son?

Resurrection Power

We know that God the Father is the source of all life. But, note what Jesus the Son says of Himself, "I am the resurrection, and the life: he that believeth in me though he were dead, yet shall he live; and whosoever liveth and believeth in me shall never die" (John 11:25, 26). God is not only the originator of life (creating the seen from the unseen) but, through Christ, He can take that which is "dead" (remember the definition of "death") and give it life. We come to know this about Christ when we focus on the literal cross and His glorious resurrection. What we fail to realize is this: Being the "Lamb slain from the foundation of the world" (Rev. 13:8), Jesus Christ lived His entire life under the law of the resurrection!

What is the law of the resurrection? Death must come before life. A seed cannot be quickened unless it dies first. Remember, death is the lack of correspondence with an environment. Christ willingly left the heavenly courts and came to earth as a babe with the same nature as you and I. As a man, how did he relate to His divinity?

"When Christ had our human nature, he was there in His divine self; but didn't manifest any of his divine self in that place. What did he do with his divine self in our flesh when he became ourselves?—His divine self was always kept back—emptied—in order that our evil, satanic selves might be kept back—emptied. Now in the flesh he himself did nothing. He says: 'Of mine own self I can do nothing.' He was there all the time. His own divine self, who made the heavens, was there all the time. But from beginning to end He himself did nothing; himself was kept back; he was emptied. Who, then, did that which was done in him? The Father that dwelleth in me, 'He doeth the works, he speaks the words'" (A.T. Jones, *The 1895 General Conference Bulletin*, p. 349).

"He undid himself, and sank himself in us, in order that God, instead of ourselves, and his righteousness, instead of our sinfulness, might be manifested in us in our sinful flesh. Then let us respond, and sink ourselves in him, that God may still be manifest in sinful flesh" (Ibid., p. 303).

Jesus Christ lived His entire life, by faith, under the law of the resurrection. He "died" to His divine self, trusting in another—His Father—to do for Him what He could not do for Himself. In His divine self He could have kept the law perfectly. We, with our sinful self,

The Law and The Gospel

cannot keep the law. To be our example, He could not use His divine self at all. Showing us we cannot use our own self either. He trusted His Father to live His life in Him. So perfectly did He keep Himself hidden, the scriptures say of Him, "No man knoweth the Son, but the Father" (Matt. 11:27). So perfectly is our self to be hidden, the world will see only Christ, which is to see the Father.

"It was a difficult task for the Prince of life to carry out the plan which He had undertaken for the salvation of man, in clothing His divinity with humanity. He had received honor in the heavenly courts, and was familiar with absolute power. It was as difficult for Him to keep the level of humanity as for men to rise above the low level of their depraved natures, and be partakers of the divine nature.

"Christ was put to the closest test, requiring the strength of all His faculties to resist the inclination when in danger, to use His power to deliver Himself from peril" (*The SDA Bible Commentary*, vol. 7, p. 930).

This is what the life of Christ will do in us as we abide by faith in Him. He will bring our sinful, evil self into submission. He will keep us from using our own power. In so doing, God the Father can again reveal Himself in us just as He did in His Son!

Death before Life

Often, when Christ's death on the cross is lifted up as our substitute—"Christ took our punishment and died for our sins" (LandMarks Magazine, June 1996, p. 13)—the mind-set of today is quick to add, "So I don't have to die for my own sins." Even when Christ is presented as the last Adam—dying "as us or instead of us" (1888 Message Newsletter, March-April 1996, p. 8)—the mind is quick to add, "So I don't have to die for my sins." The law of the resurrection is sadly being overlooked.

Listen carefully to what Waggoner says:

"There is given to every man a choice as to when he will die. Christ died for all men. We can acknowledge his death, and die in Him, and thus get His life; or on the other hand we may, if we wish, refuse to acknowledge Him, and die in ourselves. But die we must. Pay the penalty, suffer the forfeit, we must; for the law will exact the forfeit. But as I said before, we have the choice as to whether we will wait, and let the law take the forfeit from us, at a time when we will have nothing left after it is gone, or whether we will give over the forfeited life when we can take the life of Christ, and have it after we paid the forfeit" (Bible Studies on the Book of Romans, pp. 38, 39).

Christ, the last Adam, has redeemed us from the first Adam's choice to sin. As a result we will all rise from our first mortal death. But, individually we have also chosen to sin. The wages of sin is still death, and die we must. We can choose to die in Christ today by faith, or we can die out of Christ at the second death. Either way our own sinful self must die, never to be seen again. Death must come before life.

The last Adam, a quickening spirit, died as our substitute to give us resurrection from the condemnation of the first Adam's sin. The second man, the Lord from heaven, lived as our substitute to give us a perfect life, in Himself, to meet the requirements of the law. In so doing He has reconciled all of us back to God.

"When we were enemies, we were reconciled to God by the death of his Son, much more, being reconciled, we shall be saved by his life" (Rom. 5:10).

"Who hath saved us, and called us with an holy calling, not according to our works, but according to his own purpose and grace" (2 Tim. 1:9).

No matter how much knowledge we may have of the gospel story, no matter how strong we believe in Jesus Christ, no matter how well we think we obey the moral law (the Ten Commandments) it will avail

The Law and The Gospel

us nothing. Having once violated God's law of love—knowingly or unknowingly—there is nothing we can do of ourselves to get back into a right relationship with God. There is only one way, and this is found only in Jesus Christ. He died that we might have life and have it more abundantly. Only as we choose to follow Him, taking up our own cross, dying daily in Him, can we experience that life—a life that will continuously abide in Christ, a life that will put us back into a right relationship with our heavenly Father. So, how do we get out of this pit of sin, sink ourselves into Christ, and allow the Father to work in us? Let us follow Christ as He meets us where we are in the depths of our sin.

Summary

1. God's government operates like unto "natural law": constant and unchanging, no respecter of persons, always operates within divinely assigned boundaries. It is not like unto our man-made governmental laws: provisional and temporary, favors one group over another, arbitrary, based on ones will or wishes.
2. Death can be defined as a "lack of correspondence," giving it a much broader application than just the grave.
3. Being "born again" refers to our moving into Christ by faith, not His moving into us.
4. Obedience to the Ten Commandments, which we have all violated, will not save us from the death we deserve for the sins we personally have committed.
5. Obedience to the law of the resurrection is the only thing that will save us from the results of our own sins—the second death we deserve (mercy)—and at the same time bring us back into obedience to the law of God (grace).

6. Does the life of Christ reveal to us how to be obedient to the law of the resurrection?

Chapter Five

Christ Meets Us Where We Are

Because of sins committed, and its consequent burden of guilt, we have a tough time seeing how Jesus can truly relate to us and meet us where we are. After all, He never sinned! Can Jesus meet me where I am under this heavy weight of sin? Yes, He can and does! Jesus did more than just take upon Himself the results of the first Adam's disobedience, much more than simply take humanity into Himself as the last Adam:

"He was wounded for our transgressions, he was broken for our iniquities: the chastisement of our peace was upon him...and the LORD hath laid on him the iniquity of us all. He was oppressed, and he was afflicted, yet he opened not his mouth...for the transgression of my people was he stricken....Yet it pleased the LORD to bruise him; he hath put him to grief: when thou shalt make his soul an offering for sin...he hath poured out his soul unto death: and he was numbered with the transgressors" (Isa. 53:5-12).

"The guilt of fallen humanity He must bear. Upon Him who knew no sin must be laid the iniquity of us all....so great is the weight of guilt which He must bear" (*The Desire of Ages*, p. 685).

The guilt that Adam felt when he sinned, the guilt that you and I feel when we sin, Christ could not, in and of Himself, ever experience. He personally had never chosen to disobey His Father. The weight of guilt from our sins was laid upon Him. "As man He must suffer the consequences of man's sin. As man He must endure the wrath of God against transgression." (Ibid., p. 686). Sin's heaviest weight was felt in the Garden of Gethsemane and when upon the cross.

Christ in the Garden

Ellen White tells us that in the garden "Christ was now standing in a *different attitude* from that in which He had ever stood before" (Ibid., italics added). He thought differently, He felt differently, and He acted differently. He had before said, "I and my Father are one" (John 10:30), only now it seemed to Christ that there was a separation between Him and God—a separation we all know too well, but He was feeling for the very first time (Ibid., p. 687)! Jesus had before stood like a mighty cedar, now He was like a reed beaten and bent by the angry storm—just as the guilt of sin beats us down (Ibid., p. 689). Jesus had before rested solely upon God's Word and gave Satan no advantage (Ibid., p. 679); now he longed for some words of comfort from His disciples (Ibid., p. 687). How quickly we tend to run to another human being to find comfort before we seek comfort in God's Word.

"As one already glorified, He had claimed oneness with God… Now His voice was heard on the still evening air…full of human anguish" (Ibid., p. 690).

As the weight of our guilt bore down upon His soul, Jesus, the man, was losing sight of who He was as the Son of God. The depth of the sinful condition of humanity He was now experiencing dimmed His spiritual vision concerning the "unseen" truths. In Gethsemane, the Son of Man meets you and me where we are in the depths of our sin:

"The dark cloud of human transgression came between the Father and the Son. The interruption of the communion between God and His

Son caused a condition of things in the heavenly courts which cannot be described by human language" (*The SDA Bible Commentary*, vol. 5, p. 1108).

"But now with the terrible weight of guilt He bears, He cannot see the Father's reconciling face....The Saviour could not see through the portals of the tomb....He feared that sin was so offensive to God that Their separation was to be eternal" (*The Desire of Ages*, p. 753).

"God and the angels clothed themselves with darkness, and hid the Saviour from the gaze of the curious multitude while He drank the last dregs of the cup of God's wrath" (*The SDA Bible Commentary*, vol. 5, p. 1108).

"Complete darkness...enveloped the cross" (*The Desire of Ages*, p. 753). "Christ bowed His head and died, but He held fast His faith and His submission to God" (Ibid., p. 761).

Christ as Our Example

As our example, what was the level of faith Jesus exercised that enabled Him, in the midst of such darkness and despair, to submit completely to His Father?

"He had relied upon the evidence of His Father's acceptance heretofore given Him. He was acquainted with the character of His Father; He understood His justice, His mercy, and His great love. By faith He rested in whom it had ever been His joy to obey. And as in submission He committed Himself to God, the sense of the loss of His Father's favor was withdrawn. By faith, Christ was victor" (Ibid., p. 756).

By faith Christ was victorious. He stayed focused on what He could not see, rather than on what was happening around Him! He trusted in what He already knew of His heavenly parent and laid hold of a finished work—"the destruction of sin and Satan was forever made certain, that the redemption of man assured, and that the universe was made eternally secure. . . . To all these He looked forward when upon the cross He cried out, 'It is finished'" (Ibid., p. 764).

"Christ submitted to crucifixion, although the heavenly host could have delivered Him. The angels suffered with Christ. God Himself was crucified with Christ; for Christ was one with the Father. Those who reject Christ, those who will not have this man to rule over them, choose to place themselves under the rule of Satan, to do his work as his bondslaves. Yet for them Christ yielded up His life on Calvary" (*The Faith I Live By*, p. 50; *The SDA Bible Commentary*, vol. 5, p. 1108). "He had suffered death for every man" (*The SDA Bible Commentary*, vol. 5, p. 1109).

According to the principle laid out in Hebrews 7:9 and 10, God sees all humanity as being there in Christ on the cross. In Christ we all faced the wages of sin—complete separation from God. We all died and we all rose again reconciled to God. But, again, it was done only *in Christ*, by *His choices*, not by ours. We may have died in the last Adam on the cross of Calvary, 2,000 years ago, but we did not *experience* it there, and *experience it we must*!

"The Captain of our salvation was perfected through suffering. His soul was made an offering for sin. It was necessary for the awful darkness to gather about His soul because of the withdrawal of the Father's love and favor; for He was standing in the sinners place, and *this darkness every sinner must experience*" (*The SDA Bible Commentary*, vol. 7, p. 924, italics added).

Having personally chosen to sin, the law demands our personal death. What we need is a personal Savior. At some time in our lives, God will bring home to our minds the awful realization of the consequences of our own personal sins. We can allow the experience to drive us to Christ or we can turn a deaf ear, close our eyes, and face "the wages of sin" later after the 1,000 years described in Revelation 20 have ended.

"And until that time the law will faithfully perform its task of stirring up and pricking the consciences of sinners, giving them no rest until they become identified with Christ, or cast Him off altogether. Do you accept the terms? Will you cease your complaints against the law which would save you from sinking into fatal sleep? And will you in Christ accept its righteousness?" (E.J. Waggoner, The Glad Tidings, pp. 157, 158).

"'For God so loved the world, that he gave his only-begotten Son, that whosoever believeth in him should not perish, but have everlasting life.' This message is for the world, for 'whosoever' means that any and all who comply with the condition may share the blessing. All who look unto Jesus, believing in him as their *personal Saviour*, shall 'not perish, but have everlasting life.' Every provision has been made that we may have the everlasting reward.

"Christ is our sacrifice, our substitute, our surety, our divine intercessor; he is made unto us righteousness, sanctification, and redemption. . . .

"It is the righteousness of Christ that makes the penitent sinner acceptable to God and works his justification. However sinful has been his life, if he believes in Jesus as his personal Saviour, he stands before God in the spotless robes of Christ's imputed righteousness. . . .

"We stand in favor before God, not because of any merit in ourselves, but because of our faith in 'the Lord our righteousness.' . . .

"We are complete in him, accepted in the Beloved, only as we abide in him by faith.

"Perfection through our own good works we can never attain. The soul who sees Jesus by faith, repudiates his own righteousness. He sees himself as incomplete, his repentance insufficient, his strongest faith but feebleness, his most costly sacrifice as meager, and he sinks in humility at the foot of the cross. But a voice speaks to him from the oracles of God's word. In amazement he hears the message, 'Ye are complete in him.' ...

"How hard is it for humanity, long accustomed to cherish doubt, to grasp this great truth! But what peace it brings to the soul, what vital life!...

"Who can comprehend the nature of that righteousness which makes the believing sinner whole, presenting him to God without spot or wrinkle or any such thing?" (*The Signs of the Times*, July 4, 1892, also found in *Faith and Works*, pp. 105-109, italics added).

The life we lived in Christ and the death we died in Him can save us from suffering the "second death" we personally deserve, only when we sink our self into Him as He sank Himself into His Father. We are in Christ by promise, are you in Him by faith? Our evil self is to be as hidden in the divine nature as the "divine self" of Christ was hidden in our human nature. Our sinful self can be crucified today, by faith, or later at the second death in the lake of fire. But die it must.

Dying with Christ

"The great thought around which the whole Bible clusters, is death and resurrection with Christ. If we die with Him, we shall live again.

"We die with Him,--when? Now! When we acknowledge our life forfeited, and give up all claims to that life, and everything that is connected with it, that very moment we die with Christ. Now what is this giving up of our life? Life stands for everything that a man has. It stands for everything that pertains to life. What is it, then, that pertains to the life that we naturally have in ourselves? It is sin! It is the lust of the flesh, and the lust of the eyes, and the pride of life. It is envy, malice, evil speaking, evil thinking,--all these things make up the natural life....

"When we come to that place where we see that we have those

things, and are ready to give them up, and pay the forfeit, then it is that we can die with Christ, and take His sinless life in their stead. In yielding up that life of ours, we give up all these things, and when they are all given up, then we are dead with Christ. . . .

"It is necessary that we die continually, and that we continually know the power of God, and of the resurrection of Christ. . . . We must know and experience the same power that God wrought in Christ when He raised Him from the dead. . . . It is simply a matter of making the resurrection of Christ a practical thing in our own lives" (E.J. Waggoner, Bible Studies on the Book of Romans, pp. 39, 40).

"The mind of Christ is the emptying of self, is the abolishing of self, the destruction of self, the annihilation of self" (A.T. Jones, *The 1895 General Conference Bulletin*, p. 350).

"Let this mind [way of thinking] be in you, which was also in Christ Jesus" (Phil. 2:5).

"For ye are dead, and your life is hid with Christ in God. When Christ, who is our life, shall appear, then shall ye also appear with him in glory" (Col. 3:3).

"It will require a sacrifice to give yourself to God; but it is a sacrifice of the lower for the higher, the earthly for the spiritual, the perishable for the eternal. God does not design that our will should be destroyed, for it is only through its exercise that we can accomplish what He would have us do. Our will is to be yielded to Him that we may receive it again, purified and refined, and so linked in sympathy with the Divine that He can pour through us the tides of His love and power" (*Mind, Character, and Personality*, vol. 2, p. 693).

"Eternity alone can reveal the glorious destiny to which man, restored to God's image, may attain. In order for us to reach this high ideal, that which causes the soul to stumble must be sacrificed. It is through the will that sin retains its hold upon us. The surrender of the will is represented as plucking out the eye or cutting off the hand. Often it seems to us that to surrender the will to God is to consent to go through life maimed or crippled...God is the fountain of life, and we can have life only as we are in communion with Him....Only through the surrender of our will to God is it possible for Him to impart life to us.... If you cling to self, refusing to yield your will to God, you are choosing death" (*Thoughts from the Mount of Blessing*, pp. 60-62).

The Right Action of the Will

"And while Christ opens heaven to man, the life which He imparts opens the heart of man to heaven. Sin not only shuts us away from God but destroys in the human soul both the desire and the capacity for knowing Him. All this work of evil it is Christ's mission to undo. The faculties of the soul, paralyzed by sin, the darkened mind, the perverted will, He has power to invigorate and to restore. He opens to us the riches of the universe, and by Him the power to discern and to appropriate these treasures is imparted" (*Mind, Character, and Personality*, vol. 1, p. 13).

"The tempted one needs to understand the true force of the will. This is the governing power in the nature of man—the power of decision, of choice. Everything depends on the right action of the will. Desires for goodness and purity are right, as far as they go; but if we stop here, they avail nothing. Many will go down to ruin while hoping and desiring to overcome their *evil propensities. They do not yield the will to God. They do not choose to serve Him*" (*Mind, Character, and Personality*, vol. 2, p. 685, italics added).

There is an inseparable connection between "death to self" and the "right action of the will." The man of Romans 7 is exercising his will—his power of choice—but in the wrong manner. Count the number of personal pronouns in this chapter, from verse 7 to 25, to see the man's focus. Instead of choosing *whom* he will serve, he is trying to choose for himself *how* he will serve. Is this not what most of us are doing? However sincere the man is, self is still ruling through his members.

"The will is the governing power in the nature of man, bringing all the other faculties under its sway....You will be in constant peril until you understand the true force of the will" (*Testimonies for the Church*, vol. 5, p. 513).

"This will, that forms so important a factor in the character of man, was at the Fall given into the control of Satan; and he has ever since been working in men to will and to do of his own pleasure, but to the utter ruin and misery of man. But the infinite sacrifice of God in giving Jesus, His beloved Son, to become a sacrifice for sin, enables Him to say, without violating one principle of His government: 'Yield yourself up to Me; give Me that will; take it from the control of Satan, and I will take possession of it; then I can work in you to will and to do of My good pleasure.' When He gives you the mind of Christ, your will becomes as His will, and your character is transformed to be like Christ's character" (Ibid., p. 515).

Remember, Jones stated that the mind of Christ is the emptying of self. It is a mind-set that submits the will to the Father so He can work in us as He worked in His Son, transforming our character into that of Christ.

When the man we read of in Romans 7 stops fighting, in his own strength and wisdom, and simply rests in Christ, his own will in submission, he finally finds victory. Read Romans 8: 1-17, and you will find only one personal pronoun. The focus of this man is God, Jesus, and the Spirit as they are mentioned in almost every verse.

"Here is where the conflict is to be the sternest, hardest, and most fierce—in yielding the will and way to God's will and way, relying upon the gracious influences which God has exerted upon the human soul throughout all the life" (*The Signs of the Times*, February 12, 1894). "The warfare against self is the greatest battle that was ever fought. The yielding of self, surrendering all to the will of God, requires a struggle; but the soul must submit to God before it can be renewed in holiness" (*Steps to Christ*, p. 43)

Did you catch that? The battle with self has already been fought! Christ has fought that battle for every one of us. His victory is our assurance that the battle we face with self can be won. In a world that says, "I did it my way," we must fight the stern battle of yielding our will and way to God's will and way. Abiding in Christ, by faith, we find rest as we discover this battle is also a finished work. "Let this mind be in you, which was also in Christ Jesus" (Phil. 2:5)—the annihilation of self. Is this not what true Sabbath rest is all about—to rest from our work as God rested from His, to enjoy the "finished work" of God? (See Hebrews 4:3-10.)

"What you need to understand is the true force of the will. This is the governing power in the nature of man, the power of decision, or of choice. Everything depends on the right action of the will. The power of choice God has given to men; it is theirs to exercise. You cannot change your heart, you cannot of yourself give to God its affections; but you can *choose* to serve Him. You can give Him your will; He will then work in you to will and to do of His good pleasure" (*Steps to Christ*, p. 47).

"But someone may ask, when we pray "not my will, but thine be done," are we not voiding our will and refusing to exercise the very power of Choice which is part of the image of God in us? The answer to that question is a flat No!, but the whole thing deserves further explanation. No act that is done voluntarily is an abrogation of the freedom of the will. If a man chooses the will of God he is not denying but exercising his right of choice. What he is doing is admitting that he is not good enough to desire the choice nor is he wise enough to make it and he is for that reason asking Another who is both wise and good to make his choice for him. And for fallen man this is the ultimate use he should make of his freedom of will. . . .

"The true saint is one who acknowledges that he possesses from God the gift of freedom. He knows that he will never be cudgeled into obedience nor wheeled like a petulant child into doing the will of God; he knows that these methods are unworthy of God and of his own soul. He knows he is free to make any choice he will, and with that knowledge, he chooses forever the blessed will of God" (A.W. Tozer, *That Incredible Christian*, pp. 43, 44; also quoted in Lois A. Egger's *Common Sense Psychology Study Outline*, pp. 72, 73).

"So highly does God regard His handiwork that He will not for any reason violate it. For God to override man's freedom and force him to act contrary to his own will would be to make a mockery of the image of God in man. This God will never do. Our Lord Jesus looked after the rich young ruler as he walked away, but he did not follow him or attempt to coerce him. The dignity of the young man's humanity forbade that his choices should be made for him by another. To remain a man he must make his own chosen way. If his human choice took him at last to hell, at least he went there a man; and it is better for the moral universe that he should do so then that he should be jockeyed to a heaven he did not choose, a soul-less, will-less automaton" (Ibid., p. 46).

"No outward observances can take the place of simple faith and entire renunciation of self. But no man can empty himself of self. We can only consent for Christ to accomplish the work. Then the language of the soul will be, Lord take my heart; for I cannot give it. It is Thy property. Keep it pure, for I cannot keep it for Thee. Save me in spite of myself, my weak unchristlike self. Mold me, fashion me, raise me into a pure and holy atmosphere, where the rich current of Thy love can flow through my soul" (*Christ's Object Lessons*, p. 159).

What is Faith?

At the 1893 General Conference, A.T. Jones presented a study on true justification by faith versus the false (Sermon No. 12). He contrasted excerpts from an authorized Catholic work with excerpts from *Steps to Christ* by Ellen White. (Because I would highly recommend that everyone read what he has to say, I have included it in the appendix section as Appendix A.) At the end of the study, he defined faith itself from the Catholic view as compared to *Steps to Christ*. I was amazed to find that my understanding of justification by faith, as well as faith itself, at the time I read his sermon, had far too much of a Catholic flavor. Jones stated that He had had to meet the false view of faith among many Seventh-day Adventists in his day, and I find it is still held by many Seventh-day Adventists even to this day.

He read this Catholic definition of "saving faith":

"The word 'faith' in the Scripture sometimes means confidence in God's omnipotence and goodness, that He can and is willing to cure or benefit us by miraculous interposition. Mostly it refers to revealed truths, and signifies belief in them as such. No one has a right to give to the word faith a new meaning, and take it, for instance, to signify reliance on Jesus for being personally saved through this very reliance alone, unless Jesus Christ or the Apostles had, in some instance clearly attributed such a meaning to the word faith and taught the doctrine of trust in Christ for personal salvation as the only requisite for justification. No one should attach a particular meaning to the word faith, without having a good warrant in Scripture or in divine tradition.

"Now in many passages of Holy Scripture in which saving faith is plainly spoken of, by faith is not meant a trust in Christ for personal salvation, but evidently a firm belief that Jesus is the Messias, the Christ, the Son of God, that what is related of Him in the Gospel is true, and that what He taught is true" (A.T. Jones, *The 1893 General Conference Bulletin*, p. 264).

A well-known Adventist minister recently wrote the following under a subtitle "Saving faith":

"Genuine faith must be motivated by love, but it must also be a saving faith. What is saving faith?

"It is not simply trusting Christ....True saving faith is motivated by love and always includes three important elements: (1) knowing the truth as it is in Jesus; (2) believing the truth as it is in Jesus; and (3) obeying the truth as it is in Jesus. . . . Only those whose *faith is founded on a heartfelt response to gospel truth* have genuine saving faith" (Jack Sequeira, *Beyond Belief*, p. 91, italics added).

LandMarks Magazine, an independent ministries publication, defined faith as follows:

"But says one; We are sanctified by faith. Answer. We admit that we are sanctified by faith; but what is the nature of genuine faith: Does faith confine sanctification to the heart, and exclude good works? The simple definition of Bible faith is confidence in the word of God. *Faith takes hold of the truths* of God's word" (June 1998, p. 21, italics added)

By quoting these two "contemporary" references, I do not wish to point any accusing finger. I simply want to draw attention to the fact that true, genuine saving faith is not understood by many of us as it should be.

Strong's Concordance defines faith as follows:

"N.T. 4102 – persuasion, i.e. credence; morally conviction (of religious truth, or the truth-fullness of God or a religious teacher), *especially reliance upon Christ for salvation;* abstractly Constancy in such profession: by extension the system of religious (gospel) truth itself" (italics added).

Even Strong's recognizes that the main definition of faith is reliance upon Christ for salvation.

A.T. Jones quotes from *Steps to Christ*, page 63, in the chapter "Test of Discipleship":

"When we speak of faith, there is a distinction that should be borne in mind. There is a kind of belief that is wholly distinct from faith. The existence and power of God, the truth of His word, are facts that even Satan and his hosts cannot at heart deny.

"The Bible says that 'the devils also believe, and tremble;' but this is not faith. Where there is not only a belief in God's word, but a submission of the will *to Him*; where the heart is yielded *to Him*, the affections fixed *upon Him*, there is faith—faith that works by love and purifies the soul. Through this faith the heart is renewed in the image of God" (italics added).

The "object" of faith is a very real person, not just the truth about a person. You may have an absolute "belief" in the knowledge and powers that the parachute operates under. But if you do not have the "faith" to pull the cord and place yourself completely in the hands of the parachute, your "belief" avails you nothing. When you pull the cord on a parachute, your "faith" is in the chute itself. So it is with Christ. Our belief may be in the written Word of God, but our faith must be in the personal being of Jesus Christ. Our connection to Him needs to be as real to us as is the parachute to the skydiver.

In *The Ministry of Healing*, page 62, Ellen White defines not only "saving faith" but also "true faith" and "living faith," and their relationship to one another.

"To believe in Christ merely as the Saviour of the world can never bring healing to the soul. The faith that is unto salvation is not a mere assent to the truth of the gospel. True faith is that which receives Christ as a personal Saviour. God gave His only-begotten Son, that *I*, by believing in Him, 'should not perish, but have everlasting life.' John 3:16. When I come to Christ, according to His word, I am to believe that I receive His saving grace. The life I now live, I am to 'live by the faith of the Son of God, who loved *me*, and gave Himself for *me*." Galatians 2:20.

"Many hold faith as an opinion. Saving faith is a transaction, by which those who receive Christ join themselves in covenant relation with God. A living faith means an increase of vigor, a confiding trust, by which, through the grace of Christ, the soul becomes a conquering power."

Belief alone says Christ is the Savior of the world and His Father is the God of the universe. But Ellen White says faith is not just a belief in revealed truths. It is a living transaction between the individual sinner and Christ and consequently with God, thereby making Christ a "personal saviour" and His Father becomes "my Father." (See Jeremiah 3:3-4.)

Here is another definition of faith found in *Faith and Works*:

"What is faith? 'The substance of things hoped for, the evidence of things not seen' (Hebrews 11:1). It is an assent of the understanding to God's words which binds the heart in willing consecration and service to God, Who gave the understanding, Who moved on the heart, Who first drew the mind to view Christ on the cross of Calvary. Faith is rendering to God the intellectual powers, abandonment of the mind and will to God, and making Christ the only door to enter into the kingdom of heaven.

"When men learn they cannot earn righteousness by their own merit of works, and they look with firm and entire reliance upon Jesus Christ as their only hope, there will not be so much of self and so little of Jesus. Souls and bodies are defiled and polluted by sin, the heart is estranged from God, yet many are struggling in their own finite strength to win salvation by good works. Jesus, they think, will do some of the saving; they must do the rest. They need to see by faith the righteousness of Christ as their only hope for time and eternity" (p. 25).

Faith is here defined as an "assent of the understanding." Assent is defined as, "The act of the mind in admitting or agreeing to the truth of a proposition" (*Consolidated Webster Dictionary*). Faith is "not a mere assent [act of the mind in agreeing] to the truth of the gospel" (*The Ministry of Healing*, p. 62), it is the act of the mind which "binds the heart in willing consecration and service to God" (*Faith and Works*, p. 25).

What brings us to exercise this proper act of the mind? The book *Beyond Belief* states: "Faith is our human response to the objective facts of the gospel. In order to be genuine faith, this response must always be motivated by love, a heart appreciation of the gospel" (p. 90). "Only those whose faith is founded upon a heartfelt response to gospel truth have genuine saving faith" (p. 93). This statement implies that I must first have a response of love before I can exercise faith and that my faith is founded upon that response.

How does that relate to this passage from Ellen White?

"Genuine faith is followed by love, and love by obedience" (*Testimonies for the Church*, vol. 5, p. 219).

Or this one, "The precious blood of Jesus is the fountain prepared to cleanse the soul from the defilement of sin. When *you determine to take Him as your friend*, a new and enduring light will shine from the cross of Christ. A true sense of the sacrifice and intercession of the dear Saviour will break the heart that has become hardened in sin; *and love, thankfulness, and humility will come into the soul.* The surrender of the heart to Jesus subdues the rebel into a penitent, and then

Christ Meets Us Where We Are

the language of the obedient soul is as follows: Old things are passed away; behold, all things are become new. 'This is the true religion of the Bible. Everything short of this is a deception'" (*Testimonies for the Church*, vol. 4, p. 625, italics added).

Here we are told that love does not come into our soul until *after* we "determine to take" Jesus as our friend. God's love draws us to "look," then it is *our choice* to "behold." Any consequent human response of love toward God for what He has done for us is one of the "blessings" that come to us through the channel of faith; it is not a necessary requirement before we can exercise true faith. "Jesus loves to have us come to Him just as we are, sinful, helpless, dependent. We may come with all our weakness, our folly, our sinfulness, and fall at His feet in penitence. It is His glory to encircle us in the arms of His love and to bind up our wounds, to cleanse us from all impurity" (*Steps to Christ*, p. 52). Our faith is founded upon Christ's love for us, not upon our "heartfelt response" to the truth of the gospel.

It seems to be a part of our human nature to focus on the gifts that God gives us and lose sight of the Giver of the gifts. Lucifer moved his focus from Christ to himself, and the Scriptures say of him, "Thine heart was lifted up because of thy beauty, thou hast corrupted thy wisdom by reason of thy brightness" (Eze. 28:17). When he focused on all of the talents God had given him, he lost sight of the fact that he was still a dependent "created" being. The Jewish nation became so "puffed up" in all that God had given them and done for them that they failed to recognize the One who made them what they were when He came and walked among them.

Have we done the same thing with our faith? The law of God, as given on tables of stone at Sinai, is a gift. The Word of God, symbolized in the heavenly manna, is a gift. The resurrecting, transforming, power of God, as seen in Aaron's rod that budded, is a gift. All three are found in the ark of the covenant. They are hidden away, out of sight. They are not to be the focus of faith, which is also a gift. The ark is a representation of Jesus Christ, the divine human being, who made a way for us to come to the throne of God. The ark also is hidden from our view behind the veil. Christ, who was lifted up on the cross, is to be the focus of our faith. As we immerse our self into that Christ, God draws us into the hidden recesses of His sanctuary. He shows us the Christ that can only be seen by faith, the risen divine human being that stands before His throne today. In Him only do we find the true righteousness of the law, the living manna of heaven, the enlightening regenerating power to become all that He has designed us to be.

"Faith is the medium through which truth or error finds a lodging place in the mind. It is by the same act of mind that truth or error is received, but it makes a decided difference whether we believe the Word of God or the sayings of men" (*Mind, Character, and Personality*, vol. 2, p. 539).

"Truth and error are before us. God has given us sufficient evidence to determine the right way, and then he leaves us to choose for ourselves" (*The Signs of the Times*, February 16, 1882).

Faith can be related to a simple matter of choice, an "action of the will." For instance, using the man at the pool of Bethesda as an example, Christ comes to us where, and as, we are. He expresses words of hope. He gives knowledge that draws our attention to Him. Then He waits. We can choose to believe and focus upon Him, or we can look away and believe in what we see around us, what has always been.

Next, He gives us commandments to do the impossible, and He waits. Again we must choose to turn away or to listen and look steadfastly into His face as did the paralytic man. As we choose to behold, He gives wisdom and understanding, drawing out a love response in us to the love we see revealed through Him. We choose to enter into a living relationship with Him. We choose to act upon His word. This choice is made in the mind as the soul opens itself to heaven and closes itself to earth. (On earth the paralytic still cannot walk. His limbs still cannot move. But in Christ, by faith, he sees that he is made whole.)

As the choice is made to act, however contrary to what sight and circumstance may say, God gives the power, and the "soul becomes a conquering power" (*The Ministry of Healing*, p. 62). The soul does not use God's power—the soul becomes a conqueror in God's hands. The hammer does not use the arm of the carpenter—it is the arm that wields the hammer. Yield "your members as instruments of righteousness unto God" (Rom. 6:13).

"Faith is not the ground of our salvation, but it is the great blessing—the eye that sees, the ear that hears, the feet that run, the hand that grasps. It is the means, not the end. If Christ gave His life to save sinners, why shall I not take that blessing? My faith grasps it, and thus my faith is the substance of things hoped for, the evidence of things unseen. Thus resting and believing, I have peace with God through the Lord Jesus Christ" (*The SDA Bible Commentary*, vol. 6, p. 1073).

"Faith cometh by hearing, and hearing by the word of God" (Rom. 10:17)—not by "reading" but by "hearing" God speak to our hearts through His Word. Isaiah, Jesus, and Paul used the eyes and the ears as a symbol of the exercise of faith. (See Isaiah 29:10-14; Matthew 13:14-16; Mark 8:17; Acts 28:25-27; and Romans 11:8.) We all have eyes to see, but it is our choice to look, ears to hear—our choice to listen; feet to run—our choice to move; hands to grasp—our choice to reach out and lay hold.

"Faith is simple in its operation and powerful in its results. Many professed Christians, who have a knowledge of the sacred Word, and believe its truth, *fail* in the childlike trust that is essential to the religion of Jesus. They *do not* reach out with that peculiar touch that brings the virtue of healing to the soul" (*The SDA Bible Commentary*, vol. 6, p. 1074, italics added).

The Bible defines the step that comes between believing and salvation, and this is the step that many fail to exercise. It is found in Romans 10:11-14:

"For the scripture saith, Whosoever believeth on him shall not be ashamed. For there is no difference between the Jew and the Greek: for the same Lord over all is rich unto all that *call upon him*. For whosoever shall *call upon the name of the Lord* shall be saved. How then shall they *call on him* in whom they have not believed? (italics added).

Three times the word "call" is used, emphasizing its significance, and yet we tend to miss it as we focus our faith on either believing the Word or on the power to obey. What is it to "call upon him?" Paul "called" upon Caesar to decide his case. (See Acts 25:11 and 28:19.) He put his life into Caesar's hand to choose for him, and he would abide by that choice, be it unto life or unto death.

Strong's Concordance defines "call" as: "to entitle; by implication to invoke (for aid, worship, testimony, decision, etc.)." To "entitle" is to give God His rightful place of authority in and over your life. "Let this point be fully settled in every mind: If we accept Christ as a Redeemer, we must accept Him as a Ruler. We cannot have the assurance and perfect confiding trust in Christ as our Saviour until we acknowledge Him as our King" (*Faith and Works*, p. 16).

To "invoke" is defined in the *Consolidated Webster Dictionary* as "to address in prayer, to call on for assistance and protection, to call for solemnly or with earnestness." Satan "believes" but he will never "call upon the name of the Lord." Do we "trust in the Word" while actually relying on our own understanding of that Word? Or are we truly "calling upon his name," recognizing our weaknesses and our lack of wisdom? Is our faith a simple "childlike trust" in the person of Jesus? Does He rule in our life in all things? This is where prayer, especially secret prayer, comes into play. When no one else is there to see, do you still acknowledge His presence, your complete unworthiness, your absolute need, and His supreme right to rule your life in all things?

"Christ was seeking to lead them from their low condition of faith to the experience they might receive if they truly realized what He was,—God in human flesh. He desired them to see that their faith must lead up to God, and be anchored there. How earnestly and perseveringly our compassionate Saviour sought to prepare His disciples for the storm of temptation that was soon to beat upon them. He would have them hid with Him in God" (*The Desire of Ages*, p. 664).

Again, notice it is to the Father that Christ would lead us, to prepare us for the storm that lies ahead of us. A much greater level of "faith" as well as knowledge will be needed soon.

How easy it is for us to slip into the mistake of the Jews in Christ's day. "Search the scriptures; for in them ye think ye have eternal life: and they are they which testify of me. And ye will not come to me, that ye might have life" (John 5:39, 40). The heart where self is not completely surrendered will tend to trust in his knowledge of Christ, not realizing he has left the person of Christ far behind. The scriptures may tell the mind who Christ is, but only God can reveal to the heart who He is. God is drawing upon us to stretch out our faith to reach up into heaven above, to find our anchor there in the Living Word, not just the written Word.

In essence, to call upon the name of the Lord is to die to self, to exercise total trust in God, and to pray without ceasing. We are to call upon Him to aid us in our daily walk and in every situation of life. We are to seek Him for worship and to call upon Him for testimony and for every decision we have to make. We must seek Him first in all things, allowing Him to be our wisdom and our strength. Ellen White stated it so beautifully: "where there is a submission of the will to Him; where the heart is yielded to Him, the affections fixed upon Him, there is faith" (*Our Father Cares*, p. 292). Many believe, but how few "call" upon God in this manner! This is the faith Christ exercised toward His Father, to the point that Christ was so hidden we saw only the Father, we heard only the Father. Not until we become like Him shall we see Him as He is.

We have looked to nature many times to see truth illustrated; let us go there again. The part we play in cooperating with God in our salvation is revealed by this quote:

"The growth and perfection of the seed rests not with the husbandman. God alone can ripen the harvest. But man's co-operation is required. *God's work for us demands the action of our mind, the exercise of our faith.* We must seek His favors with the whole heart if the showers of grace are to come to us. We should improve every opportunity of placing ourselves in the channel of blessing. . . . We must pray that God will unseal the fountain of the water of life. And we must ourselves receive of the living water. . . . Christ commands, 'Pray without ceasing;' that is, *keep the mind uplifted to God,* the source of all power and efficiency" (*Testimonies to Ministers and Gospel Workers*, pp. 508-510, italics added).

"We are living in a day of trial, a day of probation, a day of test. God is proving His people, to see whether He can work in their behalf. . . . He wants to make us a people through whom he can reveal His grace, and He will do this if we will only give Him opportunity, if we will open the windows of the soul heavenward and close them earthward." (*The General Conference Bulletin*, March 30, 1903, par. 3).

Christ Meets Us Where We Are

Summary

1. Christ shows us the way, having lived His entire life according to the law of the resurrection.
   a. He died (ceased to correspond) to His divine self and trusted in another to live His life for Him.
   b. We must die to our evil self and trust another to live our life for us.
2. It is through the "will" that sin retains its hold on us. It is the will that must be crucified and returned sanctified—in God's control, no longer in Satan's control.
3. Faith is the choice to exercise "firm and entire reliance upon Jesus Christ" as our only hope.
4. There is a step between believing and salvation: Calling upon the name of the Lord.
   a. Giving our life into the hands of another.
   b. Acknowledging God's right to rule over us in all things.
   c. This is the step that SATAN WILL NEVER DO
   d. It is the step that WE MUST DO.
5. What makes it so difficult for us to do what we know is right in submitting the will to God?

Chapter Six

Understanding The Battle Within

"God has made every provision whereby our thoughts may become purified, elevated, refined, and ennobled. He has not only promised to cleanse us from all unrighteousness, but He has made an actual provision for the supply of grace that will lift our thoughts toward Him and enable us to appreciate His holiness. We may realize that we are Christ's possession and that we are to manifest His character to the world. Prepared by heavenly grace, we become clothed with the righteousness of Christ, in the wedding garment, and are fitted to sit down at the marriage supper. We become one with Christ, partakers of the divine nature, purified, refined, elevated, and acknowledged to be the children of God—heirs of God and joint heirs with Jesus Christ" (*Mind, Character, and Personality*, vol. 2, p. 660).

"Be ye therefore perfect, even as your Father which is in heaven is perfect" (Matt. 5:48).

"For sin shall not have dominion over you" (Rom. 6:14).

"But thou, O man of God…follow after righteousness, godliness, faith, love, patience, meekness. Fight the good fight of faith, lay hold on eternal life, whereunto thou art also called…I give thee charge in the sight of God, who quickeneth all things, and before Christ Jesus… that thou keep this commandment without spot, unrebukeable, until the appearing of our Lord Jesus Christ" (1 Tim. 6:11-14).

"He who has determined to enter the spiritual kingdom will find that all the powers and passions of unregenerate nature, backed by

Understanding The Battle Within

the forces of the kingdom of darkness, are arrayed against him. Each day he must renew his consecration, each day do battle with evil. Old habits, hereditary tendencies to wrong, will strive for the mastery, and against these he is to be ever on guard, striving in Christ's strength for victory" (*The Acts of the Apostles*, p. 476).

"By a momentary act of will, one may place himself in the power of evil; but it requires more than a momentary act of will to break these fetters and attain to a higher, holier life. The purpose may be formed, the work begun; but its accomplishment will require toil, time, and perseverance, patience and sacrifice.... All must engage in this warfare for themselves" (*Testimonies for the Church*, vol. 8, p. 313).

We have been called unto righteousness—character perfection—but we are not to think that it will be a "piece of cake" to attain this high ideal. Because of the "battle" with evil that we face every day, there is one question I have pondered over and over in my mind since becoming a Christian. "What is my part, and what is God's part?" I do not want to leave my job undone nor do I want to try and do God's work for Him. A good look at the last Adam has shown us the work that God has already accomplished for all of humanity—the provision He has already made. He is waiting ever so patiently to pour forth the *blessings* of His finished work upon us as soon as we open the doors of our hearts heavenward and close them earthward. As soon as we allow the power of God from without to come in He will bring forth the life of His Son that lies dormant in each of us. So, what is our part in this battle?

Drawing Distinctions

A clearer understanding of what my work is came when I began to draw distinctions between some very familiar Bible terms. They are (1) the carnal mind, (2) the old man, and (3) the stony heart. Most of us will use these terms as though they are interchangeable—all speaking of the same thing. I discovered they are not one and the same, although they are closely interrelated. As I studied I also found three processes at work: (1) subduing (render useless, entirely idle) and its converse—awakening, quickening, (2) eradication and implantation (put off and put on), and (3) death and resurrection (change in condition). When the distinctions were drawn and the processes properly applied, I found the nature of man, the sin problem, and the solution provided through the gospel became very clear. I hope you will think so too.

First, let us define the carnal mind. The only mention of this term is found in Romans 8:7. Here we are told that the carnal mind "is enmity against God: for it is not subject to the law of God, neither indeed can be." The carnal mind is not *at enmity* with God, it itself is the enmity. In the Geneva Bible, carnal mind is translated "mind of the flesh." Defined in the Greek it means "fleshly tendencies." This is referring to the "tendency" of the mind to think upon fleshly things. *It is not the mind that actually has carnal thoughts.* This enmity against God is further defined in James 4:4 as "the friendship of the world." Note again, it is not the "act" of being a friend of the world, but the "tendency" to be a friend of this world.

In Ephesians 2:15 we find that this enmity was in the flesh of Christ. With the way we currently define the carnal mind, we could never say that Christ had it. But drawing this distinction allows us to say, as the Bible does, that Christ had the enmity—the carnal mind—in his flesh, because it is only the "tendency" within the flesh, the "principle" of self exaltation that is against God. Like a "tendency," a principle is only the beginning, the origin or primary source, from which anything proceeds. Like a tendency it must be acted upon before it can have an impact. What did Jesus Christ do with this tendency in his flesh? Ephesians 2:15 tells us that He "abolished" it—He rendered it useless, entirely idle. (See *Strong's Concordance* #2673.) It was there in his flesh when He walked this earth, but it was never active in Him. This "tendency," this principle of living for self, never became so much as a "thought" in His mind.

Ephesians 2:16 tells us that Jesus did something else with the enmity in His flesh. He took it to the cross and it was "slain"—killed outright, put to death—in Christ. Romans 6:6 says that "our old man is crucified [impaled on a cross] with him, that the body of sin might be destroyed." At first glance we would think that the old man and the enmity in the flesh are one and the same, both being taken to the cross. But the word "destroyed" throws on a different light. It is the same word translated "abolished" in Ephesians 2:15. The old man is crucified in order that the "body of sin"—the flesh with the enmity, the carnal mind—might be rendered useless, entirely idle "that henceforth we should not serve sin" (Rom. 6:6). Romans 7:23 tells us that it is the "law of sin" in our members that holds us in bondage, fighting against the law of the mind. A principle is also a "governing law of conduct, a settled rule of action." This law (principle) of sin was active in the man of Romans 7, holding him in bondage, but was ever held inactive in the members of Jesus Christ.

When we read the word "flesh" in the Bible, we may think of the physical body itself. Ellen White draws a distinction for us in *The Adventist Home*: "The lower passions have their seat in the body and work through it. The words 'flesh' or 'fleshly' or 'carnal lusts' embrace the *lower, corrupt nature*; the flesh of itself cannot act contrary to the will of God. We are commanded to crucify the flesh, with the affections and lusts. How shall we do it? Shall we inflict pain on the body? No; but *put to death the temptation to sin*. The corrupt thought is to be expelled. Every thought is to be brought into captivity to Jesus Christ.

All animal propensities are to be subjected to the higher powers of the soul. The love of God must reign supreme; Christ must occupy an undivided throne. Our bodies are to be regarded as His purchased possession. The members of the body are to become the instruments of righteousness" (p. 127, italics added).

The physical flesh, in and of itself, cannot act contrary to the will of God, or you and I could not even exist today. But within the being of man there is a lower corrupt nature that takes in the terms flesh, fleshly, and carnal lusts. The temptation to sin, coming from the "flesh,"—this lower corrupt nature—is to be put to death, rendered idle (cease all communication with it). The animal propensities are to be subjected to the higher powers—to be held in check. It is the corrupted thought that is to be expelled—eradicated, with new thoughts to be implanted.

To sum it up, the carnal mind is simply the "tendencies" in our "lower corrupt nature" to sin—the bent to evil in the flesh, the principle of Satan's mind to live for self, waiting to be acted upon. Christ had this in His "flesh" but it was ever rendered idle in Him, ever subjected to the higher powers of His soul, while He walked this earth. On the cross he killed this enmity outright by laying down His own life, and it never rose with Him. "The last enemy that shall be destroyed is death." (1 Cor. 15:26). "Destroyed" here also means "rendered idle, completely useless." Death itself cannot be done away with, but the day is soon coming when all things that can be gathered will be gathered together in one in Christ. Then it is that sin, and its consequence of death, will never be seen again. Through faith, the enmity in our "flesh" can be rendered useless, entirely idle, during our lifetime and will not rise with those who are resurrected to meet Christ in the air.

What about the "old man"? In Ephesians 4:22 the old man is defined as our "former conversation" which in the Greek is "our past way of life." The old man is not the "tendency" to sin, it is the actual sins committed, in thought and deed. The old man is corrupt because of lusts—desires. Ephesians 2:3 further defines the old man as "fulfilling the desires [choices] of the flesh [the carnal mind] and of the mind [the deep thoughts, imaginations]." The old man is the way we live when the lusts (desires) of the flesh and the thoughts of the mind have made a union. This Christ never formed in thought or deed.

Romans 8:6 says "to be carnally minded is death." "To be" is to "enter into and to exist." It is when we allow the higher powers of the soul to enter into and exist with the tendency to sin that is in our lower nature that we "personally" become subject to death. The first Adam's choice to unite with the temptation to sin brought physical death to all humanity. Our choice to enter into union with the tendency to sin in our flesh, knowingly or unknowingly, demands our personal death—a second death. This "union" is further described in James 4:4: "Whosoever therefore will be a friend of the world" is he who chooses to enter into and exist with the "friendship of the world." When a person does this, he becomes "the enemy of God."

This old man is to be "crucified" with Christ (Rom. 6:6). Christ took our sins upon Himself on the cross and this we claim by faith as we choose to be baptized into Him. Ephesians 4:22 says we are to "put off" or to "unclothe oneself" of the old man. Ezekiel 18:31 tells us that our transgressions are to be *"cast away."* Thus we see that the old man is "formed" in us when we choose to enter into union with the enmity in our flesh—the enmity that Satan planted. It is our "character," our thoughts, feelings and consequent actions. This old man is not to be subdued, or rendered entirely idle, as is the carnal mind. It is to be "put off," "cast away," "unclothed" from us. Ephesians 4:23-24 goes on to say we are to be "renewed in the spirit" of our minds and to "put on the new man," which would be a new way of life—a new character, new motives, new thoughts, new actions.

Last, but not least, what is the "stony heart"? In Ezekiel 36:26 God says, "A new heart also will I give you, and a new spirit will I put within you: and I will take away the stony heart out of your flesh, and I will give you an heart of flesh." At first glance what is happening to the stony heart appears to be the same as happens to the old man—eradicate or put off. The following statement from Ellen White helps to clarify.

"What is the new heart? It is the new mind. What is the mind? It is the will. Where is your will? It is either on Satan's side or on Christ's side. Now it is up to you. Will you put your will today on Christ's side of the question? That is the new heart. It is the new will, a new mind. 'A new heart will I give thee.' Then let us begin right here. Conversion is simple, very simple" (*Sermons and Talks*, vol. 1, p. 210, also found in *The Battle for the Mind* by Lloyd and Leola Rosenvold, p. 25).

Ellen White ties the heart, the mind, and the will together as one in the process of conversion. We are to take the will from Satan's side and put it on the side of Christ. If we do this, we will have a new will, a new mind, a new heart. The will, mind, and heart are not being removed and replaced as the old man is nor are they being "rendered useless" as is the carnal mind. Their "union" with the flesh is being severed—broken, as the choice is made to switch sides—to take the will from Satan's side and put it on the side of Christ. "Choose you this day whom ye will serve" (Joshua 24:15).

Colossians 1:21 says that *in our mind we believe* ourselves to be alienated from God and are His enemies *because of our wicked works*. (Notice that this is not necessarily a "truth;" in fact, it can be a deception in the mind brought about by our union with the flesh.) Our wicked works testify to the union of our minds (the higher powers of the soul—the will, the heart, the spirit of the mind) with the carnal

Understanding The Battle Within

mind—the bent to evil in our lower corrupt nature. In our minds we know we have formed the old man who is a friend of the world and an enemy of God (James 4:4).

Ephesians 4:17 and 18 says that we, who have learned of Christ (verse 20), are not to walk "as other Gentiles walk in the vanity of their mind, having the understanding darkened, being alienated from the life of God through the ignorance that is in them, because of the blindness of their heart"—the stony heart. This "blindness" of the stony heart—the lack of listening to the "inner light"—makes it next to impossible for us to see who we really are in Christ by virtue of the last Adam. Even though we read in Colossians 1:20 that we are reconciled by the death of Christ, and in Romans 6:6 that the "old man" is crucified with Christ, we, as sinners, know that we deserve death, and we find it hard to believe that God truly loves us. So, how is the "stony heart" that feels alienated against God affected at the cross?

"I am crucified with Christ: nevertheless I live; yet not I, but Christ liveth in me: and the life which I now live in the flesh I live by the faith of the Son of God, who loved me, and gave himself for me" (Gal. 2:20).

The old man was crucified with Christ, to be put off and never to be put on again. Here "I" (the will, the heart, the mind, me, self) is crucified with Christ and is returned again "one" with Christ. The stony heart is taken from the flesh in that its union with the flesh is broken. The condition of the stony heart changes to "a heart of flesh"—the selfish will becomes selfless, the self-centered mind becomes Christ-centered. In Romans 6:8 we find the same thing. If we die with Christ, we shall live with Christ. *Thoughts from the Mount of Blessing* reveals that the giving of the will to God is like plucking out the eye, cutting off the hand. But, once given, its union with the flesh is broken and it is returned sanctified, one with God. Here we have death and resurrection. The one dying is also the one rising, only the "condition" changes.

We now have three distinctions and three processes:
1. Carnal mind—the *tendencies* of the flesh, lower corrupt nature, enmity in the flesh.
   - To be—rendered useless, or entirely idle, during our lifetime.
2. Old man—the *fruit of the union* of the carnal mind and the heart, will, and mind.
   - To be—put off, cast away, crucified, unclothed, and a new man put on.
3. Stony heart—the *condition of the mind*, will, heart when united with the carnal mind.
   - To be—crucified with Christ and returned sanctified (resurrected).

If you were to see the carnal mind and the old man as one and the same, then you might try "putting off" the enmity in the flesh, "putting in" the seed of Christ—you have the "holy flesh movement." Or you might try subduing your evil character, modifying it, "keeping it under" control—you now have a "works program." If you see the stony heart as the enmity in the flesh, you might try to eradicate it or subdue it rather than acknowledge "your" need to die and forfeit your life as well as your sins at the cross. This is one of Satan's greatest deceptions, developing Pharisees and Laodiceans.

The next question is, "How are these three processes put to work and in what order?" I believe the marriage illustration of Romans 7 will show us how to put off the old man, render useless the enmity in the flesh, crucify the will, and have it returned to us sanctified and selfless in Christ.

Romans Chapter Seven

Take a moment to read Romans 7:1-6. This marriage illustration is spoken to them that "know the law." It is spoken to them that recognize that the law of God is good and worthy of their obedience. Paul knows that his brethren see only the letter of the law that kills and holds in bondage. They do not yet see the spirit of the law that sustains life and allows freedom. In the illustration we are told that the law binds the woman to her husband as long as the husband is alive. Should he die then the same law now frees her to marry again. The issue here is not the law, but the woman's relationship to that law.

We understand that the woman desires to be freed from her present marriage and to be united to another. To do so before the husband dies is to commit adultery, which by God's law is punishable by death. The woman does not desire to break the law; she only desires to be set free from this binding union with her present husband so she can be free to marry another. Most expositors of this passage "kill off" the husband to set the woman free. Obviously, the present husband is not going to willingly lie down and die, and she cannot kill him for that, too, would be breaking the very law she is trying to keep. How can she be loosed from her present union with her old husband and be free to marry again without breaking the law? That is the question that is raised here.

The answer is given in Romans 7:4: "Wherefore, my brethren, ye also are become dead to the law by the body of Christ; that ye should be married to another." Let us look at the law of marriage and how it relates to us and the body of Christ. Genesis 2:24, Matthew 19:5, Mark 10:8, and Ephesians 5:31 all tell us that when a man and a woman are joined together they become "one flesh." 1 Corinthians 6:14-17 says he who joins to a harlot becomes "one flesh" with the harlot, and he who joins to the Lord is "one spirit." Now, remember, we earlier found that as Christ was raised from the grave so will we. Everyone will rise—some in the first resurrection, the rest in the second—but we shall all rise. Why? By virtue of the incarnation of Christ, we are all now members of His body—whether we know it or not. Put this with James 4:4 where we are called "adulterers and adulteresses" and what Waggoner had to say in *Bible Studies in the Book of Romans*, page 51, takes on a deep significance.

First, ask yourself, "By what right does Christ come to a married woman and propose a union with her while she is married to another, however bad that marriage might be?" By law, He has no right. Waggoner found an answer. He said that Christ can rightfully come to us and propose a union between Him and ourselves because "lawfully" he is already married to us! When the Word became flesh, He absorbed all of humanity into Himself, committing Himself to every human being in a union that He will never choose to break. As in the Hebrew custom, he paid the price for the "bride to be" to the woman's father. The commitment having been made, the "husband to be" goes to prepare a place for his new bride in his father's house. All this Christ has done. While He has been gone, preparing a place for us, it is we who have gone astray. It is we who have played the "harlot" and have joined ourselves to another.

The Bible says, "For thy Maker is thine husband" (Isa. 54:5), and "Turn, O backsliding children, saith the LORD, for I am married unto you" (Jer. 3:14).

"When we turn aside to another master, we break our vows to him, and make void the covenant; and we become adulterers, choosing the friendship and favor of others, and proving untrue to him who has died for us" (*The Signs of the Times*, August 1889).

Because of this "unlawful" union we are now in, by law we are the one's who deserve to die. When Christ died, I, being one with Him by virtue of His commitment to me, died also—*by promise*. When we consent to die in Christ *by faith*, returning to Him our own commitment to the marriage, we meet the claims of the broken law. With our death, the union with the enmity in the flesh is broken. Christ then raises us new, free to unite with the spirit of life in Christ, all according to law.

So, to sever her adulterous relationship to the old husband (from which she longs to be free), the woman herself must be the one to die. She can choose to die in Christ by faith—acknowledging a work already done in her in Christ—resting in the knowledge of who she is in Christ. Thereby she "renders idle" the claims of her old husband upon her and the fruit of that adulterous relationship; her past way of life—the old man—is also crucified. All this is hers as long as she remains united *by faith* to her "new husband"—"one spirit" with Christ. Should she return to the old husband (who will continue to seek to reunite with her) and again become "one flesh" with him, like Hosea, Christ will seek after her, calling upon her to return to the cross and reunite with Him. (How loving our true husband is!) Through the body of Christ we can, by faith, "reckon ourselves dead indeed unto sin [the old husband's claim to us rendered idle—the fruit of the adulterous union as crucified] but alive unto God through Jesus Christ our Lord" (*The Signs of the Times*, October 1, 1894). Christ will raise us anew "one spirit" with Him that we should bring forth fruit unto God.

What does this marriage illustration tell us about the condition of the man later described in the rest of chapter 7, the man who cannot do as he knows in his mind is right to do? The man of Romans 7 knows the law, that it is holy and good (verse 13). He knows the law was ordained unto life but it only condemns him unto death (verse 10). He desires to live in obedience to the law but finds himself unable to render that obedience. Like the marriage illustration, the law binds him to a relationship he desires to be free from. He knows death is the only answer—but whose?

The man first tries to free himself by "putting off" the "fruit" of this relationship. He tries to "cast away" the transgressions he has been committing. He tries to "put on" a new way of life by obeying the law. He finds that no matter how much he desires to, no matter how much he tries to live the new life, he cannot do it. Finally he cries out in desperation and despair, "O wretched man that I am! who shall deliver me from the body of this death?" This man is lamenting the "fruit" of his present relationship. The real problem is not the sins he is committing but the relationship he has to the "law of sin" in his members. Having not yet realized this fact, by what power has the man been trying to solve his problem?

Let us look for the focus of this man. Who is doing the "willing and the doing" in him? I recommend you count the number of personal pronouns—I, me, my—in Romans 7:7-25. I counted 47 is less than 20 verses! As you will soon see, his focus is himself—"I can do it." By the power of his own will, "the law of the mind," he is striving to live in obedience to God's law. The children of Israel at Sinai said, "All that the LORD hath spoken we will do" (Ex. 19:8). Could they do it? No! And neither can this man. He is discovering that the law, which he knows to be good, has become his schoolmaster—a truant officer—that condemns him. The law shows him there is *no good in him* at all and *no power in him* to do what is right. He is driven to seek another solution, and he finds it in Jesus Christ.

As in Galatians 3, the law, as a schoolmaster, has led this man to faith in Jesus Christ as his only hope. After "faith is come" he is the child of Abraham—the father of faith—and is baptized into Christ. At his baptism, (1) he enters into the death of Christ, personally meeting the penalty of the broken law; (2) the "old man" he tried so desperately

Understanding The Battle Within

to rid himself of is crucified—impaled on the cross; and (3) the union to the "law of sin" in his members is severed. He is raised a new man, united to the law of the spirit of life in Christ. His focus becomes centered on God, Jesus, and the Holy Spirit. See the focus of the man of Romans 8. As the Spirit moves upon him to unite with Christ, submitting his will to the Father, God now works in him to "will and to do of His good pleasure." He finds himself experiencing the victory and peace of Romans 8.

As related earlier, faith is more than just an intellectual belief. The Bible says, "Believe on the Lord Jesus Christ, and thou shalt be saved" (Acts 16:31), and "This is the work of God, that ye believe on him whom he hath sent" (John 6:29). Alone these scriptures could and have been misapplied to only an intellectual acknowledgement of Christ. Romans 10:12-14 added a step between believing and salvation, "Whosoever shall call upon the name of the Lord shall be saved" (verse 13). Psalm 145:18 and 19 expresses the same thought, "The LORD in nigh unto all them that call upon him, to all that call upon him in truth. He will fulfil the desire of them that fear him: he also will hear their cry, and will save them." To "call" upon the Lord is to acknowledge our need of Him and give Him His rightful place on the throne of our hearts. It is to allow Him to rule us through our conscience (the voice of God to man), subjecting our will to Him, trusting Him to do the choosing and the doing in us. (See Philippians 2:12, 13.)

The man of Romans 7 believed and he cried out and he was saved. He had been drawn of God, the law had convicted him, and his conscience was awakened to what was truth. The first-fruit of an awakened conscience is "repentance." He is "thinking differently" about God and about himself than he ever has before. He sees the holiness of God and the utter unworthiness and absolute helplessness of himself. He has come to sense his desperate need of something outside of himself to solve his bondage problem.

After true repentance comes true confession of what you are, "So then with the mind I myself serve the law of God; but with the flesh the law of sin" (Rom. 7:25). I do not believe this is a statement of what he is after he finds victory in Christ. It is the recognition of what he has discovered through this experience. In his mind he desires to serve the law of God, but in his flesh he still serves the law of sin. The conscience does not take on an active role in the life—is not "quickened"—until after a true confession is made (this process will be discussed in fuller detail later). This man of Romans 7 is confessing the "sides" of the battle that rage within each of us who have come to "know" the claims of the law upon us but find ourselves unable to keep it. The conscience is "awake" but not yet in a "ruling" position.

Notice the first part of Romans 7:25. Paul says, "I thank God through Jesus Christ our Lord." Is it possible that Paul is thanking God for this Romans 7 experience? In *Steps to Christ*, pages 35 and 36, you will find that Ellen White describes this experience as God's tender hand at work drawing us to Christ. So, let us, as Paul did, rejoice when we find ourselves experiencing the bondage and horror of Romans 7. Let us acknowledge it as a gift of repentance from God and thank Him for it. He is preparing the heart, breaking up the fallow ground, getting it ready to receive the "living law."

Also, in *The Acts of the Apostles*, page 561, Romans 7 is quoted as a part of our repentance that ever deepens as we draw closer to the throne of God. We certainly do not want to remain locked in bondage to the law of sin in our members, but when we find ourselves there, let us not sink in hopelessness as Satan would have it. Let us lift our voices in thanksgiving to God, for He has opened our eyes to see our wretchedness, or perhaps an even deeper level of our wretchedness. As we reach out the hand of faith, taking hold of and resting in Christ, we find there is no condemnation. When we consent to die, as the woman must, we find new life in Christ.

Please refer to the charts—Drawing Distinctions and The Marriage Illustration of Romans Seven—to see what I have shared with you in its simplicity. (You will find these charts in Appendix B.)

A True Self and a False Self

After coming to the understanding of the battle we fight within, as revealed in the story of the man of Romans 7, I was reading an article by Jones in *The Review and Herald*, May 20, 1902, titled "Reorganization." He stated:

"In man there is a true self, and there is the false self. The true self always empties self; the false self always exalts self. Think! When the prodigal son was off there herding the swine, and was so hungry that he was willing to pick up the husks from which the swine had sucked the juice, and see if he could not wring out some more, he 'came to himself.' Aha! The divine word is, 'He came to himself.' Always there is the true man,—the personality, the individuality, that God has created every man to be, to glorify him; for *every soul that ever came into this world is in the design of God. And the divine destiny that God has set for every soul that ever comes into this universe, is that he shall be conformed to the image of God's Son.* There is a divine design in and for each soul. And in that lies man's better self, the true self. But this other, the false, the selfish self, has taken the precedence. This other, the false, the selfish self, which is of Satan, has usurped the throne in man, and is reigning there against the man's better self always, compelling the better self to drag along in the bondage and slavery of the evil self.

"But, thank the Lord, men can be brought to the point where they will come to themselves, their real, their better selves. Do not forget that when that man, sitting there watching the swine, 'came to himself,' the first thing that he said was, 'I will arise and go to my father.' Do not forget that the Father is the One whom the true man, that better self in man, will always recognize instantly as soon as ever he awakes, and opens his eyes, and comes 'to himself.' So God sends you and me the message of the glorious gospel of Jesus Christ to bring men to themselves. And in the doing of this, by whatever means of ministration it may be that we can bring a man face to face with himself, and get him to come to himself,—O, we can always be sure that when that blessed moment comes, there is in his heart the blessed word, 'I will arise and go to my Father.' So then, *let this mind be in you which was also in Christ Jesus, who is the manifestation of that true self that annihilates that other selfish self*' (italics added).

This thought of Jones coincided with what I was learning—that there was something in us just waiting for a chance to be revealed. It also fit in nicely with the experience of the man of Romans 7 who is coming "face to face with himself."

"The only condition upon which freedom of man is possible is that of becoming one with Christ. 'The truth shall make you free;' and Christ is the truth. Sin can triumph only by enfeebling the mind, and destroying the liberty of the soul. Subjection to God is restoration to one's self,—to the true glory and dignity of man. The divine law, to which we are brought into subjection, is "the law of liberty" (*The Desire of Ages*, p. 466).

A few days after reading this article by Jones, I happened to be studying about the creation of Adam and Eve in *Patriarchs and Prophets*. The following phrase, on page 46, caught my attention: "A part of man, bone of his bone, and flesh of his flesh, she was his second self." Eve was Adam's "second self"—a first self and a

Understanding The Battle Within

second self, a true self and a false self. My mind immediately made a correlation and began to race. Could there be more to this story of Adam and Eve than the simple account of humanity's first parents' creation and fall into sin? Many stories of the Bible have deeper spiritual meanings hidden beneath the surface. The brazen serpent lifted up in the wilderness for healing from the poisonous snake bites is really the story of Jesus Christ who would be lifted up on the cross for the healing of the poisonous sting of sin. The story of the sons of Sarah and Hagar is "an allegory, for these are the two covenants" (Gal. 4:22-25).

As I opened my mind and looked deeper into the story of Adam and Eve, I found the story of man's spiritual nature as it was created, how our sinless spiritual nature became corrupt, and God's plan for restoring us to our original state. In the first few chapters of the book *Education*, Ellen White refers to three natures in man—the physical nature, the mental nature, and the spiritual (or moral) nature. After the fall she says the strength of the physical nature was weakened. The capacity of the mental nature was lessened. The vision of the spiritual nature was dimmed. Much has been said about our weak, degenerating physical bodies, and about the "untapped" capacity of our brains.

Even more has been said about our spiritual nature, only there are considerable differences of opinions as to what it is, how it operates, and what happens to it at our birth and our death. Most religious teachings will give the incarnate Son of God our weakened physical nature, and even our lessened mental capacity, but hesitate or stop cold in giving Him our fallen spiritual nature. I believe much of the mystery can be cleared up by taking a closer look beneath the surface of the story of Adam and Eve. And, by doing so, we can clearly see at what point the last Adam stepped onto the scene and the impact He had upon our fallen spiritual nature.

Defining Sin

Before going to the story of Adam and Eve, let us first take a closer look at what is causing all the confusion concerning the gospel solution to the sin problem. Obviously, whatever solution you believe the gospel offers will be determined by the understanding you have of the problem of sin. In 1986 Dennis Priebe wrote an article that appeared in the January issue of *Our Firm Foundation*. It was titled "Two Gospels Beneath the Surface," and it drew the line between the two gospels he believes can be found in Adventism today. He brought out two definitions for sin. First, "sin and guilt apply to nature, and the gospel must deal with the reality of guilt as a part of the nature of man which can never be removed until eternal life. In this view, weakness, imperfection, and tendencies are sin." Second, "sin is defined as choosing to rebel against God in thought, word, or action. In this gospel sin is our willful choice to exercise our fallen, sinful nature in opposition to God's will." He states that each definition of sin will determine your understanding of the nature of Christ, how you see justification, and how you define perfection. Whatever foundation we lay will determine the conclusions drawn.

Priebe also stated:

"As a church we have never defined clearly our beliefs in these three critical areas—sin, (nature of) Christ, and perfection . . . Because we have held contradictory views in these areas, we have been unable to clearly define our message and our mission....

"The pivotal issue which determines the direction of both systems of belief—the foundation and premise of the whole controversy—is the question, What is sin? You see, the gospel is all about how we are saved from sin. It is sin which has caused us to be lost, and the gospel is the good news of how God redeems us from sin. Now most of us have assumed for perhaps our whole lifetime that we know what sin is, but

Understanding The Battle Within

as is typically true for most things that we assume without examining them carefully, our assumptions may be just that, unproved assumptions that need careful rethinking. It is just at this point that Adventism has been challenged as having unclear and even erroneous definitions of sin which have led to erroneous positions in righteousness by faith.

"The vital question is, What is the nature of sin for which man is considered guilty, so guilty that he must die in the fires of hell unless he is rescued by the grace of God? We must be precise in defining the nature of this sin, so that we will know just what it is that the gospel rescues us from. Of what must we be forgiven? What must be healed for us to escape eternal death? When you go to see a doctor, he must first determine precisely the nature of the problem afflicting you before he can prescribe a therapy or medicine which can heal you. Just so with sin. We must know wherein our guilt lies, so that we will be able to apply the gospel to the correct illness."

I agree with Priebe in that we must be "precise in defining the nature" of sin, as well as defining sin itself, if we are to understand what the gospel is designed to do for us. Ellen White says that there is only one definition of sin: "sin is the transgression of the law" (*The Signs of the Times*, June 20, 1895; 1 John 3:4). Most believe this refers to our "actions." I recommend you look it up in the concordance. This Greek word is referring more to a condition, stating a fact, or establishing a principle. It is not a verb. If it were then why is another word depicting action tied to it in the first part of the verse when referring to the actual committing of sin? (See concordance under "trangresseth")

In 1 John 3:4 we see John drawing the same distinction as did James concerning "friendship of the world" and "to be a friend of the world" and as did Paul concerning the "carnal mind" and "to be carnally minded." Remember, the carnal mind is not the actual thinking of evil thoughts; it is only the tendency in us to do evil. When *we choose* to enter into harmony with this bent to evil, then we *commit acts of sin* and the *law of sin becomes the ruling principle* in our lives. The same kind of distinction can be drawn here in the "definition" of sin.

As we learned earlier, in the chapter "The Law and the Gospel," there are two sides to the power of gravity. The two sides are revealed by our relationship to this power. A right relationship enables gravity to benefit us. A wrong relationship allows this benefiting power to become a destroying power. The same is true of the law of God. It describes the power of God's love. When we are in a right relationship to that power (in obedience to the law), we have life. Be in a wrong relationship to that power (a transgressor of the law) and the result is death. Righteousness is the word that defines the proper relationship to the law—obedience to the law. It is the stating of a "principle." Someone who is actively in obedience to the law is said to be righteous.

Sin is simply the word that expresses a wrong relationship to the law of God's love—transgression of the law. Again, it is the stating of a "principle." Anyone who is actively disobeying the law, whether knowingly or unknowingly, is said to be a transgressor or a sinner: "Whosoever committeth sin trangresseth also the law" (1 John 3:4). Sin, as a principle, can find expression through every aspect of the wrong relationship, whether it is our sinful nature, because of Adam's wrong choice, or our own personal thoughts and actions.

The Scriptures also state: "Whatsoever is not of faith is sin" (Rom. 14:23). This scripture gets more to the heart, or the "nature," of sin. What is the inherent quality of the principle of sin that puts us on the wrong side of God's law? It is the desire to live unto oneself—selfishness and self-preservation. The essence of faith is the submission of "self" to another, trusting in another to do for us what we cannot do for ourselves. Whatsoever is not of faith is sin because faith is submission of self to Christ, and the choice to live for self makes it impossible for

Understanding The Battle Within

us to make a union with Christ. Failing to make a union with Christ makes it impossible for us to be anywhere but on the wrong side of God's law—which is sin. Anything we do that is not done through faith in Christ is sin.

The bringing in of faith takes us beyond sin simply being our "acts" of transgressing God's Ten Commandments (done by our own choices) or the "tendencies" in us to sin (coming through the sinful flesh). Our outward actions are the result of our use of the power of life God has given to us. All power is of God (Rom. 13:1). Satan and sin have no power of their own to exercise. All Satan can do is to pervert God's power, use it to destroy, and make it appear as though God, Himself, is doing it. (See the story of Job.) We can use the power of life that God has given us to stretch out an open hand and help lift up one who has fallen—an act of righteousness—or we can clench our fist, strike out, and knock someone down—an act of unrighteousness. All power is still of God. He has put it into our hands as to how we will utilize this power of life that we have. Adam had the freedom to choose how to use the power of life given him by God. He chose to live for self rather than trust in God. Thereby he chose to step on the wrong side of the law, to misuse that power, and in so doing he brought the law of sin and death into an active role, in our human nature as well as on the earth.

Today, our now fallen human nature has this principle of sin—live for self—residing in the sinful flesh. We have made many choices that allowed this principle of sin to permeate our higher powers and, therefore, we do not have the wisdom or the strength to use the power of life aright. We only have the freedom to choose who will control that power in us—God or Satan. Physically we are not strong enough to fight off sin. Mentally we do not have the capacity to understand all the depths of sin. And spiritually we cannot see the fullness of the immorality of sin. For instance, instead of seeing a loving Father who is warning us against the inevitable outworking of a principle, we tend to see a stern judge who is standing by to dish out the punishment we deserve for our personal acts in violating His law. When dealing with sin and the solution provided in the gospel, we must not limit the definition of sin to only our nature, to only our choices and consequent actions and acquired guilt, or to simply a wrong relationship. God's plan of redemption must rescue us from the nature of sin and the principle of sin, as well as all of their forms of expression.

Have you ever asked yourself what it was about sin that Christ revealed through the experience of the cross? It's true we were shown the depth of God's love—Jesus, the Son of God, willing to give up His own life to save you and me. Now let us look to see what is revealed concerning sin: (1) Satan—the so-called god of this world—moves upon men to carry out his own desires, which included killing the Son of God that he might rule as he sees fit. (2) The Jewish leaders—the so-called protectors of God's law and the sanctuary—Chose to kill the Son of God for fear of loosing their "position" over the "gifts" of God; refusing to acknowledge the "giver" of those gifts who was revealing to them their true motives. (3) The Romans—the so-called heathen—carrying out the death of the Son of God, who had been declared the King of the Jews and who presented a threat to the kingdom of Rome. (4) The disciples—Christ's followers—allowed the Son of God to die because they feared for their own lives. (5) The Jewish nation—the so-called children of Abraham, those who should have known the truth concerning the Lamb of God revealed in their years of sanctuary rituals—ignorantly stand by while their leaders manipulate the heathen Romans to kill the Son of God. (6) Pontius Pilate—the government official who finds "no fault" with this man—delivers Him up to be crucified in order to satisfy the cries of "public opinion" and to bring

Understanding The Battle Within

so-called "peace" to the region.

Do you get the picture? At the cross we not only see revealed the depth of God's love for us but we also see the depth sin will go in us against our Creator. Satan was called a "murderer" from the beginning even though at the time he first sinned I am sure he did not know to where it would lead him—but God knew. Adam and Eve simply ate a fruit from a forbidden tree, not knowing to where it would finally lead mankind—but God knew. Given opportunity (as revealed by the cross) every sinner would kill the Son of God to get his own way or to save his own life. Sin in all its aspects leads to only one thing—the death of the Son of God.

For me, the question became, "How do we get back on the right side of God's power of life?" How does our "selfish" nature become a "selfless" nature? How does the "nature of righteousness"—self-renouncing love—become the ruling "principle" in our lives, overruling the sinful nature and guiding us to make the right choices? I believe the story of Adam and Eve will greatly clarify the sin problem as it relates to man, the battle we have to fight with sin—in all its aspects—and the solution as provided by the Son of God in the gospel.

Summary

1. Drawing distinctions between familiar biblical terms reveals insights to the battle we fight within because of sin:
    - Carnal mind—*tendencies* of the flesh, lower corrupt nature, enmity in the flesh.
        - To be—rendered useless, or entirely idle, during our lifetime.
    - Old man—the *fruit of the union* of the carnal mind and the heart, will, and mind.

- To be—put off, cast away, crucified, unclothed, and a new man put on.
- Stony heart—the *condition* of the mind, will, heart when united with carnal mind.
  - To be—crucified with Christ and returned sanctified (resurrected).

2. The marriage illustration in the first part of Romans 7 reveals that it is we who have gone astray from our husband (Christ) who has declared His commitment to us and has gone to prepare a place for us. We are in adultery, and the law demands our death. If we die *in* Christ by faith, we find release from our "present" husband (the carnal mind) and deliverance from the old man (our past way of life). Through the submission of the will, the stony heart is broken up, purified, and returned an "heart of flesh."

3. The man of Romans 7 also learns this lesson of submission of the will, after fighting in his own wisdom and strength to no avail. He confesses the sides of the battle: his mind serves the law of God, but the flesh serves sin. Only by "death" can we find deliverance.

4. The step between believing and salvation that many miss is calling upon the Lord. This step means total submission of your life into God's hands, just as Paul called upon Ceasar to decide his case, be it unto life or unto death.

5. What is sin? Transgression of the law—simply a statement of fact, a *principle*, a *governing law* of conduct, a settled *rule* of action. In us it is a *tendency* to be on the wrong side of the power of love. A "transgressor" is one who is *actively* on the wrong side of the power of love. The nature, or inherent essence, of sin is to live for one's self, whereas the nature of

righteousness is to live for the good of others. With the principle of sin embedded in our flesh (which unaided we cannot resist), we must exercise faith, trusting in another to do for us that which we cannot do for ourselves: simply trusting in Christ to work His will in us.
6. In every man there is a true self and a false self. Which "self" finds its expression in you?
7. What can the story of Adam and Eve tell us about this battle we fight every day with sin?

Chapter Seven

Man's Spiritual Nature

In *The Soul and the Resurrection* by J.H. Kellogg, he speaks of two kinds of life manifested in the human body: "1. **Molecular life**, or the life of each separate constituent of the body; and 2. **Somatic life**, or the individual life resulting from the aggregate molecular life of the body" (p. 42). The molecular life is simply the life that is manifested in the cellular structure of the human body in all its different components. The molecular life of the individual cells is continuously dying and being recreated as the body grows and performs its different functions of life. This molecular life is found in all animals and plants, the cells simply differ in degree of development and organization. "Man and animals alone have the higher or somatic life. It is this life by means of which we feel, think, reason, possess all those attributes and perform all those actions which distinguish man from a vegetable" (Ibid., p. 43). This somatic life begins with the first breath taken and continues without interruption until death.

The molecular life of the cells can be studied under a microscope. It can be seen by the naked eye. The relationship of different cells and their function can be ascertained by visual scientific study. But, the somatic life itself cannot be observed under a microscope. It cannot be seen, touched, smelled, or heard separate from the molecular structure of the human body, although it can be revealed through the actions of the body as the physical body manifests the thoughts of the mind. The organ of the brain is specifically designed to take in information through the "organs" of the five senses in the body. Its function is to receive impressions from all parts of the body and to connect together all these sensations and experiences. Thought is the result of comparing all this information, originating new ideas and perceptions from the comparisons. From these thoughts the "somatic life" makes choices that affect the body's actions.

If animals also have brains with the capacity to think and make choices, wherein does man differ from the animals? "We answer, in respect to the nature of the material composing his body, man differs not at all from the lower orders of the animal creation. In organization he differs chiefly in the possession of a set of organs and faculties possessed by no other creature; viz., the moral organs and their functions, the moral faculties. ... It is the possession of a moral sense, of a conscience, which distinguishes man from beast. ... But of conscience, the power to recognize right and wrong, man is the sole possessor. ... Moral sense or conscience may be defined as an abstract recognition of right, that which leads a person to choose to do that which is good, and discard and avoid that which is wrong, *without reference to possible reward or punishment or any other self-relative motive influence*" (Ibid., pp. 64, 65, italics added). (Note that the "principle of self, self preservation" does not exist in the conscience.)

"God has given men more than a mere animal life....He has given them a conscience, and He forbids that this gift be in any way misused; it is, rather, to be exalted to the place of authority to which He has assigned it" (*Mind, Character, and Personality*, vol. 1, p. 319).

Ellen White refers to our spiritual nature as being our moral nature. The spirit is often also said to be the heart. The heart of fallen man is corrupt and needs to be cleansed. When Christ cleansed the temple, it was said to be symbolic of the cleansing of the heart. (See *The Desire of Ages*, p. 161.) The whole of human nature has three parts, body (physical), mind (mental), and soul (spirit, heart). (See 1 Thessalonians 5:23.) If the cleansing of the temple—which has three compartments—refers to the cleansing of the *heart only* then it cannot be referring to the cleansing of all three parts of our human nature, although this is the final result of the entire gospel plan. The cleansing of the temple is said to be symbolic of only one part of our human nature—the heart. The part of the temple that Christ cleansed was the courtyard. He brought silence to the temple, quieting all the noise and rabble going on in the courtyard. There are two other parts to the sanctuary—the holy place and the Most Holy Place. Is it possible that the heart itself, the spiritual nature, is threefold—that it too has three parts?

In Education pages 35 and 36, Ellen White tells us that the temple given in the wilderness was to teach the Israelites about God's glorious character and His purpose for us—to attain to that high standard of character as revealed there. She also states that the "spirit that returns to God is our character." (See The SDA Bible Commentary, vol. 6, p. 1093.) Character is made up of thoughts, feelings, and consequent actions that stem from listening to the conscience or ignoring it—being moral or immoral. If the temple is a symbol of the heart, and the temple was to reveal character, and character is the spirit of man, then would not the cleansing of the heart (the temple) be the cleansing of our character? Being the cleansing of the character would it not also be the cleansing of our spiritual nature? Again, how many compartments were in the sanctuary?

Just as the sanctuary has three parts, I have discovered that our spiritual nature is also threefold and, in the style of an allegory, the story of Adam and Eve brings this out. Beneath the surface, this biblical account of the creation and fall of our first parents very clearly shows us how God originally created the "spiritual nature" of man in

His own image—which is Spirit and is also threefold. It reveals how sin entered in and polluted the sanctuary, the heart of man. It will even give us clues as to how Christ, the last Adam, the second man, enters the polluted temple of the heart, how He cleanses it, and what He is willing and waiting to do in each one of us. First we will look at the spiritual nature of man:

As Created by God

Re-read Genesis 2 and note very carefully what we are told concerning Adam *before* Eve was created. In Genesis 2:8 we find that after God created Adam He planted a special garden and put Adam into the garden. He brought forth from the ground every tree pleasant to the sight, including the tree of life and the tree of knowledge of good and evil. This tells us that Adam saw the power and love of God—he had *the spiritual capacity for knowing God*. In verse 15 Adam was given the work of dressing and keeping the garden—he had *the power to do*. Verses 16 and 17 speak of the tree of knowledge of good and evil and God's command not to eat of it—Adam had *the power to choose*, known as "the will." In verse 19 the animals were created in the sight of and for Adam—Adam was given *dominion*. In verse 20 Adam named the animals—he had *the power to think*. He also sensed his need of a help meet—Adam had *the power to reason*.

In *The SDA Bible Commentary*, volume 1, page 1082, Ellen White says that God gave man *a heart for contemplation*. All these powers that the story reveals that Adam had are known as the "higher powers of the soul." Allegorically, Adam represents these "higher powers of the soul," which is only one-third of our spiritual nature, our first "true self." Then Eve came on the scene. She came from Adam's rib, his side—from a root word that means "halt," as in the case of Jacob who "halted upon his thigh, one sided." She was "bone of his bone, flesh of his flesh." Blood comes from the bones. She had the same life as Adam. She was the body, skin, "self" of Adam. In *Patriarchs and Prophets*, she is called Adam's "second self" (p. 46). Genesis 2:18 says she was an "help meet" for Adam—to surround, to aid, afront, the opposite part, to manifest, announce, to expose, predict, explain, praise. It sounds like she was the part of the spiritual nature that informs the higher powers of their surroundings and then helps to manifest the intents of the higher powers. Verse 24 tells us she was one flesh with Adam—two parts together as one. Allegorically, she was a second part of the spiritual nature of man—a second self—so united with Adam as to act as only one in perfect harmony.

Besides Adam and Eve, we also hear the voice of God. The conscience is said to be the voice of God to man (*Testimonies for the Church*, vol. 5, p. 120). In the biblical account, this voice speaks to Adam—not to Eve—concerning the two trees. (Keep in mind we are looking at this story as an allegory.) The conscience speaks to the higher powers of the soul—the will must be trained to obey the conscience (*Child Guidance*, p. 39). *The SDA Bible Commentary*, volume 7, page 965, tells us that the conscience is the *spiritual eye* of the mind—the "inner light." Being the light of the body it is also represented in the story as the garment of light that covered Adam and Eve's nakedness. This "inner light" radiated God's glory through them as long as they were in harmony with the voice of God. Allegorically, the voice of God is the conscience, the third part of man's spiritual nature.

We now have a threefold spiritual nature. Adam represents the part of the spiritual nature that has the power to think and do (our individuality), to reason, to choose, etc., referred to as the higher powers of the soul. He could hear the voice of God and commune with Him; He was guided by God, who is Spirit. Adam represents our first self that can understand God and relate to the spiritual world. Eve represents that part of the spiritual nature that is called the flesh, the second self, the help meet of the higher powers—to aid and to manifest the higher powers. She had a connection to the "created" things of God, as we shall soon see, and her role was to aid the first self to understand and relate to the created world around them. The third part is represented by the voice of God—the conscience—which enables us to "know" right from wrong, that special place in every human being where something of God resides, waiting patiently to commune with us every day. That place which enables us to understand and relate to the spiritual world of God.

God alone is to control the conscience (*The Desire of Ages*, p. 630). The conscience is to control the appetite, affections, desires, passions (which are represented by Eve as we shall soon see), self, and the will (which is represented by Adam). When the higher powers (Adam), the flesh (Eve), and the voice of God (conscience) were one, united in perfect harmony, the image of God was seen in the light that radiated from them, threefold but acting as one. There was peace and joy in the garden. The law surrounded them and protected them. Unfortunately, this perfect harmony did not last. The threefold unity broke down. Let us take a look at the condition of the spiritual nature:

As Fallen by the Sin of Adam

Genesis 3 gives us a deeper insight into the role that the "flesh" plays in the spiritual nature of man. Eve wandered from Adam's side. Being one with the higher powers she had the capacity to exercise them for herself in her God-given ability to relate to the created world around her. Verses 1-6 tell us a little more about our "second self," the part of the spiritual nature Eve represents. She *saw* the tree, *listened* to the serpent, *touched* the fruit, *tasted* the fruit, and most likely even *smelled* the fruit. She represents the five senses, which are said to be the "avenues of the soul."

"Guard well the avenues of the soul. Place sentinels at the eyes, the ears, the lips" (*The Review and Herald*, August 28, 1883). This part of our spiritual nature takes in information from the world around us and starts the analyzing process. Unaided by the higher powers still in harmony with the voice of God, this "second self" can easily be deceived and consequently lead to wrong choices. Eve, the flesh, did not seek out Adam, the higher powers, or God, the conscience. She thought she could handle it by herself!

She "saw that the tree was good for food" (Gen. 3:6). Was it? It may have been edible—as Satan tried to portray—in the physical sense, but *spiritually* it was not good for food. The "lust [desire] of the flesh" took precedence over the voice of God (1 John 2:16). She thought the fruit was "pleasant to the eyes" (Gen. 3:6). Again, physically it may have been very appealing, but it was not to be looked upon with desire. Wanting what she could see rather than trusting in what she could not see—God's warning concerning the tree—the "lust [desire] of the eyes" became corrupt. She believed the serpent's words and desired the fruit to make her wise. She put herself first, instead of trusting in God's word. The "pride of life" became corrupt (1 John 2:16). Satan "tempted the woman to distrust God's love, to doubt his wisdom, and to transgress his law" (*Patriarchs and Prophets*, p. 57). She took and ate of the fruit. An evil seed was planted in the flesh (*The SDA Bible Commentary*, vol. 4, p. 1143)—"an antagonistic power . . . a bent to evil, a force which, unaided, [we] cannot resist" (*Education*, p. 29).

It is true that the "physical" flesh will be affected, but here we are concerned with the "spiritual" flesh as represented by Eve. As related earlier in *The Adventist Home*, page 127, a distinction is drawn between the physical flesh and the "flesh" that refers to man's lower corrupt nature—the animal propensities, the "temptations" from within. Through acting on the voice of Satan coming through the serpent, Eve, the flesh, became "sinful flesh." Her part of the spiritual nature, the lower powers of the soul, became carnal—now within her powers laid the carnal mind, the tendencies in the fleshly part of the mind, the enmity—the bent to evil that resides in the flesh. Eve was deceived. She did not reason with Adam—the higher powers of the soul—and she did not reason with God—the voice of the conscience. She reasoned with her "self" and the serpent. She became the "false self" that Jones spoke of, as quoted earlier. *Mind, Character, and Personality*, volume 2, pages 713 and 714, reveals that Eve was hypnotized. Another mind had taken control of her mind. This part of the spiritual nature was now in the control of Satan, it was not subject to the law of God: neither indeed could it be. Applied to our lives today, the law of sin still rules—the principle of Satan's mind, live for self, controls the one-third of man's spiritual nature as represented by Eve.

Notice that Satan did not go directly to Adam, the higher powers. He went in through the "back door" so to speak—through deceiving the lower powers. He then uses the lower powers to influence the higher powers. Why not go directly to Adam? Because he knew that the higher powers were still too connected to God. So Satan set up a conflict that would weaken that relationship, and he plays the same tricks today.

Eve sought out Adam, the higher powers of the soul, the first self—the true self that was still in harmony with God. She was the "avenue" to the soul—"she became the agent of Satan in working the ruin of her husband"—Adam, the higher powers (*Patriarchs and Prophets*, p. 56). She came with her hands "filled with the forbidden fruit" (Ibid.)—the flesh was full of sin. The flesh had become the voice of Satan, speaking through the now corrupt lower nature.

James 1:14-15 says man is tempted when the lust of the flesh draws upon the will to separate from God and to join with the flesh and to follow the flesh in its desires. In volume 1 of *The SDA Bible Commentary*, Ellen White tells us that Adam was not hungry (p. 1084). Again, this was not a physical battle. This was a spiritual battle that took place in the spirit of man. Adam had to choose between the voice of God and the voice of Eve—which had become the voice of Satan. We, too, must choose between the voice of our conscience and the voice of our sinful flesh. A tremendous mental struggle commences. Remember, Eve was given as an "help meet" to Adam, to aid him in understanding his world and to manifest his thoughts.

God says to us, "Come now, and let us reason together" (Isa. 1:18). What does Adam do? *Mind, Character, and Personality*, volume 2, page 713, says that Adam reasoned with the enemy. He rested his eyes on what he could see (and feel)—Eve, his beloved flesh. Instead of resting in God's word, Adam allowed sight and circumstances to cloud his judgment. Adam chose Eve. The higher powers, having entered into union with the flesh, became "carnally minded." The "will" chose not to obey the voice of the conscience.

Likewise with us, the soul must choose to sin before iniquity triumphs over the conscience (*Testimonies for the Church*, vol. 5, p. 177). Satan requires that man disregard his conscience (*The Desire of Ages*, p. 130). The heart is made callous by stifling the conscience—forming the stony heart (*Testimonies for the Church*, vol. 8, p. 95). The lower passions blind the conscience—the spiritual eye is veiled (*Testimonies for the Church*, vol. 4, p. 31). (In sanctuary terms a veil went up between the holy place and Most Holy Place). Sin and selfishness sears, blackens, and crisps the conscience (*Testimonies for the Church*, vol. 2, p. 305). Adam was hypnotized, mind over mind. The principle of Satan's

Man's Spiritual Nature

mind—live unto self—was brought in through the sinful flesh and now controlled the higher powers of the soul, shutting out the conscience.

The garment of light that once covered them went out, "the light of the garments of heavenly innocence departed from them . . . they drew about them the dark robes of ignorance of God" (*The SDA Bible Commentary*, vol. 1, p. 1084). (Note that God did not leave them!! Their sin simply made it impossible for them to acknowledge Him.) Not a single ray of hope was left. They tried covering themselves with fig leaves—excuses for sin, an apron—because they were afraid. If perfect love casts out all fear (1 John 4:18), an imperfect love can only bring in fear. Together they reasoned that God would not really let them die (*Patriarchs and Prophets*, p. 57). The corrupt lower nature and the corrupted higher powers were "reasoning together" apart from the conscience. Darwin said that reason stands at the summit of all the faculties of the mind. He and many others do not understand the true role of the conscience. Without an enlightened conscience to guide us, we can only be guided by the mind of Satan—self rules no matter how deceived we are into believing otherwise.

In Genesis 3:8 we find that Adam and Eve heard the voice of God in the garden looking for them. God, through the conscience, is ever seeking to re-establish contact with us no matter how sinful we have become. *Patriarchs and Prophets*, page 57 says that divinity was manifested in the garden. Through knowledge of His law, God desires to bring us to a realization of our sinfulness and His holiness. The perverted higher powers and the sinful flesh, in union with one another, see only the broken law and the sentence of death. Adam and Eve, in a state of conscious guilt, saw only condemnation and in fear they hide from the voice that called out to them. What did God do? The voice of the conscience asked the higher powers, "What have you done?" The answer appears in Genesis 3:12: "The woman whom thou gavest me"—the problem is this enmity in my flesh. The flesh enticed me and I ate. The voice of conscience asked the lower powers, "What have you done?"

"The serpent beguiled me"—the devil made me do it—was Eve's reply. The things "You" created in this world I live in caused me to sin. Self protects self and casts blame upon another.

"The spirit of self-justification originated in the father of lies; it was indulged by our first parents as soon as they yielded to the influence of Satan, and has been exhibited by all the sons of daughters of Adam" (*Patriarchs and Prophets*, p. 58).

In love, God sought to convict Adam and Eve of their helplessness. The higher and lower powers were in bondage to Satan and could no longer choose appropriately for themselves. "Satan had taken them under his dominion, and there was no other power to control them. His control was absolute, and there *at that moment* was "total depravity." But God did not leave him there; he did not leave the race in that condition" (A.T. Jones, *The 1895 General Conference Bulletin*, p. 192).

The "threefold union" of the spiritual nature as God created it no longer exists. The conscience is "veiled," the higher powers are subject to the enmity in the lower powers. The lower powers are corrupt beyond repair. The situation seems hopeless to Adam and Eve, but a loving Father already has a solution. Let us look at the spiritual nature of man:

As Restored by the Last Adam

Genesis 3:14 and 15 finds God speaking hope to Adam and Eve through promises. Enmity, a principle of God's life—self-renouncing love, the law of the spirit of life in Christ—is to be placed between the seed of the woman and the seed of Satan. The seed of the woman, in our allegory, would represent the enmity in the lower corrupt nature,

Man's Spiritual Nature

for that is what is passed on to all future descendents of our first parents who joined with the voice of Satan. The seed of Satan is the seed of death (*The SDA Bible Commentary*, vol. 1, p. 1082), and this too "passed upon all men" (Rom. 5:12). *The SDA Bible Commentary*, volume 1, page 1085, says Christ stands between the living and the dead. *Patriarchs and Prophets*, page 64, says He stands between sinners and the penalty of sin. How does He do this?

One third of man's spiritual nature—the lower nature—is corrupt beyond repair because of Eve's choice to enter into union with the voice of Satan. The second one third of man's spiritual nature has been corrupted because of Adam's choice to enter into union with her. The remaining one third of the spiritual nature—the conscience—has been silenced, rendered idle. God's love suspends the death sentence upon Adam and Eve, giving the human race another chance to make the right choices.

As the last Adam, Christ maintains the gift of physical life to humanity. Death still reigns in that all are born subject to death—even the man Jesus. But, when Christ stepped into humanity, first by promise, later in reality, He put life where there is death, sustaining us physically and providing a "way of escape" for us spiritually. As the second man, the Lord from heaven, He showed us how to overcome sin, how to make the right choices, and how to escape eternal death. He did this through revealing the "law of the resurrection"—"death before life"—dying to self and allowing God to do for us that which we cannot do for ourselves. Thus He stands between the living and the dead, between sinners and the full penalty of sin—death from which there is no resurrection. So, at what point does He step into the now fallen spiritual nature of man?

"The Word was made flesh, and dwelt among us" (John 1:14). Most all will admit that Christ had our fallen physical nature, the degenerate and weakened body that was subject to disease and death. Mentally He had to learn the things of God through study of the written Word and nature, just as our minds must. When He took upon Himself our fallen human nature, to what extent did it include the now fallen spiritual nature? Galatians 4:4 and 5 states, "When the fullness of the time was come, God sent forth his Son, made of a woman, made under the law, to redeem them that were under the law, that we might receive the adoption of sons." The last Adam came into the world "made of a woman" with one third of his spiritual nature as is represented by Eve—the lower corrupt nature in our allegory. In his "spiritual flesh" dwelt the enmity (Eph. 2:15). He was made "under the law," subject to the curse of the law, which is death. The law was His schoolmaster as it is to be ours. In having to contend with a lower corrupt nature, He was led to exercise faith in God when He lived as man on this earth, just as you and I need to exercise faith in Christ.

The next comment can be easily misunderstood, so please follow me carefully. Christ came in the spiritual nature of fallen man with the lower one third of his spiritual nature as that represented by Eve *after* she ate of the fruit—He had the lower corrupt nature—the enmity in the flesh. *One third* of his spiritual nature, his higher powers, was as that represented by Adam *before* he chose to join with Eve in her transgression. Although limited in their human capacity, Jesus came with *his higher powers still free to choose*. How could this be? Jesus was made of a woman, but this last Adam had no earthly father! God was His Father, just as the first Adam could claim God as his Father. One was begotten, the other was created, but God was the direct father of both. Christ had no human father. He was "brought forth" into humanity by the Holy Spirit that moved upon Mary.

Having no earthly father, allegorically, tells us that the higher powers of Jesus' spiritual nature were free from the "bondage" of

Man's Spiritual Nature

sin as was Adam when he was created. Jesus' higher powers had no "taint" of sin and could therefore be referred to as that "holy thing." The first Adam lost his "freedom to choose" when he ate of the tree. Unlike Adam after the fall, Jesus was still free to choose to listen to and obey the voice of God through His conscience—the *one third* of his spiritual nature that the first Adam's choice had silenced. "Jesus Christ is our example in all things. He began life, passed through its experiences, and ended its record, with a sanctified human will" (*The Signs of the Times*, October 29, 1894).

As the last Adam, He came to restore to man the freedom to choose, in hopes of returning to us a sanctified will. You may be thinking that He does not meet you and me where we are if He came with a will like Adam's before the fall. Stay with me and this concern will be cleared up.

Christ stands between sinners and the penalty of death. It was the first Adam's choice to join the higher powers to the lower corrupt nature that brought death to the human race. The higher powers of Jesus Christ had to stand the test that Adam faced. The threefold spiritual nature of the first Adam, as a separate human being, still had a sinless lower nature when Eve, another separate human being, came to tempt him with the fruit. The threefold spiritual nature of Jesus Christ, on the other hand, faced the same temptation, but the lower third of His spiritual nature was corrupt, as is ours, and the middle third was limited in its capacity, as is ours, making the battle even greater for this last Adam than for the first Adam. It is a mystery how the first Adam in his sinless "threefold" spiritual nature would choose to sin. It is an even greater mystery how the last Adam, with our corrupt lower spiritual nature, could keep from sinning.

"As the Son of man, Christ would stand loyal to God. Thus it would be shown that Satan had not gained complete control of the human race, and that his claim to the world was false" (*The Desire of Ages*, p. 114).

"God broke the bond of Satan over the will of man; set man once more free to choose which authority he would follow" (A.T. Jones, *The 1895 General Conference Bulletin*, p. 192).

Christ signed the "emancipation papers" for the whole human race with His own blood. He set the "will" free to again choose for itself whose side it shall be on—God's or Satan's. Adam, prior to his fall into sin, had the freedom to choose and the power to carry out those choices. The last Adam came with the freedom to choose, but He did not use His power to carry out His choices. "To keep His glory veiled as the child of a fallen race, this was the most severe discipline to which the Prince of Life could subject Himself. Thus He measured His strength with Satan" (*Manuscript Releases*, vol. 21, p. 271). He only made one choice—"Choose you this day whom ye will serve" (Joshua 24:15). He trusted another to do for Him what He could not do for Himself. Christ, in His divinity, had power, but as a man, to be our example, He could not use His own power. He had to rely upon His Father's choices and depend upon His Father's power. He allowed His Father to work in Him "to will and to do of his good pleasure" (Phil. 2:13).

We, in our fallen condition, tend to think we have the power and wisdom to stop sinning, like the man of Romans 7, only to find we, of ourselves, cannot do as we would desire. Jesus Christ did have the power and the wisdom to keep from sinning, but to save us, He had to live as we have to live. He had to submit to another "to will and to do" for Him. How much more difficult a task was His? What we only think we can do He knew He could do, and still He had to submit. But, by His submitting, He changed the choice we have to make from "not sinning" to "whose side" will you be on.

Remember, Eve was the "help meet" of Adam. She was the part of the spiritual nature that was to aid the higher powers to understand the world they lived in and to "manifest" the thoughts and desires of the higher powers. This "help meet" was corrupted because of Eve's choice to listen to the serpent and tempt Adam to follow her in her disobedience. Jesus, as the last Adam, had to choose to not use his "flesh" as a "help meet." He had to turn to the conscience, the voice of His Father, to be His "help meet." The sinful flesh, the lower corrupt nature, always tries to rule the higher powers. Christ showed us that the Father can hold the "flesh" in check, Himself becoming our "help meet."

After 400 years of slavery, the children of Jacob believed that they were slaves to Egypt. But we discovered that they were slaves only in experience. In truth they were a free people who had been tricked, deceived into believing they were slaves. After 6,000 years of bondage to this world, we, as the offspring of the first Adam, believe ourselves, in true fact, to be slaves to sin. But the prince of this world has tricked and deceived us through the "flesh." The last Adam, having taken all humanity into Himself, set man free—free to choose which authority to follow.

Remember, Adam and Eve, after they fell, could not answer the questions of God without passing the blame. Protection of self reigned supreme. They did not have the freedom, at that moment, to choose which authority they would follow—Satan controlled the higher and the lower powers of man. Today we can make this choice. By sending His Son to dwell in humanity, God shows us that Satan no longer has complete control of the human race. The will, a part of the higher powers, is still free to choose which authority to follow, and the conscience is still able and willing to guide us into all truth.

"Since the announcement to the serpent in Eden…(Genesis 3:15),

Satan had known that he did not hold absolute sway over the world. There was seen in men the working of a power that withstood his dominion" (*The Desire of Ages*, p. 115).

When Adam (the sinless higher powers) joined with Eve (the lower corrupt nature), sin and death were not the only result. The garment of light that covered them went out. A "veil" went up between the conscience and the higher powers. The light that illuminated God's love within could no longer shine into their mind and heart. Stopped from shining inwardly, God's light could no longer shine outwardly either, it could no longer be made "manifest" through them. At that point not a single ray of hope could be found.

"Christ knew that Adam in Eden with his superior advantages might have withstood the temptations of Satan and conquered him. He also knew that it was not possible for man out of Eden, separated from the light and love of God since the fall, to resist the temptations of Satan in his own strength" (*Redemption*, p. 44).

"Fallen man, because of his guilt, could no longer come directly before God with his supplications; for his transgression of the divine law had placed an impassible barrier between the holy God and the transgressor" (*The SDA Bible Commentary*, vol. 1, p. 1086).

"Through Christ there was hope and pardon for the transgression of God's law. Although gloom and darkness hung, like a pall of death, over the future, yet in the promise of the Redeemer, the Star of hope lighted up the dark future" (*The SDA Bible Commentary*, vol. 1, p. 1084).

I believe this "impassible barrier" can be represented by the veil that separates the Most Holy Place from the holy place, and consequently from the outer court. This barrier allowed no light to pass to humanity until Christ stepped onto the scene. In the instructions given for the building of the sanctuary, the veil before the Most Holy Place did not reach to the top. It stopped short of the ceiling. Light still came

Man's Spiritual Nature

through from the Most Holy Place.

Because of Christ, the still small voice of the conscience can still be heard. The incarnation of Christ allows this third part of our spiritual nature to still have an impact upon the higher powers, even though Satan, through the flesh, tries to silence it. At Christ's death the veil in the temple was ripped apart, from top to bottom by an unseen hand. At our "death" this veil will be ripped apart, showing free access to the throne of God. If we die in Christ by faith, the veil comes down and the conscience takes its proper place as ruler of our life. If we die out of Christ, the veil will come down after the 1,000 years, as we stand outside the walls of the city that comes down from heaven and God opens our minds to where we chose Satan to rule, and rejected Christ. The glory that comes from God's throne through the conscience then will be a consuming fire to the wicked. When you think of how consumed we can become by guilt, we can understand why God allowed this veil to come between Him and us. If it were not there, guilt would totally consume us and there would be no hope.

In the temptation that Jesus faced in the wilderness, we find how the higher powers, joined to the word of God and submitted to an educated conscience, can overcome the temptations that come from the flesh (the lust of the flesh, the lust of the eyes, and the pride of life). How did He overcome? At His baptism Jesus heard these words, "This is my beloved Son, in whom I am well pleased" (Matt. 3:17). Christ enters the wilderness with these words of God fresh in His mind. Adam in the garden should also have had this thought fresh in his mind. We, at our baptism, have every right to have these words of God sounding in our minds (*The Desire of Ages*, p. 113).

Two thirds of the spiritual nature of this last Adam stood where the first Adam did when Eve came to him with her hands full of fruit. He stood free to choose which voice to listen to, His conscience speaking clearly to guide His thoughts as the temptations came through His flesh, the now fallen sinful flesh, the lower one third of His spiritual nature. He stood the test in the wilderness as every "born-again" Christian is to stand when faced with temptation, from within or without. Do keep in mind that the battle Jesus fought in the wilderness represents how to fight the battles we will face *after* we are "born again" or "abiding in Christ." It is not the picture of one who is "out of Christ" by unbelief, nor is it a picture of one who claims to be "born again" but does not yet know, or is not currently experiencing, what it is to "abide in Christ." This will be looked at shortly. Please read the chapter "The Temptation" in *The Desire of Ages* and the story in Luke 4:1-15. In summary, Satan said, "Command this stone to be made bread." Christ answered, "Man shall not live by bread alone." Here Christ is tested upon "appetite" (*The Desire of Ages*, p. 116), but do not think this refers only to a desire to eat food! I believe Christ was hungry, whereas the first Adam was not. This was a test upon all the "appetites" of the flesh for its own pleasure to the exclusion of trust in God to provide for our needs. Here Jesus overcame the "lust of the flesh."

Next, Satan showed Jesus all the kingdoms of the world and said, "Worship me and all this shall be yours." Christ answered, "Worship the Lord thy God only, and him only shalt thou serve." This was a test upon the love of the world, loving that which we see, rather than trusting in what we cannot see. Here Jesus overcame the "lust of the eyes."

Lastly, Satan took Him to a pinnacle and said, "If thou be the Son of God...It is written." Satan was really asking Him, "Show me how wise and valuable you are." Christ answered, "Thou shalt not tempt the Lord thy God." Here Jesus overcame the love of display, the desire to be important, or first, or just simply to be noticed. He overcame the "pride of life."

In the wilderness the last Adam, the man Jesus, overcame where the first Adam had fallen. Ellen White summarizes how He overcame:

"Strengthened with the memory of the voice from heaven ("This is my beloved son in whom I am well pleased"), He rested in His Father's love.

"In every temptation the weapon of His warfare was the word of God....So long as Christ held to this position, the tempter could gain no advantage" (*The Desire of Ages*, p. 120). "Jesus rested upon the wisdom and strength of His heavenly Father" (Ibid., p. 123)

Satan finally left Christ alone. "Satan trembles and flees before the weakest soul who finds refuge in that mighty name" (Ibid., p. 131). The voice of Satan, speaking through the sinful flesh, was silenced—rendered idle, for a time. In sanctuary terms, you could say Christ put up a veil between the holy place and the courtyard. He stood in the sanctity of the holy place, shutting out the noise in the courtyard. He treated the flesh as though it were already crucified, already silenced, with its power broken by the cross. Here the higher powers chose the voice of God over the voice of the sinful flesh, choosing God as His "help meet," not relying on the "flesh." Here Christ gained the victory where the first Adam failed. Here He showed us that the sinful flesh could be subdued, kept idle in us.

The voice of the conscience can guide us to the necessary words of God to meet every temptation as we choose to rest in Christ. Many tell us this experience is to be ours and is the "way" to overcome temptations and live the victorious life. But this is only *one* of the battles Christ fought. We need to know that there was more to the battle with sin than just what happened in the wilderness.

In the wilderness Jesus made "a way of escape for us" (Ibid., p. 131). "In our own strength it is impossible for us to deny the clamors of our fallen natures. Through this channel Satan will bring temptation upon us. Christ knew that the enemy would come to every human being, to take advantage of hereditary weakness . . . and by passing over the ground which man must travel, our Lord has prepared the way for us to overcome" (Ibid., p. 122).

"Temptation is resisted when a man is powerfully influenced to do a wrong action; and, knowing that he can do it, resist, by faith, with a firm hold upon divine power. This was the ordeal through which Christ passed" (*The Youth's Instructor*, July 20, 1899).

"The Majesty of heaven undertook the cause of man, and *with the same facilities that man may obtain*, withstood the temptations of Satan as man must withstand them" (*Selected Messages*, vol. 1, p. 252).

"As the Son of man, Christ would stand loyal to God. Thus it would be shown that Satan had not gained complete control of the human race, and that his claim to the world was false" (*The Desire of Ages*, p. 115).

Our higher powers in union with an enlightened conscience through an "abiding" faith will not choose to sin. "Whosoever abideth in Him sinneth not…Whosoever is born of God doth not commit sin; for his seed remaineth in him: and he cannot sin, because he is born of God" (1 John 3:6, 9). "For whatsoever is born of God overcometh the world: and this is the victory that overcometh the world, even our faith" (1 John 5:4). "His victory is ours" (*The Desire of Ages*, p. 123). Notice, again, this victory is found only by those who are "abiding in Christ." By faith, as we find rest in Jesus Christ, we can claim His victory, full and complete, today! By faith we can go forward with the victory as did Judah and the inhabitants of Jerusalem as they marched to battle with Jehoshaphat (2 Chron. 20).

By the way, there was "no man" in the courtyard on the Day of Atonement (Lev. 16:17). Sure, there were no daily sacrifices going on during the special services of that day, but, could it not also tell us that *now*, while it is the anti-typical Day of Atonement, the courtyard of our hearts, the flesh, the lower corrupt nature, is to be rendered entirely idle. Today, through faith in Christ, we can claim the sinful flesh, with all its fruit, crucified—the work of the courtyard is a "finished work" in Christ. By faith we can be in the holy place with the veil to the courtyard shutting us in. Our focus should be upon entering within the veil to the Most Holy Place—resting in the fact that the flesh (the false self, the bent to evil) has been rendered idle, the old man (our past way of life) is put off, and our first self (our will) has been crucified, and returned sanctified, with Christ.

I have shown you a picture of victorious living—the kind of life every Christian is striving for. Sad to say it is an experience we all too seldom have. Many times our *guilt* gets in the way to listening to our conscience, just as *guilt* got in the way for Adam and Eve *after* eating the fruit. What about my condition when I have knowingly committed sinful deeds, when I am full of guilt—when the voice of assurance is silenced? In the wilderness we do not see Christ struggling under a deep burden of guilt. Is there a place where Christ meets us in the pit of sin, weighed down by the guilt we bear? At times we don't feel like a "friend" of God, let alone a "son" in whom He is well pleased. Can Jesus really relate to me at times like these?

Our sense of guilt makes us want to run and hide from God, just as Adam and Eve did. We will tend to seek out "friends" for words of comfort, instead of the Word of God that seems to condemn us. This sense of guilt did not enter the experience of Adam and Eve until after the choice of Adam—allegorically, until after the higher powers chose to join with the lower corrupt nature. The story of the temptation in the wilderness shows Christ always making the right choices.

But you may say to yourself, "I have repeated the mistake of the first Adam. The higher powers of my mind are corrupted because of their union with the flesh. Many times I cannot see God as my loving

Father, I see only a Judge waiting to pass sentence upon me. I see only death looming up ahead of me. How does this last Adam meet me where I am?"

The answer is to be found in Gethsemane. Read *The Desire of Ages*, pages 685-697, very carefully in light of all that has been said thus far. "Throughout His life on earth He had walked in the light of God's presence....But now He seemed to be shut out from the light... The guilt of fallen humanity He must bear....Feeling how terrible is the wrath of God against transgression, He exclaims, 'My soul is exceeding sorrowful, even unto death'" (p. 685). Here in Gethsemane Christ enters to where Adam stood "after" he ate of the forbidden tree—where the higher powers stood "after" they joined to the sinful flesh. Here in the garden He took upon Himself our sinful nature, entering into the experience of man when the higher powers have chosen to sin. "Christ was now standing in a different attitude from that which He had ever stood before" (p. 686). Attitude is defined as "thinking, feeling, and acting." He was standing in a different "character" than ever before. He thought differently, He felt differently, He acted differently, than ever before. He was standing in the "character of fallen man," in the state of conscious guilt—our guilt, for He Himself had none. (See previous chapter titled, "Christ meets us where we are.")

"The powers of darkness were encompassing the Son of God; for the destiny of a lost world hung in the balance. *Satan was clothing him with the garments of sin.* Christ had placed himself in the sinner's stead, and he felt that a great gulf separated him from his Father. It was a moment of soul-agony for the Son of God. It was the hour of the power of darkness. Shall he drink the cup? Shall he take upon his divine soul the guilt of a lost world, and consent to be numbered with the transgressors? It was here that the mysterious cup trembled in his hand" (*The Youth's Instructor*, April 11, 1901).

Did you notice who clothed Christ in the garment of sin? It was the deceiver, the one who is a liar from the beginning. With this garment of sin upon Him, Jesus found that a sense of guilt, and its penalty of death, pressed in upon His soul. The Father seemed far from Him. He had to decide whether He would use His own power to escape the ordeal or submit no matter the cost to Himself. "The conflict was terrible" (*The Desire of Ages*, p. 687).

Submission of the will, dying to self, is where the battle is to be the hardest and the most stern we will ever fight. Three times, while weighed down with the guilt of humanity, Jesus pleaded with His Father. "O My Father, if it be possible...not as I will, but as Thou wilt" (Ibid.). He first seeks to have his own desires fulfilled, but also hopes it to be God's will. This is most often the level our prayers. "O My Father, if this cup may not pass away . . . Thy will be done." (Ibid., p. 690). "Full of human anguish," He acknowledges God's choice for Him (Ibid., p. 689). How often do we wrestle with God until our soul cries out in human anguish when we finally acknowledge God's choice for us—death upon the cross?

"O My Father, if this cup may not pass away . . . Thy will be done." Christ now prays for "His own tempted, agonized soul." He prays for strength to fulfill His mission, strength to drink "the bitter cup of humiliation and agony." Three times His humanity has "shrunk from the last, crowning sacrifice" (Ibid., p. 690). Now, one more time he prays. "His prayer now breathes only submission: 'If this cup may not pass away from Me, except I drink it, Thy will be done'" (Ibid., p.693). How few of us come this far! What brought Him to the point of total surrender of the will—even to its death?

Satan tried desperately to get Christ to focus only on what He was feeling: a sinner eternally separated from God, suffering the consequences of the broken law; the ingratitude of men who had rejected, betrayed, denied, and forsaken Him. Through sight and circumstances Satan hoped to weaken Christ's faith. But, "the history of the human race comes up before" Him (Ibid.). He saw the unseen. Transgressors left to their self must perish. He saw the helplessness of man, the power of sin, and a doomed world. His decision was made—"He will save man at any cost to Himself" (Ibid.). Could it be that we cannot truly die to self until, like Jesus Christ, our focus is on the salvation of others? When we put the salvation of others first, no matter the cost to ourselves; when we finally trust our own salvation into the hands of Christ, come what may, our prayers will breath only submission. "The law of self-renouncing love is the law of life for earth and heaven" (Ibid., p. 19).

As soon as Jesus fully surrendered to God's will for Him, an angel was sent to comfort Him. This angel pointed His eyes *upward* to a finished work: "presenting to the mind of Christ the grand results of the victory he had gained over the strong and wily foe. Christ was victor over Satan" (*Redemption*, p. 21). An angel of the Lord came to strengthen Christ to drink the cup. The angel gave Christ the assurance of God's love—still one with God, the conscience unveiled. Christ received power to again stand as a cedar—power to overcome the sinful flesh. The angel pointed Him to heaven—His will was united with God's by faith in His word. The victory over Satan that would be revealed later was won here in Gethsemane, in the secret place of prayer. Does this not tell us that this is where our battles must be fought and won—in secret prayer!?!

He leaves the Garden of Gethsemane standing tall while resting in His Father's hands. This is the battle we face when the weight of guilt from known sin weighs heavily upon our minds. This is the battle the Christian faces in different degrees during his entire walk with Christ. Those who will pass through the time of Jacob's trouble will face this battle to its fullest depth. They will not be able to bring one sin to mind, but they will have a tremendous sense of their unworthiness. Just as the fate of the world rose up before Christ, the blood of Able will cry to them from beneath the altar. For the salvation of others, they will "drink of the cup and be baptized with the baptism" (*Early Writings*, p. 283) apportioned to them, the last bit of earthliness being removed—the last bit of "self-preservation." The glory of the Lord will then arise upon them, shine all about them, and the synagogue of Satan will bow at their feet and acknowledge they were loved of God. (See Revelation 3:9.)

But what about the sinner who is being drawn to the cross for the very first time? Or the one who "feels" he has committed the "unpardonable sin"—the ones who are so full of guilt they can see no light of hope for them? How does Christ meet them? At Golgotha, upon the cross, we again find Christ unable to see through the portals of the tomb. "The guilt of every descendant of Adam was pressing upon His heart. The wrath of God against sin, the terrible manifestation of His displeasure because of iniquity, filled the soul of His Son with consternation" (*The Desire of Ages*, p. 753). For Him, at that moment, was absolute darkness, not one single ray of hope illuminated the darkness in His mind. Even nature portrayed the depth of the darkness He was experiencing, shutting Him out from human eyes. In His spiritual nature He entered into the experience of where Adam and Eve stood after they both had sinned. As He chose to become sin, in principle entering onto the wrong side of His Father's law, His higher powers were not corrupted as was Adam's when he chose to sin. The darkness that sin creates, the deceptions it plays on the mind in shutting out the light of truth, Christ experienced, only now to its fullest depth.

The same deceptions that our sins play upon our minds were played upon Christ's mind—"And you, that were sometimes alienated and enemies in your mind by wicked works" (Col. 1:21). All of His prior obedience to the law was of no value to Him then. He saw only a sinner, an enemy of God, lost and doomed to die. When we come to the cross, all of our "good works" will be of no more value than our evil works. They can give us no assurance of salvation. We know we are sinners under the sentence of death. If all of Christ's righteous deeds, carried out in full submission to God, were of no assurance to Him at the cross, then neither can the righteous deeds of even the "born-again" person be of any assurance when we meet God at the cross of Christ.

Under this heavy burden of guilt, how did He overcome? Like the sinner He had to lay hold of that which He could not see, that which He could not feel. *Faith* took hold of the "promises" made by a loving God for sinful man. He had to rely on what He had learned from the Word of God and His past experiences about the love of God and the surety of His government. He had to look beyond what He saw and felt at that moment and rest in the unseen. He simply had to submit, "Father, into thy hands I commend my spirit" (Luke 23:46).

"He was acquainted with the character of His Father; He understood His justice, His mercy, and His great love. By faith He rested in Him whom it had ever been His joy to obey. And as in submission He committed Himself to God, the sense of the loss of His Father's favor was withdrawn. By faith, Christ was victor" (*The Desire of Ages*, p. 756).

This is where the first Adam failed. This is where we all too often fail. The first Adam had heard God's word, saw and experienced His love and power, and knew the surety of God's government. Yet, he looked to Eve—the seen rather than the unseen—and he focused on what he thought he was losing rather than trusting in the God who had given him so much—in the end, he lost it all. Rather than submit his whole spirit to God, come what may, he chose to unite with his flesh.

Today, God does not require us to die to self until he first educates us through His Word. He may use the Scriptures, nature, circumstances, or whatever way He can to get through to us. He reveals His love to us in temporal matters, desiring to give us assurance that His love is there to deal with spiritual matters also. He then reveals to us His character and the surety of His government, verses the untrustworthiness and instability of sin. Not until He has given us a knowledge of Himself and of our sinfulness, bringing us to realize our need, does He expect us to trust Him and to exercise faith in Christ as our Redeemer. But the time will come to every man when he must choose whom he will serve. The still small voice of the conscience will keep calling out in the darkness of our minds until we heed its voice or silence it altogether.

We have looked at the threefold spiritual nature as it was created—all parts in complete harmony. We saw how this harmony broke down during the fall of man and how the spiritual sanctuary became polluted with a veil going up, shutting out the inner light. We looked at how the incarnate Christ also had a threefold spiritual nature. We saw Him put up a "veil" between the lower corrupt nature and the higher powers—between the courtyard and the holy place. We saw there was no veil between His conscience and His higher powers, except when Satan tried to deceive Him through the "feelings" of guilt. We've seen the similarities as well as the differences in the three parts of His spiritual nature as compared to yours and mine. We saw how the three parts of His nature operated in different experiences in His life. Now what about our spiritual nature?

As it is in You and Me Today

This allegory of Adam and Eve helps us to understand that today, because of the second Adam, we all stand, in one important sense only, where the first Adam stood when Eve came to him with her hands full of fruit. Today we are still free to choose each and every moment of every day to whose voice we will listen, to who we will submit our will.

Using Adam and Eve as an allegory, I developed four charts portraying man's spiritual nature—(1) as God created it, (2) as fallen by the sin of Adam, (3) as restored by the second Adam, and (4) as it is in you and me today. (See Appendix B.) I have also compared the information concerning our spiritual nature with the "terms" we defined earlier—see Drawing Distinctions and Romans 7—into one final chart. My hope is that you will see that God has many ways to say the same thing. So how does Christ work with the sinful fallen spiritual nature as it is in you and me today?

We found that the polluted temple Christ came to cleanse in Jerusalem is said to be symbolic of the heart of man. Have you ever noticed that the first time Christ came to cleanse the temple He entered unnoticed and unrecognized? No where are we told how long He was there "unrecognized and unhonored" before anyone took notice of His presence (*The Desire of Ages*, pp. 157-161). For me, this means the spirit of Christ's life lies unnoticed and unrecognized in us, waiting patiently for us to acknowledge its presence, and for each person this length of time is different. Suddenly something draws everyone's attention to Jesus. Again, we are not told what it was that caused them to turn to look at Him. God has many different ways of catching our attention and causing us to look to Jesus. We find that all the activity was in the courtyard where it was noisy and tumultuous. Before faith in Christ, the flesh rules, speaking loudly, creating much commotion and confusion in our minds. Instead of being a house of prayer (indicating quiet submission and reverence), the courtyard of the heart is a den of thieves (stealing from and misrepresenting God).

Our lower corrupt nature, with all its animal propensities, screams

Man's Spiritual Nature

loudly and multitudinously to be fulfilled. These cries from the flesh have found many an answering cord within our higher powers. Instead of the lower powers being subject to the higher powers (as Eve was to be subject to Adam), we find the lower powers lording it over the higher powers. Satan has usurped God's rightful place. I do not believe he did this by taking God's throne from Him. He simply silenced God's voice through what he thought was an impassible barrier, and he set up a counterfeit throne in the flesh to rule from. Or perhaps the "throne" being battled over is the governing power called "the will." Who has control of the will of man?

When I understood that our spiritual nature is threefold, I began to see that even though Satan has made inroads into our spirit, he cannot force us to sin. It is still our choice. Our biggest problem is that we think we can stop sinning by simply choosing to do so. The man of Romans 7 found that this is not the case. The good that he would do he did not do. The evil he did not want to do he did. Why? He had to learn that he should not be choosing to do what is right or wrong, but rather choosing whom he would serve: the voice of God coming through the conscience, or the voice of Satan coming through the "sinful flesh."

The demoniacs of Gadera and Capernaum teach us an invaluable lesson concerning the condition of our spiritual nature. (See *The Ministry of Healing*, pp. 91-97.) The animal propensities of their lower nature so ruled their higher powers that they literally looked and behaved as wild animals, acting as if they had no conscience. The demoniacs of Gadera were naked, which also says that to all appearances the inner light, the voice of the conscience, had gone out. But, when brought into the presence of Jesus, something in them, a "spiritual power, a perception of right, a desire for goodness" (*Education*, p. 29), was still able to recognize who Christ was and what He could do for them. From deep within the corrupted higher powers came forth the slightest hint of a whisper for help. The lower nature so controlled the body that this whisper could not be heard audibly. But the God of heaven heard it! Christ, without hesitation, answered their cry and returned the demoniacs to their "right" minds. Their "true self" had a chance to express itself. The power of the lower nature over the higher powers was broken. If God could hear their cry and deliver them, then surely He can hear your cry, even if it is not audible.

Adam was told he would have to till the soil with all its thorns and thistles. Adam, the higher powers, came from the ground whereas Eve, the lower nature, came from Adam. Because of the union the higher powers have made with the lower nature, after it became corrupt, many thorns and thistles have grown up. It will be a lifelong work to till the soil, to uproot and dig out all the thorns and thistles that have found a foot hold in the higher powers. "The sacrifices of God are a broken spirit: a broken and contrite heart, O God, thou wilt not despise" (Ps. 51:17). "Contrite" means "crushed, crumble, powdered, collapse, mutilated, ground to dust." This work is done through repentance and confession, the breaking up of the soil of the heart and the uprooting of the weeds.

Because we are all descendents of both Adam and Eve, we have a weakened physical nature, a lessened mental capacity, and spiritual vision that is dimmed. The veil is up between our conscience and our higher powers. The law of sin in the flesh has made inroads into our higher powers and all too often the flesh rules. Many of these inroads were made in ignorance, for few of us had the spiritual upbringing that Christ had. Did you know that there are no sins recorded in the Bible against Daniel, Samuel, or John the Baptist? I do not believe this means they never sinned. But I found that all three had parents who were very much aware of how special their children were to God. This is our assurance that, like Christ, our children can be overcomers in the battle with sin even at an early age, if we as parents truly understand who we are in Christ, and who they are, and raise our children accordingly.

But, let's face it, most of us never had this kind of upbringing. Many of us never even knew of God and His relationship to us, as children. And even if we did, it was usually a picture of God that was not very pleasing to a young mind. The lower nature easily made inroads to the higher powers as we were never trained to guard the avenues to the soul, the five senses, as we should. "There is none righteous, no, not one: There is none that understandeth, there is none that seeketh after God. They are all gone out of the way, they are together become unprofitable; there is none that doeth good, no, not one. . . . For all have sinned, and come short of the glory of God" (Rom. 3:10-12, 23). But does this give us an excuse for sinning? It may give us a reason for our behavior, but it is no excuse.

In my struggle to understand the sin problem and how to overcome, I came across many terms that soon became a jumbled mess in my mind. It was like I had a bunch of puzzle pieces that weren't falling into place. Pieces that had names like repentance, confession, awaken, quicken, death to self, faith, implantation, regeneration, reformation, behold and become, enlighten, etc. I took these terms to the writings of Ellen White and developed the chart titled "Two Seeds, Two Soils." It is based on the principle laid out earlier in the chapter "Our Choices" under the subheading "Christ in You by Faith." We all have been taught to see the Word of God as a seed planted in the soil of our hearts. Earlier in this book we discovered that you and I are also as a seed planted in the soil of Christ. With two seeds—the conscience (surrounded by our hardened will) and the Word of God, and two soils—our heart and Christ (in heaven), the puzzle pieces began to find their proper places. Abiding in Christ and Christ abiding in us came together as one perfect whole.

There is a quote by Ellen White where she advises that when we present truth we should keep it simple, presenting a few important points well. If this is done, God, through His Spirit, will fill in the details as the receptive mind lays hold of the fundamental truths (*Testimonies to Ministers and Gospel Workers*, p. 310). I will try to hold to this as we look at the spiritual nature as it is in man today. The work that goes on in the spiritual nature in the struggle between sin and righteousness can take volumes to discuss in detail. Yet it should be simple enough for a child to understand.

"Although the plan of salvation calls for the deepest study of the philosopher, it is not too deep for the comprehension of a child. In dying for sinners, Christ manifested a love that is incomprehensible; and in beholding this love, the heart is impressed, the conscience is aroused, and the soul is led to inquire, 'What is sin, that it should require such a sacrifice for the redemption of its victim?'" (*The Review and Herald*, April 1, 1890).

Two Seeds and Two Soils

We are in the darkness of sin, groping along, unable to turn on any lights for ourselves. It is God who is in search of us. It is He who first turns on the light. "Man has no power of himself to work out his own salvation. Salvation must be the result of cooperation with divine power, and God will not do that for man which he can do for himself. Man is wholly dependent on the grace of Christ. He has no power to move one step in the direction of Christ unless the Spirit of God draws him. The Holy Spirit is continually drawing the soul, and will continue to draw until by persistent refusal the sinner grieves away the tender messenger of God" (*The Signs of the Times*, February 12, 1894). God is constantly seeking to open our eyes by revealing to us His law, His love. Through the "inner light" that is in the conscience, God is trying to shine in His love to the higher powers. Here we make our first choice, the first exercise of faith. We can choose to be drawn or to turn away.

"Look to Christ, behold the attractive loveliness of His character, and by beholding you will become changed into His likeness. The mist that intervenes between Christ and the soul will be rolled back as we by faith look past the hellish shadow of Satan and see God's glory in His law, and the righteousness of Christ.

"Satan is seeking to veil Jesus from our sight, to eclipse His light; for when we get even a glimpse of His glory, we are attracted to Him. Sin hides from our view the matchless charms of Jesus; prejudice, selfishness, self-righteousness, and passion blind our eyes, so that we do not discern the Saviour. Oh, if we would by faith draw nigh to God, He would reveal to us His glory, which is His character, and the praise of God would flow forth from human hearts and be sounded by human voices. Then we would forever cease to give glory to Satan by sinning against God and talking doubt and unbelief. We should no longer stumble along, grumbling and mourning, and covering the altar of God with our tears" (*The SDA Bible Commentary*, vol. 6, p. 1097).

The first step is simply to believe enough to allow yourself to be drawn by God's love. Even if you have to pray the prayer, "Lord, I believe, help thou my unbelief," turn in His direction and He will draw you closer.

"My brethren and sisters, let the truth of God abide in your heart by a living, holy faith. Bible truth must be comprehended before it can convict the conscience and convert the life" (*The Review and Herald*, August, 26, 1909).

"The law and the gospel are in perfect harmony. Each upholds the other. In all its majesty the law confronts the conscience, causing the sinner to feel his need of Christ as the propitiation for sin. The gospel recognizes the power and immutability of the law. 'I had not known sin, but by the law,' Paul declares. The sense of sin, urged home by the law, drives the sinner to the Saviour" (*The SDA Bible Commentary*, vol. 6, p. 1096).

God sends forth His message to the mind of every one of His earthly children. At some point the Holy Spirit will finally be allowed to "convict" us through the conscience. A realization of truth will come home to the higher powers of the sinner. Again, a choice must be made. We can resist the conviction—kick against the pricks—or we can yield and again exercise faith, allowing the Spirit to proceed with His work.

"By his conscience every honest Jew was convinced that Jesus Christ was the Son of God, but the heart in its pride and ambition would not surrender. An opposition was maintained against the light of truth, which they had decided to resist and deny. When the truth is held as truth only by the conscience, when the heart is not stimulated and made receptive, the truth only agitates the mind. But when the truth is received as truth by the heart, it has passed through the conscience and captivated the soul by its pure principles. It is placed in the heart by the Holy Spirit, who molds its beauty to the mind that its transforming power may be seen in the character" (*Mind, Character, and Personality*, vol. 1, p. 324).

"The psalmist says, 'The entrance of Thy words giveth light; it giveth understanding unto the simple' (Psalm 119:130). When truth is working only upon the conscience, it creates much uneasiness; but when truth is invited into the heart, the whole being is brought into captivity to Jesus Christ. Even the thoughts are captured, for the mind of Christ works where the will is submitted to the will of God" (Ibid.).

Men sometimes become ashamed of their sinful ways, and give up some of their evil habits, before they are aroused to manifestly

Man's Spiritual Nature

come to Christ; but it is the power of the gospel, the grace of Christ, that is drawing them to make reformation in their conduct. An influence of which they are unconscious works upon the soul, and the conscience is quickened, and the outward life is amended. And as Christ draws them to look upon his cross, to look upon him whom their sins have pierced, the commandment comes home to the conscience. The wickedness of their life, the deep-seated sin of the soul, is revealed to them. They begin to comprehend something of the righteousness of Christ, and exclaim, 'Was all this love, all this suffering, all this humiliation demanded that we might not perish, but have everlasting life?' They then understand that it is the goodness of God that leadeth to repentance. A repentance such as this lies beyond the reach of our own powers to accomplish; it is obtained only from Christ, who ascended up on high, and has given gifts unto men. Christ is the source of every right impulse. *He is the only one who can arouse in the natural heart enmity against sin.* He is the source of our power if we would be saved. No soul can repent without the grace of Christ. *The sinner may pray that he may know how to repent.* God reveals Christ to the sinner, and when he sees the purity of the Son of God, he is not ignorant of the character of sin. By faith in the work and power of Christ, enmity against sin and Satan is created in his heart. Those whom God pardons are first made penitent" (*The Review and Herald*, April 1, 1890, italics added).

When we choose to respond to the convictions of our conscience, we are led to true repentance. The truths of God's Word find entrance into the higher powers of the soul. We begin to think differently than ever before, differently about ourselves and about the God of heaven. A sorrow for sin will arise in our hearts and a longing for the joy that Christ provides.

"If God peradventure [perhaps] will give them repentance to the acknowledging of the truth; and that they may recover themselves [become sober again, regain one's senses] out of the snare of the devil, who are taken captive by him at his will" (2 Tim. 2:25, 26).

"The God of our fathers raised up Jesus, whom ye slew and hanged upon a tree. Him hath God exalted with his right hand to be a Prince and a Saviour, for to give repentance to Israel, and forgiveness of sins" (Acts 5:31).

"We can no more repent without the Spirit of Christ to awaken the conscience, than we can be pardoned without Christ. Christ draws the sinner by the exhibition of his love upon the cross, and this softens the heart, impresses the mind, and inspires contrition and repentance in the soul" (*The Review and Herald*, April 1, 1890).

"We must have repentance toward God. Why?—because we have broken his law. We must have faith toward our Lord Jesus Christ, because he is the sacrifice for sin. And where do we get repentance?—it is the Holy Spirit that imparts repentance to us" (*The Review and Herald*, March 1, 1892).

"As the sinner is convicted of sin, he is also attracted by the love and holiness of Christ; for Jesus is drawing him unto himself. No man can originate the repentance which is essential for the saving of the soul. He can no more bring himself to repentance than he can bring about his own conversion. Repentance is born in the heart by beholding the love of Christ, who gave His life to save the sinner. It is the love of God that softens the hardest hearts" (*The Review and Herald*, September 3, 1901).

"Constantly God is laboring to make up man's deficiencies. Even repentance is brought about through the application of grace. The natural heart feels no need of repentance" (*In Heavenly Places*, p. 221).

"Repentance toward God and faith in Jesus Christ are the fruits of the renewing power of the grace of the Spirit. Repentance represents the process by which the soul seeks to reflect the image of Christ to the world" (*My Life Today*, p. 49).

"Repentance is associated with faith and is urged in the gospel as essential to salvation. . . . This repentance has in it nothing of the nature of merit, but it prepares the heart for the acceptance of Christ as the only Saviour, the only hope of the lost sinner" (*Faith and Works*, p. 99).

"The repentance required of those who seek God is that repentance that needeth not to be repented of,-a repentance manifested in a radical change of mind and heart. The heart must be brought in subjection to Christ . . . who has ascended on high, and has imparted gifts unto men. Christ said 'And I, if I be lifted up from the earth, will draw all men unto me.' When the heart and mind submit to the drawing power of Christ, the love of Jesus will lead the sinner to repentance, and as he earnestly seeks help from God, power from on high will be given him. The Saviour says, 'Let him take hold of my strength that he may make peace with me' and he shall make peace with me'" (*The Signs of the Times*, August 11, 1890).

As you can see, repentance is an essential and very important part of genuine conversion. Not only is it among the very first steps in coming to Christ, but it is a continual experience as God digs ever deeper to cleanse the higher powers—the heart, the soul, the mind, the will, self—of every foothold that sin has upon it. Using nature, Ellen White compares repentance to the tilling of the soil, the breaking up of the ground. This serves two purposes. It makes it easier to uproot the many "thorns and thistles" that have grown up, as well as prepares the soil of the heart to receive new seed. Any gardener knows that uprooting weeds and keeping the soil loose so that the water will not run off is an ongoing process throughout the growing season.

There is the potential here for us to get stuck in this "hard" experience. Many, believing that the repentance exhibited by the man of Romans 7 is the experience of a true Christian, and not "seeing" any victory in their lives, fall into the trap of thinking that we can never really overcome sin. The problem is that they are looking at the physical outworking of their lives to "see" the victory. This is not faith. Faith "is" the victory that will be revealed outwardly when truly exercised inwardly. (Remember the man at the pool of Bethesda?) For many there is not a true "heart work" taking place, and Satan seeks to deceive them. He brings them to the point of believing that as long as they are very sorry for their sin and try to do better, as long as they trust in Jesus to make up the difference, then everything will be okay. A profession of faith without the fruit thereof suits Satan just fine. (Remember the parable of the fig tree?) A look back at nature shows how erroneous this thought is.

It is not enough to break up the soil. The weeds must be removed. The soil must be cleared to prepare for the new seed. This is compared to "confession." Confession is more than just confessing our sins. To confess is to make a statement of fact. The Holy Spirit leads us to confess our sins by revealing to us our true standing before the law of God. What we tend to forget to do, when we are busy confessing our sins to God, is to also confess who we are in Jesus Christ. Looking only at our sins will weigh us down. Looking at Christ will lift the spirit above the guilt. (The Holy Spirit reproves of sin by showing us our lack of faith. See John 16:8 and 9. The focus of faith is Jesus Christ.)

The message of the two Adams is given especially to the people who must face the trials of these last days of earth's history. God knows that the trial will be great, and the promises He has for us must be just as great to meet the situation. Knowing that Christ is our parent, the promise of what we can become, and knowing that the germinating

Man's Spiritual Nature

principle of His life is in us, just waiting to be revealed, is a tremendous assurance that we can do as God has bidden us to do. What we must remember about the process of true repentance is this: the breaking up of the soil and the uprooting of weeds in preparation for new seed is all taking place in the higher powers as the hold of the flesh is being broken up. A change is taking place in the way we think and in the way we feel. It may not yet be "seen" in our physical actions. With this in mind, time has come for another choice to be made by us.

Satan, as well as God, will urge home to us a conviction of sin. The difference is this: Satan drives home our guilt—keeping our focus on our sins in an effort keep us from God or to break our hold upon Him. Remember what Satan tried to do to Christ in the Garden of Gethsemane and on the cross? God, on the other hand, presents our sins to us in their true character, urging us to keep our eyes fixed upon His Son. (Read about Jacob and the Angel in *Patriarchs and Prophets*, *The Great Controversy*, and *The Spirit of Prophecy*.) In spite of how dark our lives appear, no matter how unworthy we feel, we must look to the unseen and, with a "spiritual violence" that will not let go, lay hold of the truth as it is in Jesus—"In Him we are complete."

True confession not only uproots the weeds of the lower nature from the higher powers, it clears the King's Highway, preparing the way for Jesus to take His rightful place on the throne of our heart. True confession will "quicken" the conscience, giving it the place of authority that God ordained it should have. It will lead to the submission of the will to God's will, true death to self, and the exercise of faith that works by love and purifies the soul. Jacob had to come to the point that he ceased to struggle in his own strength. Jacob, like so many of us, was fighting to save his own life—by either trying to break the hold of the enemy (sin and Satan) upon him or by clinging to the life of Christ. Not until he relinquished his life into God's hands for better or for worse did he find himself in the arms of infinite love (*The SDA Bible Commentary*, vol. 1, pp. 1095, 1096). Then it was that he was given the determination, in God's strength, to hang on to the promises of God's Word and to not let go until he was blessed. "They that wait upon the LORD shall renew [abolish, change, put-off, pass-away] their strength; they shall mount up with wings as eagles; they shall run, and not be weary; and they shall walk, and not faint" (Isa. 40:31). (See *Thoughts from the Mount of Blessing*, p. 144 and *Christ's Object Lessons*, p. 175.)

But another pitfall lies here. Remember the story of the unclean spirit that went out from the man, decided to return to his "house" from whence he left, and found it empty, swept, and garnished? He then took seven more spirits, entered in, and the last state of the man was worse than the first. Ellen White informs us that the "garnish" in the house was "self-righteousness." At this point, following repentance and confession, Satan is ready to deceive us again. He lures us into having the form of godliness without the power thereof. He knows that death to self is the next step, and many of us will draw back. This was the condition of the Pharisees in Christ's day, and probably the Laodiceans in our day. They are poor, wretched, blind, and naked, and know it not. Perhaps many outward sins are no longer seen, but the living Christ has yet to find entrance into the heart. He still stands at the door—the veil between the Most Holy Place and the holy place—seeking entrance to the higher powers of the soul, that *He* may be the one to transform our lives. Until the will is surrendered, until self is forsaken, Christ cannot enter therein. The higher powers remain under Satan's rule, only now with a "cloak of religion."

The working of the Spirit has brought home conviction of truth and sin. In response we have experienced the gift of repentance, followed by true confession. And yet not one good seed has been planted in the garden of our hearts. The hard stony heart is being broken up, but it is not yet a living heart of flesh. The way is being prepared for His coming, but the glory of man has not yet been laid in the dust. With the "quickening" of the conscience, comes the realization of the need to submit "the will" to God. Ellen White says it so well:"It is man's part to cooperate with the divine. Here is where the conflict is to be sternest, hardest, and most fierce—in yielding the will and way to God's will and way, relying upon the gracious influences which God has exerted upon the human soul throughout all the life. *The man must do the work of inclining.* 'For it is God that worketh in you both to will and to do.' The character of the actions will testify what has been the nature of the resolve. The doing was not in accordance with feeling and natural inclination, but in harmony with the will of the Father in heaven. Follow and obey the leadings of the Holy Spirit; obey not the voice of the deceiver, which is in harmony with the unsanctified will, but obey the impulse God has given. This is what the heavenly intelligences are constantly working to have us do,—the will of our Father which is in heaven" (*The Signs of the Times*, February 12, 1894, italics added).

"God does not force the will of His creatures. He cannot accept an homage that is not willingly and intelligently given. A mere forced submission would prevent all real development of mind or character; it would make man a mere automaton. Such is not the purpose of the Creator. He desires that man, the crowning work of His creative power, shall reach the highest possible development. He sets before us the height of blessing to which He desires to bring us through His grace. *He invites us to give ourselves to Him, that He may work His will in us.* It remains for us to choose whether we will be set free from the bondage of sin, to share in the glorious liberty of the sons of God" (*Steps to Christ*, p. 43, italics added).

"What you need to understand is the true force of the will. This is the governing power in the nature of man, the power of decision, or of choice. *Everything depends on the right action of the will.* The power of choice God has given to men; it is theirs to exercise. You cannot change your heart, you cannot of yourself give to God its affections; but you can *choose* to serve Him. You can give Him your will; He will then work in you to will and to do according to His good pleasure. Thus your whole nature will be brought under the control of the Spirit of Christ; your affections will be centered upon Him, your thoughts will be in harmony with Him" (Ibid., p. 47, italics added).

"Through the right exercise of the will, an entire change may be made in your life. By yielding up your will to Christ, you ally yourself with the power that is above all principalities and powers. You will have strength from above to hold you steadfast, and thus through constant surrender to God you will be enabled to live the new life, even the life of faith" (Ibid., p. 48)."Everything is at stake. Will the human agent cooperate with divine agencies to will and to do? If a man places his will on the side of God's will, fully surrendering self to do his will, the rubbish will be cleared from the door of the heart, the defiance of the soul will be broken down, and Jesus will enter to abide as a welcome guest" (*The Signs of the Times*, February 12, 1894).

"The Spirit of God does not create new faculties in the converted man but works a decided change in the employment of those faculties. When mind and heart and soul are changed, man is not given a new conscience, but *his will is submitted to a conscience renewed, a conscience whose dormant sensibilities are aroused by the working of the Holy Spirit*" (*Mind, Character, and Personality*, vol. 2, p. 692).

This last quote drives home the phrase "There, but for the grace of God, go I." The born-again Christian is no different from the vilest heathen in the respect that the Christian has not received any new faculties that make him "better" than someone else. That is part of the "pharisaical idea" that Satan seeks to sneak in to keep "self" alive in us. A divine power from above is at work in the truly born-again Christian, to be sure. It is a power that changes us by the re-employment of the very same faculties that God has given to every human being. The only difference between the Christian and the heathen is their knowledge of God and the choices that they make in respect to that knowledge. Our choices open the way for God's power to work in us, or they shut the way and do not let God's regenerating power in.

Back to nature: the soil of the heart has been made ready to receive the seeds of the living words of God that will transform the life. But man is also said to be a seed. This process of repentance and confession, brought about by the influence of the Holy Spirit that has broken up and softened the soil of the heart, has also been working upon the will. The hardened, selfish will is the hard shell that keeps the germinating principle of the "law of the spirit of life in Christ" hidden in the conscience, keeping it dormant.

Through the two Adams we have learned that we are as a seed already planted in Christ by promise. It is not our job to plant ourselves into Christ. It is our work, by faith, to lay hold of the promise—Christ has already absorbed all of humanity into Himself. It is the work of the water of the Holy Spirit to soften that hard shell of self so that the powers of heaven—the grace that abounds all around us—may enter within and bring forth the life of Christ that lies buried there. As we, by faith, are planted in the garden of God, the powers of heaven—the Sun of Righteousness, the water of the Spirit, the nourishment of the Word of God, the atmosphere of heaven—have permission to begin their work in us. They will bring forth the image of God that we were created to reflect.

"Just as a good tree will bear good fruit, so will the tree that is actually planted in the Lord's garden produce good fruit unto eternal life. . . . *As we lay hold of Him by faith, He does the work. The believer can only trust.* As God works, we can work, trusting Him and doing His will" (*The SDA Bible Commentary*, vol. 6, p. 1080, italics added).

Until the hard shell of self is broken up and the powers of God allowed to work, there can be no implantation of the "living seeds" of God's Word in the soil of our hearts. We can deceive ourselves with our knowledge of God and the gospel. But unless the will is surrendered, the words of God are in us as the dead "letter of the law." We may have a profession of faith, a show of godliness, but the power of love and true joy in the Lord will be sadly missing, for we are not truly "abiding in Christ" by faith.

"What is justification by faith?—It is the work of God in laying the glory of man in the dust, and doing for man that which it is not in his power to do for himself. When men see their own nothingness, they are prepared to be clothed with the righteousness of Christ. . . .

"What is regeneration?—It is revealing to man what is his own real nature, that in himself he is worthless" (*Special Testimonies for Ministers and Workers*, no. 9, p. 62).

What is it to be weighed in the balances of the sanctuary and be found wanting? In *The Youth's Instructor*, July 31, 1902, we are told that "in one scale is placed his [God's] perfect, unchangeable law, demanding perfect obedience. If in the other there are years of forgetfulness, of rebellion, of self-pleasing, with no repentance, no confession, no effort to do right, God says, 'Thou art weighed in the balances, and art found wanting.'"

Notice that the life we live apart from God is on one side of the balance and without repentance, confession, and efforts to do right it cannot measure up to the law. But with true repentance, confession, and efforts to do right, our side of the scale can be weighed down,

Man's Spiritual Nature

bringing us into balance with the demanding law. "Nothing but repentance and faith can make the impure heart pure" (Ibid.). Nothing but a change in the way we think toward God and His law, as well as complete immersion into Christ by faith, can cleanse the heart and bring forth God's image in us.

Satan is ready at each step of conversion to lead us astray. There is only one solution. We must keep our eyes fixed steadfastly upon *the person* of Jesus Christ. Yes, we must see our sinfulness. Yes, we must know the law. Yes, we must continuously study the Word of God, for only by it can the conscience be educated and enlightened. Yes, we must choose to turn from sin and choose to obey God at every step. But we must keep in remembrance that we are only responding to what God is doing, that what "we must do" is only the outworking of His work in us, and that all we do comes only by the grace of Christ. Only thus can we ever hope to break the power of the false self over us, and keep the false self from again finding a place in our higher powers, overruling our "true self." We must, by faith, enter into the Most Holy Place, in heaven where Christ now is, and cooperate with Him in the work of preparing our souls to reflect the divine image. Only when the "spirit of life in Christ," that lies buried in the dormant slumbering conscience, is awakened, quickened, enlightened, educated, and given its place of authority over the higher powers can we find safety in this world where Satan seeks to rule over us.

Once we have consented to die to self, when the will is truly submitted to God, we will by faith "knowingly" abide in Christ—we will acknowledge having been planted in the Lord's garden. The Holy Spirit continues His work by putting us back through the process again, causing us to behold Christ, drawing us ever closer to Christ, deepening our repentance, making our confessions more specific, and sinking self ever further into Christ—until He has us! With our continued submission and openness to receive, all the nutrients found in the soil of Christ can find their way into our hearts. All the powers of heaven will have permission to do their work in us. Now God can implant His living principles, seeds of truth, into the soil of our heart that has been prepared to receive. These living, active principles begin to transform our characters, imperceptible to us, as we choose to continuously "behold" Him, and to "rest" in Him, by faith. (Please see the chart titled "Two Seeds and Two Soils," which you will find in Appendix B.)

There is so much more that could be said. I trust that what I have said, combined with the illustrations, will be only the beginning of a "new look" at the gospel we all love so well. What this allegory of Adam and Eve did for me was to take the many references to our spiritual nature and to "compartmentalize" them. In the story of creation, no one can confuse the voice of God with Adam, or Eve, or the serpent (Satan). And when you "allegorically" find the right "place" for the terms and aspects of our spiritual nature, as revealed in the story, it becomes clear. Remember, truth can afford to be fair. It has nothing to fear in standing up and being tested. Ellen White admonishes us to "agitate, agitate, agitate" (*Testimonies for the Church*, vol. 5, p. 708). By this she does not mean to create chaos and confusion. She means we should not be afraid to take a good hard look at what we believe and why we believe it. We must know for ourselves what is truth because God Himself has revealed it to us, not because our church expounds it, our minister preaches it, our teachers taught it, our parents have always held it, or our spouse believes it. We must know what truth is because God has said it to us in the deepest recesses of our own hearts.

I know this is what the Lord has personally said to me. I am one of those people who like to have all the pieces in place, not before I believe, but to strengthen my belief. Each detail that God opened to my view and then put into place only drew me closer to Him. No matter how deep I dug, He was there. No matter how confusing things became, He cleared them up in His time and way if I simply waited upon Him. Our work is to "behold," and He will work the "become" in us.

"It is the Holy Spirit, the Comforter, which Jesus said He would send into the world, that changes our character into the image of Christ; and when this is accomplished, we reflect, as in a mirror, the glory of the Lord. That is, the character of the one who thus beholds Christ is so like His, that one looking at him sees Christ's own character shining out as from a mirror. *Imperceptibly to ourselves* we are changed day by day from our own ways and will into the ways and will of Christ, into the loveliness of His character. Thus we grow up into Christ, and unconsciously reflect His image.

"Professed Christians keep altogether too near the lowlands of earth. Their eyes are trained to see only commonplace things, and their minds dwell upon the things their eyes behold. Their religious experience is often shallow and unsatisfying, and their words are light and valueless. How can such reflect the image of Christ? How can they send forth the bright beams of the Sun of Righteousness into all the dark places of the earth? To be a Christian is to be Christlike.

"Enoch kept the Lord ever before him, and the Inspired Word says that he 'walked with God.' He made Christ his constant companion" (*The SDA Bible Commentary*, vol. 6, p. 1097, italics added).

The Personal Presence of Christ

"It is fellowship with Christ, personal contact with a living Saviour, that enables the mind and heart and soul to triumph over the lower nature. Tell the wanderer of an almighty hand that will hold him up, of an infinite humanity in Christ that pities him. It is not enough for him to believe in law and force, things that have no pity, and never hear the cry for help. He needs to clasp a hand that is warm, to trust in a heart full of tenderness. Keep his mind stayed upon the thought of a divine presence ever beside him, ever looking upon him with pitying love. Bid him think of a Father's heart that ever grieves over sin, of a Father's hand stretched out still, of a Father's voice saying, 'Let him take hold of My strength, that he may make peace with Me, and he shall make peace.' Isaiah 27:5" (*Christ's Object Lessons*, p. 388).

Jesus must become to us as our very best and closest friend. When I was in the eighth grade, I was quite infatuated with Abraham Lincoln. I read everything I could about the man. The one thing I always regretted was not having had the opportunity to actually meet this famous president. We may know all about Jesus and the life He lived and what He has gone to heaven to do, but how many of us can say we have actually "met" Jesus and have talked to Him "face to face" as one does with a very dear and close friend? Is He your constant companion?

"*The soul that is brought into personal contact with Christ, becomes a holy temple unto the Lord*; for Jesus is made unto the believer wisdom, righteousness, sanctification, and redemption. *He who has fully surrendered to God has a consciousness of Christ's saving presence.* He is a possessor of spiritual patience, and has the rest of soul that comes from learning of Him who is meek and lowly of heart. Trusting in Jesus to be his efficiency and righteousness, his soul is filled with a pleasant contentment" (*The Review and Herald*, December 4, 1894, italics added).

"Christ has provided means whereby our whole life may be an unbroken communion with himself; but *the sense of Christ's abiding presence can come only through living faith*. There must be a personal consecration to him. Self must be hid with Christ in God; then the grace received will be constantly imparted as a grateful offering to God. In this union Christ identifies himself with man before God and the heavenly universe. 'But as many as received him, to them gave he power to become the sons of God, even to them that believe on his name.' Our sins are reckoned to Christ. His righteousness is imputed to us, and we are made the righteousness of God in him. Because of his atoning sacrifice, our prayers go up to the Father, laden with the fragrance of Christ's character, and, one with Christ, we are accepted in the Beloved" (*The Review and Herald*, September, 18, 1900, italics added).

So, how does Christ become a very real and personal presence in the soul?

"The work of the Holy Spirit is immeasurably great. It is from this source that power and efficiency come to the worker for God; *and the Holy Spirit is the Comforter, as the personal presence of Christ to the soul*. He who looks to Christ in simple, child-like faith, is made a partaker of the divine nature through the agency of the Holy Spirit. When led by the Spirit of God, the Christian may know that he is made complete in Him who is the head of all things. As Christ was glorified on the day of Pentecost, so will he again be glorified in the closing work of the gospel, *when he shall prepare a people to stand the final test,* in the closing conflict of The Great Controversy" (*The Home Missionary*, November 1, 1893, italics added).

"The disciples returned to Jerusalem rejoicing, not that they were deprived of their Master and Teacher, for this was to them a cause for personal mourning rather than joy. But Jesus had assured them that he would *send the Comforter, as an equivalent for his visible presence*" (*The Spirit of Prophecy*, vol. 3, p. 256, italics added).

Just how close is this connection to Christ supposed to be?

"Jesus says, 'I am the vine, ye are the branches' (John 15:5). *Can we conceive of a more intimate relation than this implies? The fibers of the branch are identical with those of the vine.* The communication of life, strength, and nourishment from the trunk to the branches is unobstructed and constant. . . . Such is the believer's relation to Christ, if he abides in Christ and draws his nourishment from Him. *But this spiritual relation between Christ and the soul can be established only through the exercise of personal faith.* 'Without faith it is impossible to please him' (Hebrews 11:6); for *it is faith that connects us with the power of heaven, and brings us strength for coping with the powers of darkness.* 'This is the victory that overcometh the world, even our faith' (1 John 5:4). Faith familiarizes the soul with the existence and presence of God, and, living with an eye single to the glory of God, more and more we discern the beauty of His character, the excellence of His grace. Our souls become strong in spiritual power; for we are breathing the atmosphere of heaven, and realizing that God is at our right hand, that we shall not be moved. We are rising above the world, beholding Him who is the chief among ten thousand, the one altogether lovely, and by beholding we are to become changed into His image" (*Selected Messages*, book 1, p. 334, italics added).

To what extent is He to be near to us each day?

"Amidst the solemn majesty of the mountain solitudes Moses was alone with God. Everywhere the Creator's name was written. Moses seemed to stand in His presence and to be overshadowed by His power. Here his self-sufficiency was swept away. In the presence of the Infinite One he realized how weak, how inefficient, how short-sighted, is man.

"Here Moses gained that which went with him throughout the years of his toilsome and care-burdened life—a sense of the personal presence of the Divine One. . . ."Moses did not merely think of God, he saw Him. God was the constant vision before him. Never did he lose sight of His face.

"To Moses faith was no guesswork; it was a reality. He believed that God ruled his life in particular; and in all its details he acknowledged Him. For strength to withstand every temptation, he trusted in

Him" (*Education*, p. 63).

"Christ therefore is a personal Saviour. We bear about in our body the dying of the Lord Jesus, which is life and salvation and righteousness to us. *Wherever we go, we bear the abiding presence of One so dear to us; for we abide in Christ by living faith.* He is abiding in our hearts by our individual, appropriating faith. We have the companionship of the divine Jesus, and as we realize his presence, our thoughts are brought into captivity to him. *Our experience in divine things will be in proportion to the vividness of our sense of his companionship.* Enoch walked with God in this way; and Christ dwells in our hearts by faith when we appreciate what he is to us, and what a work he has wrought out for us in the plan of redemption. Then we shall be most happy in cultivating a sense of this great Gift of God to our world, and to us personally" (*The Signs of the Times*, September 3, 1896, italics added).

In my search, I discovered an explanation of how the "presence" of Christ can be in us, "dormant, unnoticed, and unrecognized," and yet be a "living, dwelling" presence in us when the Holy Spirit works through our exercise of faith. Listen carefully to these next references.

"Man's way is to devise and scheme; God implants a principle. . . . Christianity has a much broader meaning than many have hitherto given it. It is not a creed. It is the word of Him that liveth and abideth forever. It is a living animating principle, that takes possession of mind, heart, motives, and the entire man" (*Testimonies to Ministers and Gospel Workers*, pp. 420, 421).

"Where God has implanted a principle, our life and actions together are simply an expression of that principle. And if God's principle is not there, the principle of the devil is there" (A.T. Jones, *The 1897 General Conference Bulletin*).

"Men will never be truly temperate until the grace of Christ is an abiding principle in the heart.... Circumstances cannot work reform. Christianity proposes a reformation in the heart. What Christ works within, will be worked out under the dictation of a converted intellect" (*Temperance*, p. 102).

"The understanding, the will, the affections, must be yielded to the control of the word of God. Then through the work of the Holy Spirit *the precepts of the word will become the principles of the life*" (*The Ministry of Healing*, p. 514).

"Actions reveal principles and motives" (*Testimonies for the Church*, vol. 5, p. 103).

We are to be controlled by duty and principle, not by feelings. (See *Testimonies for the Church*, vol. 2, p. 435.)

Remember, the conscience acts only upon principle—what is right, what is good—with no reference to consequences. Faith does not make facts; it only lays hold of them.

"When His words of instruction have been received, and have taken possession of us, Jesus is to us as an abiding presence, controlling our thoughts and ideas and actions. . . . The words of Christ are spirit and life. . . . He dwells in us by the word of truth" (*Testimonies to Ministers and Gospel Workers*, p. 389).

"*The character* of the persecution changes with the times, but *the principle—the spirit* that underlies it—is the same that has slain the chosen of the Lord ever since the days of Abel" (*Thoughts from the Mount of Blessing*, p. 29).

Here character, principle, and spirit are tied together as one. Our spirit is made up of principles that make up our character. Words to describe principle are "beginning; commencement; a source of origin; the primary source from which anything proceeds; a governing law of conduct; a settled rule of action; a motive; an element; an agency; etc." Spiritualism tries to put into man a real, living "spiritual" being, something that has existence of its own in or out of the body. Pantheism tries to present God as "merely" a principle leaving out His ability to be "personally" with us. Truth says God, a real self-existing being, implants His principles into man, the Holy Spirit animates these principles, and through our exercise of faith, they become the controlling influence in us, and through the Holy Spirit, they are to us as the personal presence of Christ to the soul.

"It is through faith in Jesus Christ [the real living Being who walked this earth and now stands in heaven for us] that the truth is accepted in the heart, and the human agent is purified and cleansed.... *He has an abiding principle in the soul, that enables him to overcome temptation.* . . . unless truth is planted in the heart, it cannot control the life" (*The SDA Bible Commentary*, vol. 7, p. 951, italics added).

"Truth is an active, working principle, molding heart and life so that there is a constant upward movement" (*Mind, Character, and Personality*, vol. 2, p. 784, italics added).

"*Faith is the medium through which truth or error finds a lodging place in the mind.* It is by the same act of mind that truth or error [right or wrong principles] is received, but it makes a decided difference whether we believe the Word of God or the sayings of men. When Christ revealed Himself to Paul and he was convinced that he was persecuting Jesus in the person of His saints, he accepted the truth as it is in Jesus. A transforming power was manifested on mind and character, and he became a new man in Christ Jesus. He received the truth so fully that neither earth nor hell could shake his faith" (*Mind, Character, and Personality*, vol. 2, p. 539).

This is why there must be a continuous searching of the Word of God for truth. The Pharisees knew the Scriptures of their day inside out, yet Christ said they did not know Him. It is only through faith in Christ and the work of the Holy Spirit that these truths can be brought from the intellect into the soul, bringing to us a sense of the personal presence of Christ. The Spirit can only work as we by faith allow it to. The Pharisees did not exercise any faith in Christ. They were too busy living unto themselves. They desired to uplift themselves instead of Christ. The principles of Satan ruled them, under a cloak of religion.

"Under God, Adam was to stand at the head of the earthly family, to maintain the principles of the heavenly family. This would have brought peace and happiness. But the law that none 'liveth to himself' (Romans 14:7), Satan was determined to oppose. He desired to live for self. He sought to make himself the center of influence. It was this that had incited rebellion in heaven, and it was man's acceptance of this principle that brought sin on earth" (*Counsels to Parents, Teachers, and Students*, p. 33).

"May the Lord help us to die to self, and be born again, *that Christ may live in us, a living, active principle*, a power that will keep us holy" (*Testimonies for the Church*, vol. 9, p. 187, italics added).

Only as Christ "abides" in the soul—dwells in the heart by faith, a living active principle, a power to keep us holy—can we ever hope to overcome sin. But, He can only abide in us as we by faith abide in Him. (See Ephesians 3:14-21.)

"It is the grace [a principle] that Christ implants in the soul which creates in man enmity against Satan. Without this converting grace and renewing power, man would continue the captive of Satan, a servant ever ready to do his bidding. But *the new principle in the soul creates conflict where hitherto had been peace*. The power which Christ imparts, enables man to resist the tyrant and usurper. Whoever is seen to abhor sin instead of loving it, whoever resists and conquers those passions that have held sway within, *displays the operation of a principle wholly from above*" (*The Great Controversy*, p. 506, italics added).

"When the truth is held as truth only by the conscience, when the heart is not stimulated and made receptive, the mind [the mental nature] only is affected. But when the truth is received as truth by the heart [the spiritual nature], it has passed through the conscience and captivated the soul by its pure principles. It is placed in the heart by the Holy Spirit, who reveals its beauty to the mind, that its transforming power may be seen in the character" (*The Review and Herald*, March 29, 1906).

Once the principles of truth are received by the higher powers, through the Holy Spirit, the thoughts of the mind are changed and the life shows these changes by our outward actions. The lower nature loses its hold upon the higher powers, and the conscience—the light of the body—begins to shine, not only in the chambers of the mind but outwardly in our character. This next statement brings us back to the cleansing of the temple, to the place where we started in the cleansing of our spiritual nature.

"Pure and undefiled religion is not a sentiment, but the doing of works of mercy and love. This religion is necessary to health and happiness. It [the pure principles of truth] enters the polluted soul-temple, and with a scourge drives out the sinful intruders. Taking the throne, it consecrates all by its presence, illuminating the heart with its bright beams of the Sun of Righteousness. It opens the windows of the soul heavenward, letting in the sunshine of God's love [also a principle]. With it comes serenity and composure. Physical, mental, and moral strength increase, because the atmosphere of heaven, as a living, active agency, fills the soul. Christ is formed within [a living, active principle, a power], the hope of glory" (*The Review and Herald*, October 15, 1901).

"It is our privilege to open our hearts, and let the sunshine of Christ's presence in. My brother, my sister, face the light. Come into actual, personal contact with Christ, that you may exert an influence that is uplifting and reviving. Let your faith be strong and pure and steadfast. Let gratitude to God fill your hearts. When you rise in the morning, kneel at your bedside, and ask God to give you strength to fulfil the duties of the day, and to meet its temptations. Ask Him to help you to bring into your work Christ's sweetness of character. Ask Him to help you to speak words that will inspire those around you with hope and courage, and draw you nearer to the Saviour" (*Sons and Daughters of God*, p. 199).

Summary

1. God said, "Let *us* make man in *our* image" (Gen. 1:26, italics added). God is Spirit and threefold in nature—Father, Son, and Holy Spirit. Man is said to be the temple of God. The sanctuary has three compartments—the courtyard, holy place, and Most Holy Place
2. The story of Adam and Eve can be seen as an allegory of the "spiritual" nature of man, which is seen to also be threefold in nature.
3. Seeing our spirit as threefold enables us to see that God never left us alone at the fall, even though all became dark and Satan appeared to take control through the flesh. Something of God patiently "waits" in us to be brought forth, just as the life principle "waits" in the fertile seed.
4. Seeing the human nature as threefold enables us to see how the Son of God could come as Adam before the fall, with one third of His spirit—His higher powers—still in close connection to His Father, the voice of His conscience. And also as Adam after the fall with one third of His spirit, the sinful flesh, containing the seed of Satan, as all humanity does.
5. Seeing our spirit as threefold enables us to see how Satan and

Man's Spiritual Nature

sin can appear to have complete control over our human nature and how it can appear to be impossible to overcome sin in this lifetime, but the life of the man Jesus proves otherwise.

6. Satan sought to usurp God's place over the higher powers of man by taking control of the "flesh." Through the second Adam, God sets man's will free—free to choose whom he will follow, whom he will listen to: the voice of Satan in the flesh or the voice of God in the conscience. The man Jesus shows this to be true and possible for every human being.

7. The life principle of our Creator still lies in each of us, dormant until the time comes that we acknowledge the coming of Christ in our flesh and the power of His resurrection.

8. Only in the soil of Christ can we meet the penalty we deserve and rise again (a seed cannot be quickened except it die). Only in Christ can we be nourished by the "living" Word of God, so that we may arise and shine and give glory unto God.

9. So, where do we go to find this vital and necessary connection to our Lord and Savior, Jesus Christ?

Chapter Eight

Rising To Where Christ Is

"No other life was ever so crowded with labor and responsibility as was that of Jesus; yet how often He was found in prayer! . . . Again and again in the history of His earthly life are found records such as these: 'Rising up a great while before day, He went out, and departed into a solitary place, and there prayed.' 'Great multitudes came together to hear, and to be healed by Him of their infirmities. And He withdrew Himself into the wilderness, and prayed.' 'And it came to pass in those days, that He went out into a mountain to pray, and continued all night in prayer to God.' Mark 1:35; Luke 5:15, 16; 6:12.

"In a life wholly devoted to the good of others, the Saviour found it necessary to withdraw from the thoroughfares of travel and from the throng that followed Him day after day. He must turn aside from a life of ceaseless activity and contact with human needs, to seek retirement and unbroken communion with His Father. As one with us, a sharer in our needs and weaknesses, He was wholly dependent upon God, and in the secret place of prayer He sought divine strength, that He might go forth braced for duty and trial. In a world of sin Jesus endured struggles and torture of soul. In communion with God He could unburden the sorrows that were crushing Him. Here He found comfort and joy.

"In Christ the cry of humanity reached the Father of infinite pity. As a man He supplicated the throne of God till His humanity was charged with a heavenly current that should connect humanity with divinity. Through continual communion He received life from God, that He might impart life to the world. His experience is to be ours" (*The Desire of Ages*, pp. 362, 363).

It is in the hours of secret prayer that the soul makes a living connection with divinity. Only by faith can we grasp who we are in Christ. Only by faith can we see ourselves in Him, seated in heavenly places with Him. When faith can lay hold of these promises, as though they are a living reality, the glory of God will shine about us, in us, and through us. We too will be charged with that heavenly current that connects humanity with divinity.

Secret Prayer

"It is impossible for the soul to flourish while prayer is not a special exercise of the mind. Family or public prayer alone is not sufficient. Secret prayer is very important; in solitude the soul is laid bare to the inspecting eye of God, and every motive is scrutinized. Secret prayer! How precious! The soul communing with God! Secret prayer is to be heard only by the prayer-hearing God. No curious ear is to receive the burden of such petitions. In secret prayer the soul is free from surrounding influences, free from excitement. Calmly, yet fervently, will it reach out after God. Secret prayer is frequently perverted, and its sweet designs lost, by loud vocal prayer. Instead of the calm, quiet trust and faith in God, the soul drawn out in low, humble tones, the voice is raised to a loud pitch, and excitement is encouraged, and secret prayer loses its softening, sacred influence. There is a storm of feeling, a storm of words, making it impossible to discern the still, small voice that speaks to the soul while engaged in its secret, true, heartfelt devotion. Secret prayer, properly carried out, is productive of great good. But prayer which is made public to the entire family and neighborhood is not secret prayer, even though thought to be, and divine strength is not received from it. Sweet and abiding will be the influence emanating from Him who seeth in secret, whose ear is open to answer the prayer arising from the heart. By calm, simple faith the soul holds communion with God and gathers to itself divine rays of light to strengthen and sustain it to endure the conflicts of Satan. God is our tower of strength" (*Testimonies for the Church*, vol. 2, p. 189). (The entire section where this quote is found is well worth reading!)

Secret prayer—when no one is looking to see how pious we are, when no one is near to impress with what we know, when it is just ourselves and our faith—reveals the truth concerning our relationship with God and just how real He is to us. Here is the place where we seek to draw nearer to God and He comes near to us. Here is the place where our weakness is exchanged for His strength. Our will is given over to His will, our sins given up for His righteousness. Here, humbly bowing before the King of the universe, our faith is to be strengthened to meet the trials of each day, to be fortified with victories gained while on bended knee. How many of us stay on our knees in silence before Him until we "know" He has spoken to us? How often do we stay and wrestle with Him until we "know" we have the blessings of His promises? For many of us it is far too seldom.

"Prayer and faith are closely allied, and they need to be studied together. In the prayer of faith there is a divine science; it is a science that everyone who would make his lifework a success must understand. Christ says, 'What things soever ye desire, when ye pray, believe that ye receive them, and ye shall have them.' Mark 11:24. He makes it plain that our asking must be according to God's will; we must ask for the things He has promised, and whatever we receive must be used in doing His will. The conditions met, the promise is unequivocal.

"For pardon of sin, for the Holy Spirit, for a Christlike temper, for

Rising To Where Christ Is

wisdom and strength to do His work, for any gift He has promised, we may ask; then we are to believe that we receive, and return thanks to God that we have received.

"We need look for no outward evidence of the blessing. The gift is in the promise, and we may go about our work assured that what God has promised He is able to perform, and that the gift, which we already possess, will be realized when we need it most.

"To live thus by the word of God means the surrender to Him of the whole life. There will be felt a continual sense of need and dependence, a drawing out of the heart after God. Prayer is a necessity; for it is the life of the soul. Family prayer, public prayer, have their place; but it is secret communion with God that sustains the soul life" (*Education*, pp. 257, 258).

Science is knowledge coordinated, arranged, and systematized. In the prayer of faith, there is a divine science. Many claim they do not know how to pray. Many of us pray only to meet our immediate temporal needs. The prayer of faith is dependent upon knowing God's Word. Faith then lays hold of God's promises and claims them as its own. Faith acknowledges there is a very real God behind those promises who cannot lie—there is a heavenly Father just waiting to bestow the blessings of all His promises upon the believing one, a loving Father just waiting to give the gift of His Spirit to His children. Faith does not wait to see if God has given the gift before believing it is his. Faith lays hold of the facts, the truth as it is in Jesus, and then rises to face its daily duty, knowing the blessing will be there when it is needed.

There was a special request I took to prayer one afternoon. I quoted God's promise to Him, claimed it as my own by faith, and then thanked Him for it. My "thank you" seemed to fall flat on the floor before me. I tried again. I repeated to God His own Word, His promise as found in His Scriptures. Through my faith in Jesus Christ as my Savior, I claimed the promise as my own. I thanked Him that I had now received the gift. Again my thanks fell down around me. Frustrated, but not daunted, I tried again. Several times, over and over, I claimed the promise; yet each time I thanked Him I knew something was wrong. Finally, I asked the Lord to help me understand.

I sensed that I was not yet believing the promise was mine, something was yet lacking for my faith to truly lay hold of the promise and not let go. Once again I presented my request before God. This time, even before I could quote the scripture, I heard the promise spoken to me! It was not an audible voice, but it came from deep within. I knew I had not spoken those words. I *knew* God had spoken them to me. "Faith cometh by hearing the word." Now I *knew* the promise was mine and could thank Him through tears of pure joy. He showed me that it is not enough just to know His promises and that it was not my faith that gained the promises for me. I needed to know Him who had already paid the price to make those promises mine. I needed to commune with Him—to take time to listen to Him, as with a dear friend or a loved one. It was not my faith that made the promise mine; Jesus' faith had already done that. He wanted my faith to lay hold of much more than just the promise I held up to Him. He wanted to be much more to me than just a "provider" of my needs. He wanted me to cry out to Him as my personal Father, and not just seek after Him for the gifts He had to offer (Jer. 3:3, 4)!

"Not until through faith and prayer the disciples had surrendered themselves fully for His working was the outpouring of the Spirit received. Then in a special sense the goods of heaven were committed to the followers of Christ. . . . The gifts are already ours in Christ, but their actual possession depends upon our reception of the Spirit of God.

Rising To Where Christ Is

"The promise of the Spirit is not appreciated as it should be. Its fulfillment is not realized as it might be. It is the absence of the Spirit that makes the gospel ministry so powerless. Learning, talents, eloquence, every natural or acquired endowment, may be possessed; but without the presence of the Spirit of God, no heart will be touched, no sinner be won to Christ. On the other hand, if they are connected with Christ, if the gifts of the Spirit are theirs, the poorest and most ignorant of His disciples will have a power that will tell upon hearts. God makes them the channel for the outworking of the highest influence in the universe" (*Christ's Object Lessons*, pp. 327, 328).

The true prayer of faith should never be hurried or spoken rashly or loudly. It is a time when there should be silence in the soul, an inner quietness that waits patiently to hear God speak. I think that when we refuse to leave the place of solitary prayer until we know we have made a connection with divinity, until we know the Spirit of the Lord has come to us, we shall have found the way to take the kingdom by violence as did Jacob. The battle he fought was while he was in prayer. The battle of faith, I believe, must be fought on our knees in secret prayer. As each battle is fought and won, we can go forth with the necessary victory to meet the trials of the day. Through the Holy Spirit, we can face each day with a realization of the personal presence of a very personal Savior by our side.

"It was in the mount with God that Moses beheld the pattern of that wonderful building which was to be the abiding place of His glory. It is in the mount with God—in the secret place of communion—that we are to contemplate His glorious ideal for humanity. Thus we shall be enabled so to fashion our character building that to us may be fulfilled His promise, 'I will dwell in them, and walk in them; and I will be their God, and they shall be My people.' 2 Corinthians 6:16 (*Education*, p. 258).

Christ is Our Only Hope

"The Lord can do little for his people, because of their limited faith. The ministers have not presented Christ in his fullness to the people, either in the churches or in new fields, and the people have not an intelligent faith. They have not been instructed as they should have been, that Christ is unto them both salvation and righteousness. The love that Christ manifested in taking human nature, in bearing insult, reproach, and the rejection of men, in suffering crucifixion on the cross, should be presented in every discourse. It is Satan's studied purpose to keep souls from believing in Christ as their only hope; for the blood of Christ that cleanseth from all sin is only efficacious in behalf of those who believe in its merit, and who present it before the Father as did Abel in his offering.

"The offering of Cain was an offense to God, because it was a Christless offering. The burden of our message is not only the commandments of God, but the faith of Jesus....

"When the Lamb of God was crucified on Calvary, the death knell of Satan was sounded; and if the enemy of truth and righteousness can obliterate from the mind the thought that it is necessary to depend upon the righteousness of Christ for salvation, he will do it. If Satan can succeed in leading man to place value upon his own works as works of merit and righteousness, he knows that he can overcome him by his temptations, and make him his victim and prey. Lift up Jesus before the people. Strike the door-posts with the blood of Calvary's Lamb, and you are safe" (*The Review and Herald*, September 3, 1889, italics added).

Jesus knew how difficult it would be for His disciples after He was gone. He gave them assurance that He would not leave them "empty handed." In fact, the gift He had in mind for them, and for us, could not come, and would not be appreciated, until He went away. We know that

Rising To Where Christ Is

Jesus Christ is the "hope" of the Christian, but did you know the word "hope," in reference to Christ, cannot be found in the four Gospels? Could it be because "hope that is seen is not hope" (Rom. 8:24)? It was necessary for Jesus to go away to strengthen our faith, to stretch out the longings of the heart to as high as the heavens in search of Him, and to see the unseen.

"Nevertheless I tell you the truth; It is expedient for you that I go away: for if I go not away, the Comforter will not come unto you; but if I depart, I will send him unto you. And when he is come, he will reprove the world of sin, and of righteousness, and of judgment. Of sin, because they believe not on me; Of righteousness, because I go to my Father, and ye see me no more; Of judgment, because the prince of this world is judged" (John 16:7-11).

The Comforter convicts of sin by showing us sin in its true character—our lack of faith. He thereby encourages us to fix our hold upon Christ. The accuser is the one who tries to focus our attention on every wrong thing we think and do in order to weaken and break our hold upon Jesus. Seeing the sins we have committed is necessary to show us our need, but do not let them, through guilt, drive a wedge between you and your Savior as Satan would have it.

The Comforter convicts of righteousness by pointing our eyes up to a risen Savior, not to the law and not even to Christ who walked this earth as our example. Don't get me wrong, these are to be studied and meditated upon to be sure, but only in the light of whom Christ now is in heaven, where we see Him no more except through the eyes of faith. Christ's work on earth is a finished work. The righteousness we seek is already ours in the Christ who now stands in heaven. Have we risen to be there in Him by faith?

The Comforter will reprove the world of judgment by revealing that the prince of this world has been judged. Satan is a conquered foe;

his case has been tried; the decision has been made; he has no more power over us than that which we give him through our own ignorance and fear. "In the world ye shall have tribulation: but be of good cheer; I have overcome the world" (John 16:33). "Christ has conquered the powers of earth; and shall we be afraid of a world already conquered?" (*The Great Controversy*, p. 610). There is nothing to fear in the judgment if the Comforter has been our earthly companion.

Christ came to this world, and He lived a righteous life through total submission to the will of His Father. He chose to serve His Father—His Father made all His choices for Him. He did not come to save Himself. He came to save you and me. When will we learn that it is Christ's righteous life that saves us? In Christ, His righteousness is our righteousness. As our faith lays hold of and rests in that one all encompassing fact, as our only means of salvation, we will willingly yield our members as instruments into God's hands. Then He can come to you and me and work in us to reveal His righteousness. To save us? No! Like Christ, any righteousness revealed in us is only for the salvation of others and for the glory of God. Our works earn us no credit; they have no merit toward our own salvation. Our life simply testifies to the world and the unfallen universe the One we have chosen to rule over us. Let us put our eyes squarely upon Jesus Christ. Shall we not practice the "obedience of faith" (Rom. 16:26)? Let us "fight the good fight of faith" (1 Tim. 6:12)."'The faith of Jesus.' It is talked of, but not understood. What constitutes the faith of Jesus, that belongs to the third angel's message? Jesus becoming our sin-bearer that he might become our sin-pardoning Saviour. He was treated as we deserve to be treated. He came to our world and took our sins that we might take his righteousness. And faith in the ability of Christ to save us amply and fully and entirely is the faith of Jesus" (*Selected Messages*, book 3, p. 172).

"When he stood where we are, he said, 'I will put my trust in Him;'

Rising To Where Christ Is

and that trust was never disappointed. In response to that trust, the Father dwelt in him and with him and kept him from sinning. Who was He?—We. And thus the Lord Jesus has brought to every man in this world divine faith. That is the faith of the Lord Jesus.—That is saving faith. Faith is not something that comes from ourselves, with which we believe upon him; but it is that something with which he believed,—the faith which He exercised, which He brings to us, and which becomes ours, and works in us,—the gift of God" (A.T. Jones, *The 1895 General Conference Bulletin*, p. 270).

"If you are willing to learn meekness and lowliness of heart in Christ's school, He will surely give you rest and peace. It is a terribly hard struggle to give up your own will and your own way. But this lesson learned, you will find rest and peace. Pride, selfishness, and ambition must be overcome; your will must be swallowed up in the will of Christ. The whole life may become one constant love sacrifice, every action a manifestation, and every word an utterance of love. As the life of the vine circulates through stem and cluster, descends into the lower fibers, and reaches to the topmost leaf, so will the grace and love of Christ burn and abound in the soul, sending its virtues to every part of the being, and pervading every exercise of body and mind" (*The SDA Bible Commentary*, vol. 5, p. 1091).

"All that any man in the world has to do in order to be saved, is to believe the truth, that is, to recognize and acknowledge facts, to see things just as they actually are, and to confess them. . . . This is the only true confession of faith" (E.J. Waggoner, The Glad Tidings, p. 88).

Vision of a Finished Work

If God's glory is to arise and shine (Isa. 60:1) upon God's people on this earth, it must first arise and shine in us, in Christ, by faith. We need to behold ourselves in Him as He now stands in our human nature before the very throne of God. In Revelation 14:4 we find that the hundred forty four thousand are said to "follow the lamb withersoever he goeth." In 1 John 2:6 we are commanded to "walk, even as he walked." If we are to finish the work that God has given us to do then we must lift our eyes toward heaven and away from this earth. We must believe the truth, recognize and acknowledge the facts, see things just as they actually are, confess them, and then choose to "walk, even as he walked"—as one already glorified, claiming our "oneness" with the Father in Christ Jesus. (See *The Desire of Ages*, pp. 690, 691.)

"God has wrought out salvation for every man, and has given it to him; but the majority spurn it, and throw it away. The Judgment will reveal the fact that full and complete salvation was given to every man, and that the lost have deliberately thrown away their birthright possession. Thus every mouth will be stopped" (E.J. Waggoner, The Glad Tidings, p. 22).

In the story of Esau we are told that "for a dish of red pottage he parted with his birthright, and confirmed the transaction by an oath. A short time at most would have secured him food in his father's tents, but to satisfy the desire of the moment he carelessly bartered the glorious heritage that God himself had promised to his fathers. His whole interest was in the present. He was ready to sacrifice the heavenly to the earthly, to exchange a future good for a momentary indulgence.

"'Thus Esau despised his birthright.' In disposing of it he felt a sense of relief. Now his way was unobstructed; he could do as he liked. For this wild pleasure, miscalled freedom, how many are still selling their birthright to an inheritance pure and undefiled, eternal in the heavens! (*Patriarchs and Prophets*, p. 179).

"Because of his indifference to the divine blessings and requirements, Esau is called in Scripture a 'profane person.' Verse 16. He represents those who lightly value the redemption purchased for them by

Christ, and are ready to sacrifice their heirship to heaven for the perishable things of earth. Multitudes live for the present with no thought or care for the future. Like Esau they cry, 'Let us eat and drink; for tomorrow we die.' 1 Corinthians 15:32....How many, even of professed Christians, cling to indulgences that are injurious to health and that benumb the sensibilities of the soul....

"Multitudes are selling their birthright for sensual indulgence. Health is sacrificed, the mental faculties are enfeebled, and heaven is forfeited; and all for a mere temporary pleasure—an indulgence at once both weakening and debasing in character. As Esau awoke to see the folly of his rash exchange when it was too late to recover his loss, so it will be in the day of God with those who have bartered away their heirship to heaven for selfish gratifications" (Ibid., pp. 181, 182).

Ellen White recognizes that the heirship of heaven is the birthright possession of every human being, just as the Bible reveals this fact. In Isaiah 14:17 we are told that in the last days Satan "opened not the house of his prisoners." This refers to those who have not accepted Christ and will not rise when He comes again to take His people home. The marginal reading of my Thomas Nelson, KJV Bible says, "Or, did not let his prisoners loose homewards." Did you catch that? Heaven is the home even of those who do not rise when Christ returns! They will have chosen this earth as their home and Satan will have the right to hold them in the grave, but in Christ heaven was their true home. Heaven is your home today. The choice is yours as to whether or not you will ever see the home that Christ has prepared for you. Unfortunately, that inheritance guaranteed to us through Christ will not be valued by multitudes of people who live only for the present life. Too late they will wake up to their loss.

This idea of waking up too late brings to mind an episode of Mission Impossible, a TV program that aired several years ago. The mission was to entrap a man into making a confession of a crime he had committed. The man was kidnapped and kept under heavy security with the pretense that it was for his own protection. He was told that someone was seeking to take his life and the only way they could continue to protect him was to admit to his crime. It took several days to get the man to believe in what was happening to him. Finally they gained his trust, and the man wrote out his confession. That night he went to sleep a contented and happy man. He awoke the next morning to find the confession missing from the nightstand and the guard no longer at his door; in fact, no one was around. He went down the corridor to a door that had always been locked and it now opened easily. Upon stepping through the door, he found himself in a very large hanger, and he knew he had been "entrapped, deluded, decoyed, tricked" (definition of "enticed" in James 1:14). His effort to save himself now proved to be his death warrant. Satan's mission is to entrap us, to give us a sense of security, and to lull us to sleep as to the time we live in, for he knows that when we wake up it will be too late.

    This world we live in is one big delusion created by Satan's lies. A mixture of truth and error bombards our senses every day. He has devised many avenues that give the illusion of peace and safety. Some are very clever counterfeits of the truth. There is no way under heaven by which we may be saved other than by Jesus Christ. In Him salvation is already ours. Any attempt on our part to be saved in any other way will only be to throw away our "birthright possession." By faith we need to catch the vision of a finished work in Christ and, by faith, lay hold of it as a true fact in us in Christ. As we choose to act upon that fact, in total submission to Christ, God will be enabled to manifest His finished work in us for the world to see. Soon, I pray, it can truly be said of us:

    "Here are they that keep [guard (from loss or injury) by keeping

Rising To Where Christ Is

the eye upon (*Strong's Concordance,* p. 203)] the commandments of God, and the faith of Jesus" (Rev. 14:12). Many interpret the word "keep" in this verse as obedience to the law—the Ten Commandments—as revealed on the two tables of stone. It is true that God's final remnant will be obedient, but this verse is acknowledging their high regard for the law of God. I believe that when we, by faith, see what Ellen White saw, as noted in the following quote, our focus will no longer be upon two tables of stone. Instead, we will seek to "guard by keeping the eye upon" the living law as manifested in Jesus Christ.

"In the ark, beneath where the angels' wings were spread, was a golden pot of Manna, of yellowish cast; and I saw a rod, which Jesus said was Aaron's; I saw it bud, blossom and bear fruit. [Numbers 17:8.] And I saw two long golden rods, on which hung silver wires, and on the wires most glorious grapes; one cluster was more than a man here could carry. And I saw Jesus step up and take of the manna, almonds, grapes, and pomegranates, and bear them down to the city, and place them on the supper table. I stepped up to see how much was taken away, and there was just as much left; and we shouted Hallelujah—Amen" (A Word to the Little Flock, p. 16).

Ellen White saw the bowl of manna and Aaron's rod that budded. But she did not see two tables of stone. In their place she saw two large bundles of living grapes, hanging upon silver wires attached to two golden rods. I believe what she saw was a living depiction of faith that works by love. She saw the fruit of the Spirit, hung upon silver wires of obedience that stem from the golden rods of faith and love, to be found only in the personal Savior who stands as the Lamb slain before the throne of God in heaven above.

It is interesting to note that the Lord required half a shekel of silver as the ransom for every first-born Israelite (Ex. 30:11-16). He explained that He considered it "an atonement for your souls." The poor were to give no less, nor were the rich to give more. Wealth makes no difference when the Judge ponders the cases of men or women for redemption. All are equally sinful in His eyes. But today we "are not redeemed with…silver…but with the precious blood of Christ" (1 Peter 1:18, 19). Silver thus suggests redemption based on the perfect obedience of the Savior who gave His life as the ransom for the lost (Leslie Hardinge, With Jesus in His Sanctuary, pp. 81, 82).

May we guard by keeping the eye upon this view that Ellen White had of the living law and ever keep our eyes fixed upon Jesus, who is the fulfillment of the law. May we learn to partake of that life now, manifesting the fruit of the Spirit here on earth, that we may be fitted to partake of it at the great supper in heaven above.

There is still much for us to learn. When a light is turned on, we see things we did not see before. Spotlights are used to draw attention to certain areas, and they bring out details hard to see. The message that began to sound in 1888 was like a spotlight. It was designed to cause us to see things from a new perspective, to reveal to us details that were hidden from view. Unless we use that light, we will be left in the darkness of misunderstanding.

"There is much light yet to shine forth from the law of God and the gospel of righteousness. This message, understood in its true character [thoughts, feelings, and actions], and proclaimed in the Spirit, will lighten the earth with its glory" (*Manuscript Releases*, vol. 2, p. 58).

Several years ago my 13-year-old son and I had been at a meeting where new light was being presented and there was very strong opposition expressed in words and feelings. As we were driving home, he shared with me the following insight: "I see a ladder that reaches from earth to heaven. The believer in Christ is on this ladder, climbing up to heaven. New light is like a higher rung on the ladder, and we are to reach up and take hold of it. In order to move upward, we must take our feet off the rung below. Sometimes we are afraid to move. I think we forget that Christ is the ladder and that the rungs are only steps."

When we are first drawn to Christ, we are given a vision of Him hanging upon the cross. There we learn of God's love toward us, and we find freedom from guilt and a promise of power to overcome. Next we behold Him in His "sacrificial" life upon this earth. There we learn to know what He expects of us and is capable of doing in and through us. Now we need to learn to behold Him as He is in heaven above. He is still the "Lamb slain" but now He stands in "glorified humanity" before the throne of God. We need to learn to walk on this earth, "even as he walked," "as one already glorified," claiming our "oneness" with God as revealed in Jesus Christ, for He is our Example. (See *The Desire of Ages*, p. 690 and John 17.)

Each view of Christ's life is to be a stepping stone toward heaven. Like the rungs on the ladder, they can easily become a stumbling block if we cling to what we know and refuse to move forward. He came down from heaven to reach us where we are in our sinful human nature upon this sin-cursed earth. Will we now, by faith, come up to Him where He is in His divine human nature in heaven above? Soon Christ will move from the temple in heaven to this earth. I want to be among those who follow Him out of the temple by faith, so that when we see Him in reality, descending upon the cloud, we will cry, "Lo, this is our God; we have waited for him" (Isa. 25:9).

"We are living in the most solemn period of this world's history. The destiny of earth's teeming multitudes is about to be decided. Our own future well-being, and also the salvation of other souls, depends upon the course which we now pursue. We need to be guided by the Spirit of truth. Every follower of Christ should earnestly inquire, 'Lord, what wilt thou have me to do?' We need to humble ourselves before the Lord, with fasting and prayer, and to meditate much upon his Word, especially upon the scenes of the Judgment. We should now seek a deep and living experience in the things of God. We have not a moment to lose. Events of vital importance are taking place around us; we are on Satan's enchanted ground. Sleep not, sentinels of God; the foe is lurking near, ready at any moment, should you become lax and drowsy, to spring upon you and make you his prey" (*The Great Controversy*, p. 601).

Satan seeks to discourage us and cause us to fall. God gives us hope and longs to hold us up, to keep us from falling. To whose voice will you listen? What course are you following?

"Satan is an accuser, and is making the case of Israel appear as desperate as possible. He presents before the Lord their faults and failures, hoping that they will appear so dark in the eyes of Christ that he will render them no help in their great need. Joshua, aware of the imperfections of Israel, stands under condemnation, clothed with the filthy garments of sin, while Satan is pressing upon his soul a sense of guilt that makes him almost helpless" (*The Watchman*, September 25, 1906).

Joshua, the high priest, standing before Christ, is also a representation of God's people in the last days. Known sin brings home a sense of guilt and drives a wedge between us and God. This is Satan at work. He desires us to feel helpless and consequently to lose all hope. If we will simply turn to Christ in spite of how we "feel," we will find Satan's work a deception and discover that Christ is ever present to help.

"Satan was charging the people of God with all his attributes, and presenting before them the sins he had instigated them to commit. Satan clothed their characters with his own filthy garments of sin, and nothing was lost in his reckoning of their misdeeds. But these souls who were represented as wearing the black robes of Satan's weaving in his hellish loom, were not an appropriate representation; for they had repented of their transgressions. The Lord who searcheth

Rising To Where Christ Is

the heart and understandeth the imagination of the thoughts, had set their sins before them, and had given them the promise: 'If thou seek him, he will be found of thee; but if thou forsake him he will cast thee off forever.' The Lord, the everlasting God, is ever present to observe, inspect, and examine all things. The hearts of all are read as an open book. 'The eyes of the Lord run to and fro throughout the whole earth'" (*Manuscript Releases*, vol. 7, p. 202).

"If you would stand through the time of trouble, you must know Christ, and appropriate the gift of his righteousness, which he imputes to the repentant sinner. Human wisdom will not avail to devise a plan of salvation. Human philosophy is vain, the fruits of the loftiest powers of man are worthless, aside from the great plan of the divine Teacher. No glory is to redound to man; all human help and glory lies in the dust; for the truth as it is in Jesus is the only available agent by which man may be saved. Man is privileged to connect with Christ, and then the divine and the human combine; and in this union the hope of man must rest alone; for it is as the Spirit of God touches the soul that the powers of the soul are quickened and man becomes a new creature in Christ Jesus. He was manifested to bring life and immortality to light. He says, 'The words that I speak unto you, they are spirit and they are life.' The psalmist declares, 'The entrance of thy words giveth light; it giveth understanding unto the simple'" (*The Ellen G. White 1888 Materials*, p. 1073).

When Adam transgressed God's command, the earth was broken away from heaven. A loving Father sent forth His Son to bridge this gap—to reconnect the "island" of earth to the "continent" of heaven. (See *The SDA Bible Commentary*, vol. 1, pp. 1084, 1085, 1095.) When the Son had finished His work and was about to return to His Father, He let us know we would not be left alone. He sent forth a Comforter, whose work it is to guide us into all truth, bringing to our minds all that Christ said and did. When we by faith sink ourselves into Christ then He has us! Through the Holy Spirit, Christ will become a very real presence within the soul. If we know Christ is near, we can be sure the Father is also near, for they are one. All power in heaven and earth are just waiting to assist us in our everyday struggles as well as in the hour of temptation that is fast coming upon this earth. May we learn the lesson of Isaiah 40, may we hear the voice of the one crying in the wilderness, and may we respond as God has designed we should:

"Comfort ye, comfort ye my people, saith your God. Speak ye comfortably to Jerusalem, and cry unto her, that her warfare is accomplished, that her iniquity is pardoned: for she hath received of the LORD's hand double for all her sins.

The voice of him that crieth in the wilderness, Prepare ye the way of the LORD" (verses 1-3).

"The voice said, Cry. And he said, What shall I cry? All flesh is grass, and all the goodliness thereof is as the flower of the field: The grass withereth, the flower fadeth: because the spirit of the LORD bloweth upon it: surely the people is grass. The grass withereth, the flower fadeth: but the word of our God shall stand forever.

"O Zion, that bringest good tidings, get thee up into the high mountain; O Jerusalem, that bringest good tidings, lift up thy voice with strength; lift it up, be not afraid; say unto the cities of Judah, Behold your God!" (verses 6-9).

"But they that wait upon the LORD shall renew [put off] their strength; [then] they shall mount up with wings as eagles; they shall run, and not be weary; and they shall walk, and not faint" (verse 31).

God's Word is full of warning against the consequences of violating His law, but it is also full of comfort and hope for the one who has transgressed His law. It is my prayer that the thoughts of my mind and the meditation of my heart are acceptable in the sight of the Lord, my

Strength and my Redeemer. May the words of my testimony be used by His Spirit to guide you into an even deeper relationship with "him that is able to keep you from falling, and to present you faultless before the presence of his glory with exceeding joy" (Jude 24).

In closing, allow me to share with you the outpouring of my heart as I became aware of the nearness of Christ to me when I did not know He was already there.

NEVER ALONE

You came when I was so alone.
You lifted me up from deep despair.
Guilt, anger, pain, all fled away;
And then I knew, You were there.

You took my hand, and step by step,
You let me see how much You care.
I learned to accept, even me,
And thus I knew, You were there.

I thought my heart would burst for Joy!
Such a feeling must be rare!
No greater Friend can there be found,
Then when I know, You are there.

You gave up all to be with me,
No greater love is there to share!
At the cross, I willingly die;
Because I know, You are there.

Comfort Ye My People

Love you gave. Love in me was sown,
As all my sin and grief You bear.
We became one, and then I saw:
That you had ALWAYS been there!

From first life, in my mother's womb,
Through every day's woe and care.
What sorrow I must have caused You;
I did not know, You were there.

"I'll never leave thee nor forsake thee."
This Your Word is everywhere.
How patiently You have waited,
To think! You were always there!

Thy rod and staff now comfort me,
A pilgrim in life's thoroughfare.
Another country, I do seek;
Eternally, we'll be there!

"To the only wise God our Saviour, be glory and majesty, dominion and power, both now and ever. Amen" (Jude 25).

Appendix A

"The Third Angel's Message-No. 12"

The following excerpt was written by A.T. Jones and is titled "The Third Angel's Message-No. 12." It was published in *The 1893 General Conference Bulletin*.

"I have here a book entitled, Catholic Belief. It bears the imprimatur of John Cardinal McCloskey, Archbishop of New York...and comes into this country with the approval of the hierarchy in this country.

"I shall read some from it. And, that you may have the two things—the truth of justification by faith and the falsity of it—side by side, I will read what this says, and then what God says in *Steps to Christ*. It is in the Testimonies also and all through the Bible, of course. I want you to see what the Roman Catholic idea of justification by faith is, because I have had to meet it among professed Seventh-day Adventists the past four years right straight through. These very things, these very expressions that are in this Catholic book, as to what justification by faith is and how to obtain it, are just such expressions as professed Seventh-day Adventists have made to me as to what justification by faith is.

"I want to know how you and I can carry a message to this world, warning them against the worship of the beast, when we hold in our very profession the doctrines of the beast. Can it be done? (Congregation: "No.") And so I call your attention to this tonight so you may see just what it is, and so that, if possible, knowing what it is to start with, knowing that it is papal, knowing that it is the beast, you will let it go because it is that, even if you are not ready to believe in justification by faith, indeed, even if you cannot see that, as some are unable to, as God gives it. Now, if we find out that it is papal, I hope those who have held that, or expressed it at any rate, whatever they have held, will be willing to let it go any way. On page 74 of this work I read as follows:"'In the case of grown-up persons, some dispositions are required on the part of the sinner in order to be fit to obtain this habitual and abiding grace of justification.'

"He has got to prepare himself for it. He has got to do something to make himself fit to receive it. As I read each statement from this book, I shall then read the opposite of it. So now, on pages 26 and 27 of *Steps to Christ*, I read as follows: [paging may differ depending on your copy of *Steps to Christ*]

'If you see your sinfulness, do not wait to make yourself better. How many there are who think they are not good enough to come to Christ. Do you expect to become better through your own efforts?... There is help for us only in God. We must not wait for stronger persuasions, for better opportunities, or for holier tempers. We can do nothing of ourselves. We must come to Christ just as we are.' (And Romans 4:5).

"This is justification by faith. That other thing is justification by works. This is of Christ; that is of the devil. One is Christ's doctrine of justification by faith; the other is the devil's doctrine of justification by faith. And it is time that Seventh-day Adventists understood the difference. (Congregation: "Amen!")

"Again from the Catholic work:—

"'A man can dispose himself only by the help of divine grace, and the dispositions which he shows do not by any means effect or merit justification: they only prepare him for it.

"'No, I don't believe in justification by works, but we have got to so something in order to be prepared for it. We have got to show our good intentions any way. We have got to make some good resolutions before we start, any way; something to prepare us for it.'"What does God say? On page 33 of *Steps to Christ* I read:"'He is wooing by his tender love the hearts of his erring children. No earthly parent could be as patient with the faults and mistakes of his children, as is God with those he seeks to save.'

"He does what? 'Seeks to save.' This is God's way. Oh, no, He waits until men prepare themselves to be saved. That is Satan's way. "'No one could plead more tenderly with the transgressor. No human lips ever poured out more entreaties to the wanderer than He does. All His promises, His warnings, are but the breathing of unutterable love. When Satan comes to tell you that you are a great sinner, look up to your Redeemer and talk of His merits. That which will help you is to look to His light. Acknowledge your sin, but tell the enemy that "Jesus Christ came into the world to save sinners," and that you may be saved by His matchless love.' (And John 3:16).

"This is justification by faith. That is justification by works. This is Jesus Christ. That is Satan.

"Then in this Catholic work it goes on to tell a list of things that you must do in order to have these dispositions: 'An act of faith . . . an act of fear of God, an act of hope . . . an act of repentance . . . a resolution to approach the Sacrament of Penance.'

"These are things that will prepare you to be justified to be saved. On page 76 of this same work, I read:"'We stand in continual need of actual graces to perform good acts, both before and after being justified.'

"Good acts must be performed before we are justified, in order to fit us for it.

"'The good acts, however, done by the help of grace before justification are not, strictly speaking, meritorious, but serve to smooth the way to justification, to move God.'

"They 'serve to move God.' That is just the hard, iron spirit the devil asserts was in the Lord when He started, in heaven; that God was a tyrant; that God does not want His people to be free, His creatures to be free, that He sits there and wants everything to go just so without any reason, judgment, freedom, or anything of the kind. He has to be 'moved' by His creatures. That is the doctrine that Satan has put into the idea of sacrifice from that time until now. God appointed sacrifices to show to man, to convey to man, what God is willing to do for man, that God is making sacrifice for him. But Satan whirled it around and man has got to do this in order to get God into good humor, that the Lord is angry with him and the Lord wants to punish him and now we have got to sacrifice to pay Him off so He will not hurt us, and we have to 'move' Him to justify us.

"Let us read what the Lord says on that, *Steps to Christ*, pages 57 and 58. Speaking of the parable of the prodigal son and how that, when the wanderer was yet a great way off, the father had compassion on him and ran and fell on his neck and kissed him, it says:"'But even this parable, tender and touching as it is, comes short of expressing the infinite compassion of the heavenly Father. The Lord declares by His prophet, "I have loved thee with an everlasting love; therefore, with loving-kindness have I drawn thee." While the sinner is yet far from the Father's house, wasting his substance in a strange country, the Father's heart is yearning over him and every longing awakened in the soul to return to God is but the tender pleading of His Spirit, wooing, entreating, drawing the wanderer to His Father's heart of love.

"'With the rich promises of the Bible before you, can you give place to doubt? Can you believe that when the poor sinner longs to return, longs to forsake his sins, the Lord sternly withholds him from coming to His feet in repentance? Away with such thoughts! Nothing can hurt your soul more than to entertain such a conception of our heavenly Father.'

"Who wants to hurt our souls? (Congregation: "Satan.") Who wants most to hurt the soul? Satan. What could more hurt the soul than that doctrine in that book that we must put ourselves into dispositions, into frames of mind, and make good resolutions and all these things in order to 'move' God to take pity on us and save us. What could more hurt the soul than to think that God sternly holds off the sinner until the poor lost soul does something to move Him? What more hurtful thing could a person believe? The Lord's answer is: 'There is nothing can hurt your soul more than such a conception.' Then, where alone can that doctrine come from? (Congregation: "Satan.") Yet that is passed off under the title and under the idea of justification by faith! There is no faith in it. Away with it, saith the Lord. And let all the people say, Amen.

"Again I read from Catholic Belief:—"'But if with the assistance of actual grace, good works are done by a person who is in a state of justifying grace, then they are acceptable to God and merit an increase of grace on earth and an increase of glory in heaven.'

"What saith the Lord? Page 61, *Steps to Christ*. And this is in the chapter entitled 'The Test of Discipleship.' It is talking to those who are disciples; it is talking to the same persons to whom that other book talks. What does it say?

"'While we cannot do anything to change our hearts or to bring ourselves into harmony with God, while we must not trust at all to ourselves or our good works, our lives will reveal whether the grace of God is dwelling within us.'

"You see then, God's idea is that when He is there, He will show

Himself through us. The other, Satan's idea, is that after we have got the Lord converted, then we do some good work that is 'meritorious,' and we will be safe in this world; we will have 'an increase of grace' on this earth, 'and an increase of glory in heaven.' That is the very foundation of the merits of the 'saints,' from which the pope draws indulgences to give to those who have not enough merit of their own.

"Now that which I have just read from this Catholic work is in a chapter on justification, preaching the straight doctrine of justification. Here (page 365) he reviews the doctrine of justification by faith, in condemnation of Protestants who believe it. Let us see, brethren, whether we shall be Protestants or Catholics. Let us see whether we shall believe in Jesus Christ or Satan. That is what we need to understand now, and know now we understand it, before we start in to give the third angel's message. I read:

"'As in revolutions the leaders try to gain the people over by the bait of promised independence, so at the time of the so-called reformation—which was a revolution against church authority and order in religion—it seems that it was the aim of the reformers to decoy the people under the pretext of making them independent of the priests, in whose hands our Saviour has placed the administering of the seven Sacraments of pardon and of grace.'

"'They began, therefore, by discarding five of these Sacraments, including the Sacrament of Order, in which Priests are ordained, and the Sacrament of Penance, in which the forgiveness of sins is granted to the penitent....They then reduced, as it appears, to a mere matter of form, the two Sacraments they professed to retain, namely, Holy Baptism and the Holy Eucharist. To make up for this rejection they enable each individual to prescribe for himself, and procure by himself the pardon of sin and divine grace, independently of the priests.'

"Elder Jones: Is this true doctrine? Is it true that a man can approach God by himself, independently of the priests? (Congregation: "Yes.") What saith the Lord? *Steps to Christ*, p. 117:

"'The relations between God and each soul are as distinct and full as if there was not another soul for whom He gave His beloved Son.'

"Thank the Lord. Now I read on in the Catholic book:

"'Independently of priests and of the sacraments, they invented an exclusive means, never known to the Church of God, and still rejected by all the Eastern Churches and by the Roman Catholics throughout the world, by which the followers of Luther ventured to declare that each individual can secure pardon and justification for himself, independently of priests and sacraments.'

"'They have framed a new Dogma, not to be found in any of the Creeds, or in the Canons of any General Council; I mean, the new dogma of Justification by Faith alone, or by Faith only.'

"That is the 'new dogma' that is condemned by the papacy; this is not in any of the creeds which she has. On page 366 I read again:

"'By adding the word alone, Protestants profess to exclude all exterior, ceremonial, pious, or charitable works, works of obedience or of penance, and good moral acts whatever, as means of apprehending justification, or as conditions to obtain it.'

"'Oh, yes, you have got to do something to pave the way; you have got to do something to get out of that place where you are,' so that you can be justified. You must lift yourself up part of the way, and then the Lord will be moved and will receive you and justify you. That is Satan's doctrine. Shall we be Protestants or Catholics? That is the question. (Congregation: "Protestants.") Shall we proclaim the third angel's message against the worship of the beast and his image? or shall we be a part of the beast and his image ourselves? That is the question. For the image is the image of the beast in this point as well as in all else, even though it profess to be Protestant. It is apostate Protestant. On page 367 of the Catholic book I read the following:

"'To do these acts with the view of being justified is, they say, like giving a penny to the queen to obtain from her a royal gift.'

"What saith the Lord? Page 51, *Steps to Christ*:"'This is the lesson which Jesus taught while He was on earth, that the gift which God promises us, we must believe we do receive, and it is ours.'

"Then which is Christianity? (Congregation: "The last.") But the Catholic Church says that this is Protestantism. It is true. Thank the Lord!

"But we continue reading from this Catholic work:

"'Come as you are, they add; you cannot be too bad for Jesus.'

"Thank the Lord that this is not Catholic doctrine. Thank the Lord it is no part of the beast or his worship nor the image and his worship. Let us put them together. What saith the Lord? Page 27, *Steps to Christ*:"'We can do nothing of ourselves. We must come just as we are.'

"Again, on page 55, *Steps to Christ*:"'Jesus loves to have us come just as we are, sinful.'

"What is 'sinful?' (Congregation: "Full of sin.") Does Jesus love to have us come to Him just as we are, full of sin? (Congregation: "Yes.") Does He? (Congregation: "Yes, sir.") Let us be Protestants. Let us have the third angel's message, which is the gospel of Jesus Christ.

"'Jesus loves to have us come just as we are, sinful, helpless, dependent. We may come with all (how much? "All.") our weakness, our folly, our sinfulness, and fall at His feet in penitence. It is His glory to encircle us in the arms of His love and to bind up our wounds, to cleanse us from all impurity. . . . None are so sinful that they cannot find strength, purity, and righteousness in Jesus, who died for them.'

"That is the gift of God. That is His gift—a free gift without money, without price, and I take it gladly and everlastingly thank Him for it. This is the Lord's idea of justification by faith. The other is Satan's idea. Let us read from the Catholic book again:

"'Through faith alone in His promise, they (Protestants) assert, you can and should accept Christ's merits, seize Christ's redemption and His justice; appropriate Christ to yourself, believe that Jesus is with you, is yours, that He pardons your sins, and all this without any preparation and without any doing on your part.'

"Good! Thank the Lord, that is Protestantism! and Catholics know that it is Protestantism. Do you know it? On page 53, *Steps to Christ*, let us see what the Lord says:"'It is the will of God to cleanse us from sin, to make us His children, and to enable us to live a holy life. So we may ask for these blessings, and believe that we receive them, and thank God that we have received them. It is our privilege to go to Jesus and be cleansed and to stand before the law without shame or remorse.' Eph. 1:3.

"(Congregation: "Amen.") Without any need of doing penance? (Congregation: "Yes.") Thank the Lord.

"Now the Catholic book again:-

"'In fact, that however deficient you may be in all other dispositions which Catholics require, and however loaded with sins, if you only trust in Jesus that He will forgive your sins and save you, you are by that trust alone forgiven, personally redeemed, justified, and placed in a state of salvation.'

"Now let us read on page 33, *Steps to Christ*, again:

"'When Satan comes to tell you that you are a great sinner, look up to your Redeemer, and talk of His merits. That which will help you is to look to His light. Acknowledge your sins, but tell the enemy that "Jesus Christ came into the world to save sinners, and that you may be saved by His matchless love." Jesus asked Simon a question in regard to two debtors. One owed his lord a small sum, and the other owed him a very large sum, but he forgave them both, and Christ asked Simon which debtor would love his lord the most. Simon answered, "He to whom he forgave most." We have been great sinners, but Christ died that we might be forgiven. The merits of His sacrifice are sufficient to present to the father in our behalf.'

"Are they, in fact? (Congregation: "Yes sir.") Good! There is a great deal more in this Catholic work that I will not take time to read now. It goes on to define what faith is. Now think carefully, because I have met people all the way along who think that this very thing is faith which this Catholic book calls faith. I read page 368:

"'The word "faith" in the Scripture sometimes means confidence in God's omnipotence and goodness, that He can and is willing to cure or benefit us by some miraculous interposition. Mostly it refers to revealed truths, and signifies belief in them as such. No one has a right to give the word faith a new meaning, and take it, for instance, to signify reliance on Jesus for being personally saved through this vey reliance alone, unless Jesus Christ or the Apostles had, in some instance clearly attributed such a meaning to the word faith and taught the doctrine of trust in Christ for personal salvation as the only requisite for justification. No one should attach a particular meaning to the word faith, without having a good warrant in Scripture or in divine tradition.'

"'Now in many passages of Holy Scripture in which saving faith is plainly spoken of, by faith is not meant a trust in Christ for personal salvation, but evidently a firm belief that Jesus is the Messias, the Christ, the Son of God, that what is related of Him in the Gospel is true, and that what He taught is true.'

"On page 370, it defines faith, and I will read that before reading the opposite."'These texts, all of which refer to saving faith, prove beyond a doubt that not trust in Christ for personal salvation, but the faith of the creed, the faith in revealed truths.'

"Now what is faith according to that? 'The faith of the creed.' They simply draw up a statement of stuff that they call the doctrine of God and then you believe that and do your best and that passes for justification by faith. Whether the creed is drawn up in actual writing or whether it is somebody's idea that they want to pass off by a vote in a General Conference, it makes no difference in principle, the creed is there and subscription to it is just that kind of faith. And there are people here who remember a time—four years ago [1888]—and a place—Minneapolis—when three direct efforts were made to get just such a thing as that fastened upon the third angel's message, by a vote in a General Conference. What somebody believed—set that up as the landmarks and then vote to stand by the landmarks, whether you know what the landmarks are or not, and then go ahead and agree to keep the commandments of God and a lot of other things that you are going to do, and that was to be passed off as justification by faith.

"Were we not told at that time that the angel of God said, 'Do not take that step; you do not know what is in that'? 'I can't take the time to tell you what is in that,' but the angel has said, 'Do not do it.' The papacy was in it. That was what the Lord was trying to tell us, and get us to understand. The papacy was in it. It was like it has been in every other church that has come out from the papacy; they would run a little while by faith in God and then fix up some man's idea of doctrine and vote to stand by that and vote that that is the doctrine of this church and then that is 'the faith of the creed,' and then follow it up with their own doing.

"Is there anybody in the house who was there at that time that cannot see now what that was back there? Then, brethren, is it not time to cut loose, if it takes the very life out of us? It will take the very life out of us; it will crucify us with Jesus Christ. It will cause such a death to sin as we never dreamed of in our lives before. It will take all that papal mind out of us, all that iron spirit out of us, and it will put there the divine, tender, loving mind of Jesus Christ, that wants no creed, because it has Christ Himself.

"Well, let me read that again and then the contradiction of it here. It seems as though one book was written for the other. Brethren, which of the books shall we follow? Ah, *Steps to Christ*. That is what it is, and then it is steps with Him; when we have stepped to, then it is steps with Christ. Now, I will read that over again and then read the opposite:

"'Now, in many passages of Holy Scripture in which saving faith is plainly spoken of, by faith is not meant a trust in Christ for personal salvation, but evidently a firm belief that Jesus is the Messias, the Christ, the Son of God, that what is related of Him in the gospel is true, and that what He taught is true.'

"That is Catholic 'faith.' Now what is the Lord's definition, His idea of faith? Page 69, *Steps to Christ*:"'When we speak of faith, there is a distinction that should be borne in mind. There is a kind of belief that is wholly distinct from faith. The existence and power of God, the truth of His word, are facts that even Satan and his hosts cannot at heart deny.'

"Did not the evil spirits tell Jesus that he was the Christ? (Congregation: "Yes.") Then the devils, Satan and his hosts, do believe in the existence and power of God, that His word is true, and that Jesus is the Messias, the Christ, the Son of God. Satan and his hosts believe all that. But that is not faith. How much power is there in their belief to work good in their lives? None at all. They have no faith. But just this is the Catholic faith, isn't it? What kind of faith is that then? That is satanic faith. That is all it is, satanic belief, as this puts it; but yet the papacy passes it for faith. And whosoever passes that for faith is a papist even thou he profess to be a Seventh-day Adventist. But I read on from *Steps to Christ*:"'The Bible says that "the devils also believe, and tremble," but that is not faith. Where there is not only a belief in God's word, but a submission of the will to Him; where the heart is yielded to Him, the affections fixed upon Him, THERE IS FAITH.'"That is the truth of justifying faith; that is righteousness by faith; that is a faith that works, thank the Lord--not a faith that believes something away off, that keeps the truth of God in the outer court, and then seeks by his own efforts to make up the lack. Not that. No, but faith that works. It itself is working; it has a divine power in it to manifest God's will in man before the world. That is righteousness by faith--the righteousness which faith obtains, which it receives, and which it holds--the righteousness of God.

"I continue reading from *Steps to Christ*:"'Faith that works by love and purifies the soul. Through this faith the heart is renewed in the image of God.'

"I do not need to read any more, as this is enough to show the contrast and the time is far gone. This is enough to show that the papal doctrine of justification by faith is Satan's doctrine; it is simply the natural mind depending upon itself, working through itself, exalting itself and then covering it all up with a profession of belief in this, that, and the other, but having no power of God. Then, brethren, let it be rooted up forever."

The following excerpt was written by A.T. Jones and is titled "The Third Angel's Message"—No. 13. It was published in *The 1893 General Conference Bulletin*.

"The last study we had here was an effort to get as plainly as possible before this people, the difference between satanic belief and the faith of Jesus Christ; the difference between justification by works under the heading of justification by faith—the difference between that and justification by faith as it is. That was the effort; that was the aim. And you will remember how it was done. And that brought us to the subject that is ever before us now: that we must have the teaching of righteousness according to righteousness. And this can be, as we have found, only according to God's idea of righteousness and not our own, and in order to have God's idea of righteousness instead of our own, we must have the mind…of Jesus Christ. Whoever has not the mind of Christ itself, whoever has not yielded up himself and all that he has and is and received the mind of Christ instead, does not know, and he cannot know what righteousness by faith is; he cannot know what justification by faith is. He may profess it; he may assent to it; he may claim it, but he cannot know it, for no man can know it with the natural mind.

Appendix B

Many Ways to Say the Same Thing

What I have found in my study is that many times the same thing is being said over and over again, only in several different ways and through multiple stories and object lessons. Each may focus on a specific aspect: what it is and how it affects us. Or the focus may present a certain perspective: such as our personal view as a sinner seeking salvation, an overall view in context of *The Great Controversy*, or even God's view as He seeks to bring the controversy to an end. But the same story, the gospel story, is being played out again and again. What I have done in this book is try to share the story as I have come to see it, focusing on what God has already done for us and our own personal experience as we fight the battle with self and fight the good fight of faith.

On the following pages are several charts where I have taken the information shared in this book and simplified it. When I understood the distinctions between the carnal mind, the old man, and the stony heart, and the three processes thus revealed, the marriage illustration of Romans 7 became easy to grasp, and the significance of the battle of the man of Romans 7 found its proper relevance. Because the stories in Romans 7 bring more understanding and further insight as to how these "distinctions" play out in our personal desire for salvation from sin, I have placed these charts facing each other so they may be easily compared.

Next, there are four charts depicting the spiritual nature of man as revealed allegorically in the story of Adam and Eve. Our spiritual nature as created and as fallen are placed facing each other, making it easy to see just what happened when Adam and Eve sinned. The next two charts—our spiritual nature as restored by Christ and as it is in you and me today—also face each other. Together they show how the second Adam came to the polluted temple of humanity, what He did for us, and what must be done to change our spiritual nature.

The chart on the two seeds and two soils explains what is our work and what is God's work as we struggle to die to self and come into alignment with God's will. Finally, I have included a comparison of all the charts. It again shows that the terms defined in the chapter "Drawing Distinctions" can be found in Romans 7, both in the marriage illustration, and again in the battle of the man of Romans 7. As an allegory, Adam and Eve shed even more light on these terms and their application to us on a spiritual level. Breaking down the spiritual nature into three compartments has helped me to better understand the fight we face within. It has helped me to understand that there is more than one "process" that must be applied and to the appropriate aspect of our nature, or we end up failing and not knowing why. It also lets me know that God has never left us alone, and it gives me the assurance that this battle with evil can and will be won. God will bring sin to an end, in His people and on this earth, never to rise again.

Is it really necessary for you to understand everything that I have tried to reveal here? No, it is not. A simple child-like faith is all that is needed. But, for most of us, "adulthood" has gotten in the way. So, it is my hope, and simple prayer, that these charts will enable you to clearly see that the Lord has many ways to say the same thing. He is trying every way He can to get His message of love across to us. I hope these charts will help you.

I am one who has wrestled with these things because I like to dig

Many Ways to Say the Same Thing

deep and to know how things work. What I have shared here is for those who desire to understand WHY they still sin, in spite of all their good intentions and efforts to do what is right, and WHY the man Jesus seemed to live a righteous life so easily and we seem to falter at every step. It is my belief that when we know how our spiritual nature works, God's plan of salvation becomes clear, and the part we play is revealed. Knowing that there is that of God in us (a perception of truth, a desire for goodness), as well as that of Satan (a bent to evil), and that we (our power of choice) stand in the middle, and that the fight is over who will rule our will, has helped me tremendously.

Today, God is in need of a people who will "follow Jesus withersoever He goes." To do this, to the extent that God now needs, will require us to know who Jesus was—His nature as a human being—to know how He lived a righteous life, to know how He maintained His relationship to His Father, and to know how He remained true on the cross when He thought His Father had forsaken Him. How can we know with assurance that we can "drink of the cup He drank" and remain true, if we do not know how He did it?

DRAWING DISTINCTIONS

CARNAL MIND	STONY HEART	OLD MAN
Enmity, not subject to the Law of God	Powers of the soul: individuality,	Children—fruit of the flesh
Mind of the flesh	Power to think and do, the mind, the	Former conversation, way of life
Friendship of the world	Heart, the will—power of choice, self	Fulfilling lusts of the flesh and
Tendency; bent to evil in the flesh	Reason, capacity to know God	Thoughts of the mind
Lower corrupt nature	"In" the flesh—in "union" with the flesh	"To be" a friend of the world
Law of sin—voice of Satan	AT enmity with God—enemy of God	Adultery, disobedience
False man—second self	Hardened—blind, conscience silenced	"To be" carnally minded
Principle "live for self"	Selfish—marriage to flesh; flesh rules	END IS DEATH
TO BE ENTIRELY IDLE RENDERED USELESS	TO BE TAKEN FROM THE FLESH GIVEN TO GOD—SELF MUST DIE RETURNED SANCTIFIED	PUT OFF, UNCLOTHE IMPALE ON A CROSS

⇅ ⇅ ⇅

SPIRITUAL MIND	HEART OF FLESH	NEW MAN
Light in every man; that of Christ	Powers of the soul: individuality,	Fruits of the Spirit
Lying dormant in the conscience	Mind, heart, the will, self, reason,	New conversation, way of life
Desire for goodness	Capacity to know God	Walk in spirit, fulfilling desires of the
Perception of Truth	Powers quickened and enlightened	Spirit, the enlightened conscience
Spiritual Tendencies	Hardened will softened, broken	"To be" a friend of God
Law of spirit of life in Christ	"In" the spirit—in "union" with Christ	Righteousness, obedience
Eye of the mind	AT ONE with God	"To be' spiritually minded
Voice of God	Self-less—united to Christ, Spirit rules	END IS ETERNAL LIFE
AWAKENED, QUICKENED PUT IN PLACE OF AUTHORITY	EVER SUBJECT TO GOD, TO AN ENLIGHTENED CONSCIENCE	PUT ON, CLOTHE WITH RENEWED IN THE MIND

Many Ways to Say the Same Thing

MARRIAGE ILLUSTRATION OF ROMANS 7

OLD HUSBAND ---------marriage--------- WOMAN ---------marriage--------- ANOTHER MAN
One flesh, flesh rules. Self becomes selfish   *One spirit, spirit rules. Self becomes selfless*

OLD HUSBAND	WOMAN	ANOTHER MAN
Law of sin and death (in the flesh)	Self, our individuality	Law of spirit of life (in the conscience)
Body of sin—Lusts of the flesh	(power to think and do)	Christ (light that lights every man)
Enmity—carnal mind	The will (power of choice)	Spiritual tendencies
Lower corrupt nature	The stony Heart	Power of the Resurrection
TO BE RENDERED IDLE	TO BE GIVEN TO GOD	TO BE RENDERED ACTIVE

FRUIT OF MARRIAGE *(Self must die with Christ)*   *(Self raised new with Christ)* FRUIT OF MARRIAGE

Evil deeds, transgressions	The woman is in adultery with her present husband.	Righteous deeds
Disobedience	The law says she must die. She can CHOOSE to	Obedience
OLD MAN	die in Christ, by faith, and her Old Man, her past	NEW MAN
Former conversation	way of life, would be crucified with her. The	New way of life
To be carnally minded	UNION with the old husband is broken, rendering	To be spiritually minded
Selfish	him powerless over her. Christ, her true husband,	Self-less
TO BE PUT OFF	raises her to live again in union with Himself.	TO BE PUT ON
END IS DEATH	TO BE CRUCIFIED – TO BE RAISED NEW	END IS ETERNAL LIFE

In Christ the sinful flesh (carnal mind) was abolished (rendered idle) and was slain (killed outright) at the cross. As in Christ, by faith the sinful flesh can be rendered idle in us during our walk on this earth and will be killed outright at our physical death, not to rise in the first resurrection. The woman can choose not to die in Christ by faith, but DIE SHE MUST. If not IN Christ, than OUT of Christ, still united to her old husband who will rise with her at the second resurrection, to face the penalty of the

THE SPIRIT OF MAN
"THE SANCTUARY OF THE HEART"

CREATION: Genesis, chapter 2 and 3

MADE IN THE IMAGE OF GOD

THE EARTH	COURTYARD	HOLY PLACE	MOST HOLY PLACE
THE GARDEN OF EDEN	EVE—2nd SELF	ADAM—1st SELF	VOICE OF GOD
Created perfect Created in sight of Adam Created for Adam	Flesh of his (Adam's) flesh Senses—avenue to the soul: See, hear, touch, taste, smell "Help-meet" for 1st self: to surround, to aid, predict, explain, praise	Capacity to know God Higher powers: To think and to do To will—Power of choice To reason Heart, affections	Conscience God alone controls Commands to obey Warns of disobedience Light of the body Spiritual eye of the mind
God meets with Adam here in the garden	One with higher powers Exercises higher powers	Given dominion Power to recognize and overcome sin	To control appetite, affections, desires, passions, self, and the will, the power of choice

PLAN OF SALVATION—OBEY AND LIVE—GOD RULES

Inward light radiated as a garment of light around them

Many Ways to Say the Same Thing

THE SPIRIT OF MAN
"THE SANCTUARY BECOMES POLLUTED"

THE FALL: Genesis, chapter 3

GOD'S IMAGE DEFACED

THE EARTH	COURTYARD	HOLY PLACE	MOST HOLY
VOICE OF SATAN	EVE—2nd SELF	ADAM—1st SELF	VOICE OF GOD
Lies, deception False promises, Tempts to distrust God's Word	Senses deceived: Lust of the eyes, lust of the flesh, pride of life. Reasons with Satan, not Consulting Adam—1st self	Great mental struggle. Must choose between voice of God and voice of Satan (coming through Eve) Reason exalted over conscience	Conscience—disregarded blackened, seared by sin. Light of the body goes out
Takes dominion from Adam	Hands "full of fruit" Evil Seed Implanted	Higher powers subject to the flesh Becomes "Stony Heart"	Convicts of sin and death Spiritual vision dimmed
Now Prince of this world Garden of Eden shut to Adam and Eve	Flesh becomes sinful flesh, "bent to evil"—tendencies to sin—the carnal mind. IS enmity, not subject to the law of God	AT enmity with God: "To be" carnally minded, the power of choice—the "will" in bondage "Soul" in a state of conscious guilt	Image of God not seen (God does not leave them Promises of restoration)

FLESH RULES—SIN WHEN IT IS FINISHED BRINGETH FORTH DEATH

Dark garments of ignorance drawn about them

233

THE SPIRIT OF MAN
"CHRIST ENTERS THE POLLUTED TEMPLE"

INCARNATION: Christ becomes man

IMAGE OF GOD RESTORED

THE EARTH	COURTYARD	HOLY PLACE	MOST HOLY
VOICE OF SATAN	2nd SELF—HUMAN	ADAM—1st SELF–DIVINE	VOICE OF GOD
Lies, deception, False promises Tempts to distrust God' Word, to doubt God's goodness	Born of a woman, sinful flesh—enmity in his flesh—lust of the eyes, lust of the flesh, pride of life. Made under the law, subject to death	No earthly father, God is His father, just as first Adam. Higher powers as originally created. The "will" not in bondage, but free to choose whose voice to listen to, as was 1st Adam	Conscience—light of the body, spiritual eye of the soul, educated by study of the Word Rules by permission
Claim to world proven false	*"Sinful flesh" submitted to His Father*	*Higher powers subject to the conscience—"called upon God"*	*God speaks the words God does the works*
Does not have complete control of the human race	*Rendered idle during His life Slain at the cross Does not rise in Christ*	*Exercises faith and submission to His Father Dies to His "Divine Self"*	*Conscience rules Christ's "help-meet" Image of God restored*

PLAN OF REDEMPTION—TRUSTING HIS FATHER TO DO FOR HIM

Revealed the glory of God to a dying world, death cannot hold him—resurrection.

Many Ways to Say the Same Thing

THE SPIRIT OF MAN
"WHO DWELLS IN THE TEMPLE OF YOUR HEART?"

YOU AND ME: As we are today

WHOSE IMAGE IS SEEN UPON YOU?

THE EARTH	COURTYARD	HOLY PLACE	MOST HOLY
VOICE OF SATAN	2nd SELF—LOWER NATURE	1st SELF—HIGHER NATURE	VOICE OF GOD
Prince of this world	Avenue to the soul—the	Higher powers weakened	Conscience--eye of the
Principles of this world	five senses easily deceived,	State of conscious guilt	soul, perception of truth
Pleasures of this world	IS enmity against God	AT enmity with God	desire for goodness
	carnal mind—evil tendencies,	No power to overcome sin	Spiritual tendencies
	Lower animal passions	The will—still free to choose	Light of the body
Tempts to distrust God, to love this world	Comes to the higher powers with hands full of sinful desires	Who "dwells in your heart? Who has control of your will?	Convicts of sin, righteousness, judgment
Prince of this earth is a conquered foe	*To be rendered idle Slain at the cross by faith*	*Submission of will to God Heart yielded to Christ Crucified and returned*	*Conscience rules To be our "help-meet" Image of God restored*

PLAN OF REDEMPTION—TRUSTING GOD TO DO FOR YOU WHAT YOU CANNOT DO

Arise and shine, for the glory of God *has risen* upon you *in Christ*

Comfort Ye My People

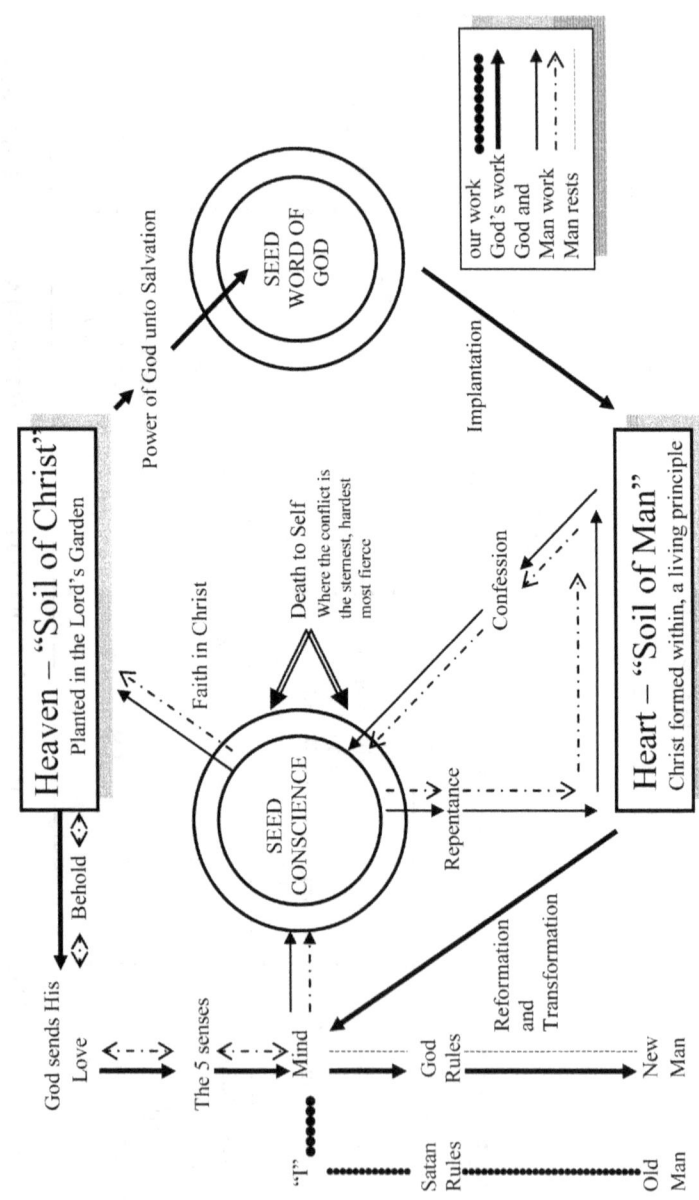

Many Ways to Say the Same Thing

Two Seeds and Two Soils

God sends His Love
God initiates salvation by sending to us a message of his love.

The 5 Senses
This is the "avenue to the soul" through which God's message passes to reach the mind.

Mind
This is the intellect. Here we make a choice to listen or to reject God's message.

Reject and "I" takes precedence, Satan rules, the old man is formed. *Listen* and the holy spirit moves truth into the conscience.

"Seed" Conscience
Surrounded by the "hard shell" of self. Holy spirit "awakens" slumbering conscience—conviction of truth, choice to "kick against the pricks" or to receive.

Repentance
"First-fruit" of awakened conscience. Roman's 7 experience, softening of the heart. Breaking up the soil—loosening the hold of the lower nature upon the higher powers of the mind.

Confession
Uprooting the weeds. Confessing sin, as well as the truth as it is in Jesus. The clearing of the king's highway. The heart turning from sin and towards righteousness.

Death to Self
This is the point where most of us stop. Here is where the conflict is to be the sternest, the hardest, and the most fierce. This is the "plucking out of the eye, the cutting off of the hand." When the "hard shell" of self is broken, the will has submitted to God, and the conscience is "quickened."

Faith
Abiding in Christ—submission of the will to him, the heart yielded to him, the affections fixed upon Him. Christ is our supreme preference. We have perfect reliance upon Him.

Christ receives our entire consecration—giving up all, and open to receive all. Seeing ourselves as already planted in the garden of the Lord, by faith.

Behold
Our "work" is to continue to fix our eyes upon God. As we do this the process repeats and goes ever deeper.

He puts us through the steps again, and again, till He has "every bit" of us hidden in Him by faith.

Power of God unto Salvation
Faith has opened the door for God to work. We experience the blessings of a "finished work"—the mind of Christ, the faith of Christ, God's grace and His love.

"Seed, Word of God
The "hard shell" of the dead letter of the law breaks away and the living spirit of the law comes home to the heart—the divine nature, new motives.

Implantation
God plants the living principles of His word into our hearts—the higher powers.

Heart, soil of man
Christ is formed within, a living abiding principle, a power unto holiness.

Reformation and Transformation
New principles in the mind. This change is unconscious, imperceptible. God rules and a new man is seen.

Many Ways to Say the Same Thing

Drawing Distinctions	Adam and Eve	Romans 7	Spiritual Nature	Sanctuary
Carnal mind, IS enmity, bent to evil in the flesh, seeks to rule, law of sin, sinful tendencies	*Eve after* eating of the fruit Becomes the *sinful "flesh"* Now the false "second" self Hands full of fruit	*Old Husband*, who holds the woman in bondage	*Lower corrupt nature*, enmity in the "flesh", law of sin in our members, animal passions	*Courtyard* of the heart, (altar of sacrifice is found here)
TO BE RENDERED IDLE—CANNOT INHERIT THE KINGDOM OF GOD				
Stony heart—AT enmity, in union with the "flesh", hardened, blind, conscience silenced	*Condition* of 1st self once Adam joins to Eve, ignoring the law of God, hiding from God, excuses for sin	*Woman* (in adultery)	*Higher powers* of the soul, the will, mind, heart, united to the carnal mind—Law of self preservation rules	*Holy place* of the heart, curtain is open to the courtyard
TO BE CRUCIFIED WITH CHRIST—1st SELF MUST CONSENT TO DIE				
TO BE RETURNED SANCTIFIED—1st SELF RAISED NEW IN CHRIST—SELFLESS				
Heart of flesh, the will choosing to serve God, in union with enlightened awakened conscience	*Condition* of 2nd Adam, Choosing to serve God, in the spirit, AT ONE with God	*Woman* reunited to her true husband	*Higher powers* of the soul, united to Spirit of life in Christ, self-less, Spirit rules with a sanctified will	*Holy place* of the heart, curtain open to the Most holy place

Many Ways to Say the Same Thing

Drawing Distinctions	Adam and Eve	Romans 7	Spiritual Nature	Sanctuary
Eye of the mind, Christ in you the hope of Glory, spiritual tendencies	*Voice of God* speaking to Adam, convicts of sin, Law of God written in every heart	*New husband*, spirit of life, law of the resurrection	*Conscience*, spiritual power in every heart: perception of truth, desire for goodness	*Most holy place* of the heart—ray of divine light
TO BE AWAKENED, QUICKENED, PUT IN PLACE OF AUTHORITY				
Old man—past way of life, former conversation, *to be* a friend of the world	*Result* of 1st Adam choosing Eve, eating of the wrong tree, disobedience to the law	*Children*—fruit of the marriage, "oh wretched man that I am"	*Character* formed when the will chooses sin, *To be* carnally minded	*Sinner* in need of forgiveness and the blood of Christ
TO BE PUT OFF—CAST AWAY				
TO BE PUT ON—CLOTHED WITH				
New man—new way of life, new conversation, *To be* a friend of God	*Result* of 2nd Adam choosing God, keeping "Eve" (his flesh) in subjection, obedient to the law, mind of Christ	*New Children*—fruits of the spirit, Righteousness	*Character* formed when the will chooses Christ *To be* spiritually minded	Become a son of the high priest, *laver experience*

We invite you to view the complete
selection of titles we publish at:

www.LNFBooks.com

or write or email us your praises,
reactions, or thoughts about this
or any other book we publish at:

TEACH Services, Inc.
P.O. Box 954
Ringgold, GA 30736

info@TEACHServices.com

www.ingramcontent.com/pod-product-compliance
Lightning Source LLC
Chambersburg PA
CBHW060156190426
43199CB00043B/2409